SIR GUY CARLETON

SIR GUY CARLETON

From a painting in the Public Archives of Canada

SIR GUY CARLETON
(LORD DORCHESTER)

By A. G. Bradley

UNIVERSITY OF TORONTO PRESS

Copyright, Canada, 1966
by University of Toronto Press
Reprinted 2014
ISBN 978-1-4426-5221-7 (paper)

PUBLISHER'S NOTE

A. G. Bradley was an English writer and historian, who lived for a time in the United States and Canada, and subsequently wrote a number of books on Canadian topics, including *The United Empire Loyalists: Founders of British Canada* (1932).

This biography was first published in the famous Makers of Canada Series in 1907, and re-issued in 1926 with supplementary notes incorporating later research by A. L. Burt. When it first appeared it was reviewed by William Wood, who described it as "a really good book on one of the greatest makers of the Empire."

PREFACE

The conquest of Canada, while it solved one problem, created another. It removed a great cause of worry to the old colonies but added a source of perplexity to the mother country. Hitherto the British Empire had grown chiefly by peaceful expansion rather than by conquest. Now, at one stroke, it was enlarged by the addition of a new territory which was not a new country. It had been settled by another European colonizing people who possessed a civilization quite different from that of Britain and just as old. What was to be done with Canada? The acquisition of Acadia, fifty years earlier, had given a little foretaste of this problem and the result had not been happy. The problem would have been serious enough had the American tragedy not developed and had France been Britain's friend instead of her secret or open foe.

The solution was the combined work of governors in Canada and the board of trade and secretaries of state at home. Two ideas at once thrust themselves forward—to wean the Canadians from their old allegiance, and to give the country a British character by attracting an English-speaking population and establishing British institutions. It was natural that the governor being on the spot, should think chiefly of winning

SIR GUY CARLETON

the French population. With all his Scottish ardour, Murray, the first governor, applied this policy in Canada and pressed it at home. But this was a mere beginning; he was recalled before civil government had been established two years. Carleton, who now found himself in Murray's shoes, followed on in his steps. His success was much greater. He was not tripped up, nor was he checked like Murray, for he lacked his explosive temper and was secure in the confidence of the home government, which Murray never enjoyed. Moreover, his purpose was strengthened by the failure of the hope of an English-speaking population and by the gathering of the storm cloud to the south. Before the latter broke on the shores of the St. Lawrence, the Quebec Act had been passed, the Roman Catholic Church had been won, and Britain, through her representative Carleton, was revealed to the French in Canada as a liberal and sympathetic conqueror. Though the Americans were repulsed before the walls of Quebec, the crisis had not fully passed. The entry of France on the American side of the war placed a great strain upon the new loyalty of the Canadians, and Haldimand, who succeeded Carleton, felt as if he were sitting on the edge of a volcano. Few native Britons have been embued with a stronger sense of duty and devotion to their country than this adopted son from Switzerland, and he followed straight along the path which Carleton had pursued.

PREFACE

One mistake they both made, and the discovery of this is one of the reasons for the addition of notes to these chapters which were written twenty years ago. In giving a constitution to Canada in 1774, the British government sought to mould it to the character of the population which was overwhelmingly French, but had no design of sacrificing the English-speaking minority, as has sometimes been said. The Quebec Act established French civil law for the French landowners, and royal instructions to the governors directed the continuance of the rights of *habeas corpus*, trial by jury for civil matters, and English commercial law for the English minority. Both were to be satisfied. This was quite possible because the English minority had little interest in land tenure and the French majority had no more concern with commerce. But this balanced constitution was never realized. Only the part enacted by the British parliament was put in force. The other part was killed by the disobedience of Carleton and Haldimand.

Though the injustice thus suffered by the minority was unnecessary, it was the natural counterpart of the strong French policy of these two governors, and the value of this policy cannot be overestimated. It laid to rest the fears which the Canadians had harboured for their religion and their racial integrity. The French of Canada were the first to enjoy that liberty to other races

SIR GUY CARLETON

which is such a large part of the secret of strength of the modern British Empire.

When Carleton returned as Lord Dorchester, the whole face of things had changed. With the failure of the first hopes for an English population, the prospect had gradually dawned of Canada remaining to all time French in character though British in allegiance, and for almost a quarter of a century it had remained solidly French. Now a new future opened out. With the coming of the Loyalists, it was plain that Canada was to be English as well as French in character—a country with a dual nationality. A new policy was urgent and Dorchester came out to find it. The new policy was embodied in the Constitutional Act. But this, though it was based upon material which he collected, was neither his work, nor did it please him. Inspired by his commission as governor-general over the North American colonies which had survived the American wreck, and by the plan of his chief justice, William Smith, he urged the federation of all British North America. But the secretary-of-state was deaf to this prophetic proposal.

There is a wealth of material for the life of Haldimand from his arrival in America at the opening of the Seven Years' War. He was a great collector of papers, as the two hundred and thirty-two volumes in the British Museum testify. The materials for the life of Dorchester are much

PREFACE

scantier. His papers were all burned after his death by direction of Lady Dorchester. Though his official correspondence has been preserved with other state papers, it is insufficient and has to be checked with other documents. This is a slow task, but it is particularly important because of Dorchester's character. Haldimand's character was almost transparent in its simplicity; Dorchester's was not. Haldimand never tried to cover up his mistakes; Dorchester always did. Since Haldimand has been cleared of the aspersions cast by Du Calvet, subsequent investigation has found little to correct and has been limited to filling out the picture. With Dorchester it is different. In some particulars the traditional interpretation has had to be reversed. The purpose of the notes, in the preparation of which both published and unpublished material has been used, is to add the fruit of later research, and the reader is advised to refer to them because the original text, excepting some minor changes, has not been altered.

A. L. BURT.

University of Alberta, August 15th, 1925.

CONTENTS

CHAPTER I
RETROSPECT 1

CHAPTER II
THE NEW GOVERNOR 29

CHAPTER III
THE QUEBEC ACT 57

CHAPTER IV
CARLETON'S MARRIAGE . . . 75

CHAPTER V
MONTGOMERY AND ARNOLD . . . 95

CHAPTER VI
LAST DAYS OF THE SIEGE . . . 127

CHAPTER VII
THE EVACUATION OF CANADA . . . 141

CHAPTER VIII
ADVANCE INTO THE ENEMY'S COUNTRY . 153

	Page
CHAPTER IX	
CARLETON SUPERSEDED BY BURGOYNE	171
CHAPTER X	
PREPARATIONS FOR PEACE	191
CHAPTER XI	
DORCHESTER'S RETURN	221
CHAPTER XII	
THE CANADA ACT	251
CHAPTER XIII	
A NEW SITUATION	269
CHAPTER XIV	
CLOSING YEARS	281
APPENDICES	313
INDEX	329

SIR GUY CARLETON

CHAPTER I

RETROSPECT

BEFORE introducing to the reader the soldier-statesman who is the subject of this memoir, it seems advisable to give a short sketch of existing conditions in the country which he was called upon to govern. Indeed it is almost necessary thus to prepare the ground for the advent of our proconsul, so that the reader may properly understand the kind of furrow he had to break. One may affirm too with perfect safety that the great lull which fell upon Canada at the close of the stir and turmoil of the Seven Years' War and the downfall of French power on the St. Lawrence, presents few attractions to the mind of a reader exhilarated by the glamour of those dramatic incidents. Most of us, on closing that page of history which influenced the future of two hemispheres far more than Waterloo, have felt little inclination to concern ourselves with the immediate fortunes of a few thousand war-sick and isolated French-Canadians. The historical student has turned more readily to the greater problems that so soon began to agitate the people of those British provinces after their safety had been secured by the fleets and armies of the mother country. Most people have a vague, but sufficiently accurate notion,

SIR GUY CARLETON

that the French-Canadians were left practically undisturbed in their laws and religion, and that to this wise and benevolent policy they responded with a due measure of loyalty and affection. But it is necessary here to be a little more precise and to indicate some of those complications inevitable to such new conditions, and the difficulties which beset the administrators of the conquered province from its first occupation.

Canada had been surrendered to Amherst by Lévis on the fall of Montreal in 1760. But the war with France in Europe was only closed by the peace of two years later, when the colony was formally ceded to the British Crown. Throughout this interval Canada was under a purely military rule, administered by a governor in Quebec with others nominally subordinate to him at Three Rivers and Montreal respectively. The chief authority, however, still lay with the commander-in-chief at New York, a position retained by Amherst. But for all practical purposes General Murray may be regarded as the administrator of Canada until the peace, as he was also its first actual governor subsequently to it. Murray had been one of Wolfe's three brigadiers at the Battle of the Plains. He had remained in command at Quebec and ably defended it against the French throughout the following winter. He was a good soldier and well versed in the military and civil conditions of North America, and withal an able, sensible and extremely

WOULD CANADA BE RETAINED

just man with a good knowledge of the French language.

These three years of military rule were, of course, regarded as a mere temporary expedient. No one knew positively whether Canada would be retained or restored at the treaty which would follow the approaching peace. The country was then regarded by British colonists as of no value for agricultural settlement, while its commercial statistics were contemptible. Its importance seemed mainly strategic; it was a foothold whence the dreaded power of France might menace the western continent. However, there were a few, how few must always be the marvel of us moderns, who saw the handwriting on the wall and who understood the temper of the average American colonist: his intense localism and aloofness from the political and social atmosphere of the mother country, his growing impatience of every form of restriction—and some were really galling, originating outside his own provincial legislature. A few prescient Englishmen, and more Frenchmen, displayed an indifference to the possession of Canada for the same reason, but from opposite motives. With the French power firmly seated on the St. Lawrence, it is safe to say that no thoughts of independence would have germinated to the south of it. But these warning voices were scarcely heard at the time—significant though they are to read of nowadays in the light of our later knowledge.

SIR GUY CARLETON

Murray's temporary government had been merciful and successful within its limitations. Both he and his officers won by degrees the hearts and the confidence of their late antagonists. They administered the law fairly and justly and did everything in their power to mitigate those sufferings, inevitable at the close of a devastating war, which in this case had been aggravated by the monstrous frauds and corruption of Bigot and his gang. Even the British soldier out of his poor pittance was not backward with such assistance as he was able to offer. When an order had gone out, however, in the autumn of 1761 to the garrisons in North America that the soldier was to pay four pence a day for his rations, hitherto provided by government, a serious mutiny broke out in Quebec. Fearful of the contagion spreading to other garrisons, Murray and his officers threw themselves into the breach with fine coolness and daring, and at the imminent peril of their lives, quashed a rising among these veteran troops, who as contemporary accounts tell us, were "mad with rage" at what they deemed a gross injustice. This intervention elicited the special gratitude of the king.

At this time too the great Indian rising known as "Pontiac's War" broke out. All the western Indians who had been actively or passively attached to the French went on the war-path. The old French forts from Michilimackinac in the far north-west to the Ohio valley, now mainly occupied by small British garrisons, had been treacherously attacked

PONTIAC'S WAR

and most of them had fallen. There had been much massacre and bloodshed. The frontiers of the middle provinces were threatened as they had been threatened after Braddock's defeat. Pontiac was an able and crafty leader of his race and had opened the war at Detroit, the defence of which important post by Major Gladwin is a memorable episode in North American history.

The French traders and settlers round these remote posts had no doubt some hand in fomenting discontent. The commanding influence and tact of Sir William Johnson succeeded in quieting the serious discontent of the Six Nations whose territory lay between the settlements and the West. If they had risen the situation would have been serious indeed. Their grievances were genuine enough, for the land greed of the British colonists, from highest to lowest, led to the most unscrupulous and dishonest methods of acquiring patents to Indian lands, the most flagrant among which being that of plying the Indians with liquor and securing their signatures to deeds when drunk. The provinces were loud in their claims to manage their own Indian affairs so long as it was a matter of mere land grabbing, but when the vengeance this awakened threatened their frontiers they called to the Crown to protect them and grudged every shilling and every man they were asked to contribute. Pontiac's War, however, had been mainly instigated by the French influence in the western country and had been further en-

SIR GUY CARLETON

couraged by the lack of friendly recognition and attention which the Indian's dignity required as part of the price of his friendship.

The war lasted for three years and occupied several British regiments, but was indifferently supported by the colonists whom it chiefly concerned. The gallant Swiss colonel, Bouquet, of the 60th was its guiding spirit. His masterly marches through the Alleghany forests on the track of the unfortunate Braddock and the heroic Forbes, and yet a hundred miles deeper into the wilderness than they, his hotly fought and successful actions with outnumbering Indian warriors on their own grounds, are among the best performances of a British officer and British regulars in the American wars. The war was not finished till 1765. But when Bouquet had done with them the western Indians from Michilimackinac to the Mississippi had no longer any shadow of a doubt but that King George, and not King Louis, was now their father. Colonial legislatures passed eloquent addresses of thanks to the soldier, the gentleman, and the scholar who had delivered them from their terrible foes. And they might well have included Johnson in their eulogies, for his ceaseless efforts had alone prevented four thousand Iroquois warriors from joining in the fray. Bouquet was made a brigadier, but that was the limit of recognition a grateful king and government accorded him. Though only forty-six his health would seem to have been undermined, and death closed his honourable life in

THE TREATY OF PARIS

the years of his last and most important service. He died at his new command in Florida and added another grave to those of the "unremembered dead" whose services England overlooked then and has long forgotten, because they were given not in the glare of the footlights but on the remote and unfamiliar stages where the work of empire has been so largely done. Students, however, have not forgotten Bouquet, for many volumes of papers connected with his long service in America lie ready to their hand in the British Museum. He bequeathed them to his friend and executor, General Haldimand, another Swiss officer of the same famous corps, who has himself contributed almost as voluminously to the contemporary literature of the period. It is surely a curious reflection that to the literary zeal and foresight of these two loyal, foreign-born officers, we are indebted for the largest mass of contemporary evidence left by any persons connected with this period in North America.

The Treaty of Paris in 1763 decided the retention of Canada by Great Britain, and it was immediately followed at the close of the same year by a proclamation of George III regarding his new governments in North America. We are only here concerned with that of Quebec, which excluding Nova Scotia and of course Newfoundland, covered the whole of what was then regarded as Canada. In the far north the Hudson's Bay Company, then as for a century later, held its solitary reign. Concerning the

SIR GUY CARLETON

title to the territory now roughly occupied by the provinces of Quebec and Ontario, though the latter was still a wilderness, there was no doubt. But it is easy to forget that after the cession of Canada the whole of the western country from Lake Erie southward behind the Alleghanies and as far as the New Orleans settlements up the Mississippi, ceded by the same treaty to Spain, was included in the king's new province. French settlement then extended no farther westward than the Island of Montreal. Modern Ontario and the vast west behind and to the south of it was occupied by the Indian nations, and thinly sprinkled with fortified trading-posts whose French defenders were now displaced by British garrisons.

The new ordinance confirmed the French inhabitants, or "new subjects" as they were called, in the full exercise of their religion as already promised at the surrender. It directed the substitution of the English criminal code for the more merciless French usages, an innovation already practically made and gladly accepted by the mass of the French inhabitants. In the matter of the civil code the proclamation was more vague, directing that English law should be followed so far as was compatible with the nature and customs of the people. This tentative clause was probably wise and even inevitable, but it gave rise to much of the misunderstanding and confusion with which the earlier governors had to grapple. The proclamation

INITIAL DIFFICULTIES

went on to invite English-speaking people, or the "king's old subjects," to make their home in his new dominion, promising them, when the time should be ripe, all the benefits and blessings of British institutions and representative government. The French population at this time numbered about seventy thousand. The English for a long time scarcely exceeded four hundred, entirely confined to the two small cities of Quebec and Montreal, which contained between them a population of some seventeen thousand souls. The English settlers were mainly composed of traders and miscellaneous people of lower degree, with a few disbanded soldiers and half-pay officers, who had followed the army.[1] The majority were from the American colonies, and their numerical insignificance did not prevent them from at once endeavouring to establish the axiom that the country was to be administered entirely by themselves.

Murray was now appointed governor and captain-general of Canada. During his military governorship he had already experienced much trouble from the overweening pretensions of this small faction. He was now, like his successors, to experience much more. This difficulty will be so prominent in these pages that it will be enough to say here that it was aggravated by the fact of the British residents being, upon the whole, inferior representatives of their nation, while among the mass of unlettered

[1] See appendix A.

SIR GUY CARLETON

and reactionary French-Canadians there were several hundred persons of the seigniorial class, men, generally speaking, of polite manners and sufficient education, and accustomed to the respect accorded to a more or less exclusive caste. Murray and his officers had not unnaturally established good relations with the leading representatives of this small *noblesse*,[1] while with those not immediately in contact with him, as well as with the religious bodies and the peasantry the former had earned a general reputation for kindness, justice and integrity of purpose. In spite of the soreness of recent defeat, British rule was perhaps never quite so popular as when Murray, who had won the confidence of the French-Canadians during his dictatorship, retained it through the thornier period which distinguished the inauguration of civil government.

The number of the Canadian *noblesse* who returned to France has been frequently exaggerated. It seems to have been well under three hundred, including women and children, and many of these were actually officers serving in the French army, who followed their regiments. Amherst at the surrender in 1760 had granted religious freedom, but refused French law,[2] and had allowed eighteen months for all those unwilling to accept such terms to wind up their affairs and return to France. The question of civil law was of great importance to a

[1] See appendix B.
[2] See appendix C.

SEIGNIORIAL TENURE

reactionary population wedded to immemorial custom. No wonder royal proclamations were timid of definition. But the general construction put upon the ordinance by the English authorities at Quebec was that of an English code. It was soon found, however, that to disturb the French laws of land tenure and inheritance, with which the whole seigniorial system of the province was bound up, was to invite chaos. Still more, any attempt at innovation was ignored. So the government was virtually compelled to acquiesce in the old custom so far as these more vital matters were concerned.

It is possible that there may be readers who need reminding that the land system of Lower Canada was of a quasi-feudal nature; that the country was partitioned into large estates held of the French Crown by a resident *noblesse* created during the past century and a half for this specific purpose. These seigniories were occupied by the peasantry or *habitants* at trifling rents, with the reservation of mill privileges and the payment of certain dues to the lord on sales or succession, and other transactions common to feudal or manorial custom. The seigniors held their estates rather in the sense of trustees for the people than as military fiefs. Though they had been the natural leaders of the militia of the colonies, the "militia captains" responsible for the force were specially selected persons in various districts, seigniorial rank not of necessity carrying military rank.

SIR GUY CARLETON

If the *noblesse* bore a partial resemblance, as was inevitable, to that of older countries, the peasantry, on the other hand, were more independent and well-to-do than those of France, as testified by a score of contemporary writers. A considerable fraction of the population were occupied as *coureurs de bois* in the fur trade, but the majority lived under the conditions here briefly indicated, along the banks of the St. Lawrence from Montreal to Gaspé. Those seigniors who had sufficient means, however, seem like their bigger prototypes in France, and with better reason, to have spent much of their time at one or other of the two cities, while many of them in the late régime had held offices of various kinds in Quebec or Montreal, which added to their income.

Inadequate as is this slight sketch of a wide and complex subject it describes the situation sufficiently to give the reader some notion how widely different were the ideas of French and English colonists on the subject of land tenure. The latter, then as now, accustomed to acquire as much land in actual freehold as he had money to pay for, to buy and sell, barter or exchange it at a moment's notice, was confronted on coming to Canada, particularly if he came from the colonies, with a system that seemed to his restless and irreverent and material soul, barbarous and mediæval. From his office or shop in Quebec he clamoured for an application of the English land laws, not because he wanted to

THE QUESTION OF CIVIL LAW

become a land owner, but because as a true Briton, he thought the French laws ridiculous and suggestive of tyranny, just as he considered Roman Catholics as outside the pale of human justice.

But all attempts to enforce English civil law in matters connected with property rebounded from the adamantine walls by which French customs were encircled, leaving scarcely any impression. Murray with his broad sympathies and sound sense soon discouraged the attempt and a little later it was formally abandoned. Two civil officers were sent out from England, a chief-justice and an attorney-general,[1] to inaugurate and supervise one of the most complicated judicial problems that the wit of man could have been asked to solve. They were hopeless failures, neither of them knowing any French or any law, and they were in due course dismissed. As regards the general government, Murray had been empowered by royal instruction to nominate a council of eight members authorized to make laws and ordinances. This he had done, including in the number one French-Canadian.[2] The new courts were formally established in 1764. There was a court of king's bench holding its sessions at Quebec twice a year for trying civil and criminal cases according to English law—with an appeal to the governor in council in amounts over three hundred pounds and to the

[1] See appendix D.
[2] See appendix E.

SIR GUY CARLETON

king in amounts over five hundred pounds. There was a court of common pleas, holding bi-annual sessions, to determine according to equity, having regard to English laws, and to try cases above the value of ten pounds. Trial by jury might be resorted to if demanded by either party, and there were to be no religious disqualifications.[1] Lastly justices of the peace were appointed throughout the province.

The French in spite of their confidence in Murray were greatly perturbed at the prospect of a change to laws they knew nothing of, administered in the courts in a language they did not understand and by people who did not understand theirs. Not one in fifty could read or write and their very ignorance made them the more fearful. The attitude of the handful of British who had come among them was not of a kind to win their hearts, or wean them from their old customs. Murray describes them in one letter to the home government as "men of mean education, either young or inexperienced, or older men who had failed elsewhere," in another as "licentious fanatics." One might suspect even this shrewd soldier of over-heated language if Carleton had not in his turn treated his British-Canadian subjects to somewhat similar flowers of speech in his confidential despatches.

Here is the first presentment of the grand jury, the spokesmen of the handful of "licentious fanatics" who had come in to make money and regen-

[1] See appendix F.

THE FIRST GRAND JURY

erate Canada at the same time, and the reader may gather something of their point of view. They called for the better observance of the Sabbath Day and declaimed against the ordinary festivities of the Roman Catholic country they had transferred themselves to. They furthermore put it on record that a learned clergy was required to preach the Gospel in French and English. They demanded that no ordinance should be passed by the governor in council without consultation with themselves, and that the public accounts should be laid before them twice a year. They also represented the ordinances of the governor in council creating courts of judicature in the provinces as unconstitutional. Having hit at the government they then fired a shaft at the army, declaring it unfitting that its officers should exercise any judicial authority. Finally they protested against Roman Catholics sitting on juries in their own law courts, as it was "in flagrant violation of our most sacred laws and liberties and tending to the entire subversion of the Protestant religion." They also referred to Canada, which was as old as Virginia, as an infant colony. This piece of presumption on the part of a quarter sessions grand jury in hectoring and reprimanding the governor and council, accompanied by pretensions to represent the colony, took away the breath of the presiding justice, Samuel Gridley, who snubbed them soundly. As for Murray he was justly enraged at this irregular attack on his administration. He sent home

SIR GUY CARLETON

despatches giving the names of the signatories who represented, he declared, about two hundred of their race and faith in Quebec and Montreal, not ten of whom were freeholders, and who aspired to absolute dominion over eighty thousand of the king's new subjects. Moreover, six French-Canadian grand jurors who understood no English had been fraudulently induced to join in the presentment and now petitioned the king stating in what manner they had been deceived. The result of all this was a royal reprimand to these intolerant busybodies and a further announcement of His Majesty's intentions to see complete justice done in every way to his new French subjects.

Murray now thought it advisable to send a representative to London to explain the situation to the British government, and accordingly selected Cramahé, the most efficient member of the council —a Swiss by birth but an officer in the British army by profession. The British merchants countered this by despatching one of their own number to propagate their version of Canadian affairs in London. The British community slowly increased to between four and five hundred. They gathered all the trade of the colony into their hands, the French showing little aptitude for it, but being persons for the most part of little or no capital and not many scruples, such impetus to business as they created was qualified by the friction they stirred up; for they seem to have spared no pains in letting the

DISLIKE OF THE ARMY

French know their opinion of their customs, habits and religion, and on the other hand to have taken little trouble to acquire the language of the country they traded in. Their relations with the military were quite as unfortunate, imbibed apparently from the American colonies where the troops who protected the country in time of war were flouted in peace as the pestilent minions of autocratic rule.

No barracks had as yet been built in Canada and billeting was an unfortunate necessity. The British merchants, and from example many of the urban French inhabitants, adopted such a bitter attitude towards the army that the resentment of the soldiers was very naturally aroused and a good deal of unpleasantness evoked. The magistrates were drawn mainly from the small British civilian class who were deeply imbued with the new spirit of antimilitary republicanism born of the removal of the French terror from their borders. They passed severe sentences on the little frolics of exuberant privates, and this with an unctuous malevolence that was doubtless galling to the men whose devotion alone had made a career in Canada possible for these eighteenth century Bumbles. The officers shared in an odium quite unmerited in their case and not merely resented by themselves but by the better class among the French, with whom they seem to have been distinctly popular. The British community then went so far as to forward a petition to the Crown for Murray's recall, signed by twenty-one persons. In this precious document they declared that they had submitted patiently to arbitrary military rule where they had expected to enjoy the blessings of British liberty, which in plain English meant a monopoly of authority over their French fellow-subjects and a legislative assembly chosen from themselves alone. A somewhat characteristic complaint against the much harassed governor was his remissness in attending church. This petition was supported by the London merchants for whom they acted as principals or agents, and whose knowledge of the complexities of the situation must have been even less than that of their present day descendants, which is saying much. A counter petition was promptly forwarded by the French seigniors defending Murray in eloquent language, describing him as the victim of a cabal, expressing the highest esteem for his justice and his good qualities, and praying for his retention. The friction with the military gave rise to a regrettable incident in Montreal at the close of 1764, which caused much heat and excitement throughout the colony, and as its effects lasted long after Carleton had assumed the governorship a brief outline of it seems necessary here.

It so happened that one Walker, a leading trader and magistrate in Montreal, English by birth, but Bostonian by recent habitation, had been extremely forward in securing the severe sentences passed upon the soldiers. He was a notoriously sour and bad-tempered person and deeply imbued with

THE WALKER OUTRAGE

those feelings of dislike towards everything monarchical or military then gathering strength in the province he had come from. The trouble arose out of a billeting order in the execution of which a certain Captain Fraser had assigned another officer, Captain Payne, to rooms in the house of a French-Canadian, which he himself had just vacated. In this house it so happened there lodged a magistrate, on which account the owner claimed exemption; but Fraser argued that the exemption applied only to the actual houses of magistrates, not to those where they happened to be lodging. Captain Payne, however, positively declined to move, upon which a warrant was issued against him, and on his proving obdurate he was summoned before the magistrates and promptly committed to gaol. After lying there for some days he applied to the chief-justice of the province for a *habeas corpus* and was set at liberty. But the resentment felt by the garrison at what was conceived to be an outrage and an insult was prodigious. Fraser wrote to Murray that unless these magistrates were deposed he would himself resign. The justices, however, showing no signs of contrition, but rather the reverse, the garrison lodged a formal complaint. Feeling ran very high and Murray summoned the magistrates concerned to wait on him at Quebec; but before they could start an event occurred which brought matters to a crisis and wrought up the whole colony to a high pitch of excitement.

SIR GUY CARLETON

Walker was the most active of the offending magistrates, and a plot was hatched by persons unknown to punish him. One night, while at supper with his wife, a number of masked men entered his house and assaulted him in most ferocious fashion, among other deeds cutting off a piece of his ear. The incident was of course serious, but the stir it created through the colony was out of all proportion, for it seemed certain that it must have been the work of some members of the garrison, and the faction opposed to them had an extraordinary opportunity for vindicating their treasured prejudices. All contemporary accounts declare that a panic seized the colony, and that every one expected to be robbed and murdered in his bed. When a soldier entered a shop we are told he had a pistol presented at his head until he completed his purchase. Even the French-Canadians, mostly neutral in these quarrels, took alarm. The noise of it reached England and the Crown offered a reward of a hundred guineas with a free pardon for any information leading to the conviction of the offenders. The victim himself offered a like sum for the discovery of the despoiler of his ear, while the inhabitants of Montreal offered another three hundred pounds. These large rewards were absolutely without effect, and it was not till two years afterwards, soon after Carleton's arrival, that anything transpired and a greater stir than ever was created of which we shall hear in due course. These events took place at the close of 1764.

THE RELIGIOUS QUESTION

In that year the governorship of Montreal and Three Rivers had been abolished. Haldimand held office at the latter place and Burton at Montreal, where he had given, and continued to give, Murray some trouble by refusing to recognize his authority. Indeed Murray appears to have regarded the disturbances there as partly due to lack of a firm hand.

A few weeks after the Walker outrage there was more friction than ever between the troops and the magistrates. A number of men of the 28th were committed to gaol with vindictive harshness, and feeling ran so high that a mutiny was feared and Burton deemed it necessary to acquaint Murray. Upon this the latter at once proceeded to Montreal, and affirmed that he found the inhabitants in fear of their lives and that a guard was mounted nightly at Walker's door. He spent some weeks in the town endeavouring to restore confidence and harmony and in prosecuting inquiries into the Walker mystery, which proved, as already intimated, fruitless. Before leaving he made arrangements for substituting another regiment for the 28th, which was already under marching orders.

The question of their religion, now that all hope of restoration to France was over, gave the French-Canadians many tremors and the British government much concern. Throughout the British colonies the liberal policy of the Crown in this particular had been freely censured, and it became one of the leading grievances in their indictment of the mother

SIR GUY CARLETON

country when the colonies began to formulate them. The government, however, stood firm on this point. There were many difficulties connected with its actual settlement. By the terms of surrender in 1760 free exercise of religion was granted "till the king's pleasure should be known." The king's pleasure was of course expressed in the treaty of three years later, and ordained that his new Roman Catholic subjects might profess the worship of their religion according to the rights of the Romish Church "so far as the laws of Great Britain permitted," a concession, however, which scandalized the British colonies and yet did not fully ease the minds of the indulged Canadians. Clericalism was a weighty force in the life of French Canada and the last sentence seems to have frightened its leaders. Moreover there were some practical difficulties. There had been no bishop, for instance, in the country since the surrender. An unqualified refusal had been given by the Crown to any further introduction of priests from France, for it was an obvious inference that they would strive to maintain the bonds of sentiment between the mother country and its lost colony, and in case of war would be dangerous agents. There now seemed to the Canadians some fear of their supply of priests running out, and Murray reported that it was the rising generation whose souls they were mainly anxious about. The leading ecclesiastics of Quebec petitioned the Crown, suggesting that priests should be introduced from other countries

MURRAY'S DEPARTURE

than France, or that a bishop should be elected by themselves. After much discussion the latter suggestion was adopted and Monseigneur Briand was selected by the British government from three or four candidates, and was consecrated in Paris. He arrived about the time of Murray's departure in 1766.

The Jesuits too about this time were expelled from France, and the few that were in Canada as well as their considerable property became the subject of much controversy. Another trouble arose from the fact that a great deal of the old paper money issued by the French in the late war was still held in Canada, and though its redemption was a condition of the treaty the French government had shuffled a good deal in the matter and had caused the Canadians much anxiety and some loss. The English traders in Canada made considerable profits in buying up this paper from those who were forced to sell, though Murray did his best to prevent such sacrifices by opening an office for registrating the notes. The total amount of this paper in circulation was seventeen million livres.

The discontent of the British community with Murray found expression from time to time in letters of complaint to prominent persons in England which, added to the disturbance in Montreal, prompted the home government to summon him to London in an inquiring rather than a censorious mood, so far as one may learn. He arrived in the summer of 1766, leaving Colonel Irving, the senior

SIR GUY CARLETON

member of the council, as his deputy. He never returned though he retained his governorship for a time.[1]

After reaching London Murray published a written report addressed to Lord Shelburne. As an account of the colony by the man who had been responsible for its government for six years and who had on the whole acted with judgment and wisdom, a brief summary of his picture of it will be no bad introduction to the advent of his successor.

After an exact enumeration of the statistics of the country as to land, population, live stock and so forth, which having been collected by himself shows much praiseworthy effort, he treats of the British Protestant population, most of whom were "followers of the army, of mean education, or soldiers disbanded at its reduction. All have their fortunes to make and I hear few of them are solicitous about the means where the end can be obtained; in general the most immoral collection of men I ever knew and of course little calculated to make the new subjects enamoured with our laws, religion and customs, far less adapted to enforce these laws and to govern."

The Canadians on the other hand, the report declares, had been accustomed to arbitrary and military government, and were a frugal, industrious, moral race of men who from the mild treatment they received from the king's officers who ruled the country from the surrender of the colony

[1] See appendix G.

MURRAY'S REPORT

till the treaty of 1763, when civil government was declared, had greatly got the better of the natural antipathy they had to their conquerors. Murray here describes "the numerous *noblesse* piquing themselves much on the antiquity of their families, their own military glory and that of their ancestors, and though not rich, nevertheless in a situation, in a country of abundance where money is scarce and luxury unknown, to support their dignity. Their tenantry who pay only an annual quit rent of a dollar for a hundred acres are at their ease and comfortable. They had been accustomed to respect and obey their *noblesse*, their tenancies being in the feudal manner."

They had shared with the officers the dangers of the battlefield, and their natural affections had increased in proportion to the calamities overtaking both in the conquest of the country. As they had been taught to respect their superiors, Murray tells us, they were shocked at the insults which their *noblesse* and the king's officers had received from the English traders and lawyers since civil government was instituted. It was natural to suppose them jealous of their religion, for it had been the policy of the French government to keep them in a state of extreme ignorance. Few could read, and printing had not been permitted. Their veneration for the priesthood was in proportion to their ignorance. The clergy were illiterate and of mean birth, and now that fresh recruits from France were forbidden

SIR GUY CARLETON

Murray considered that the order would gradually sink in quality provided they were not exposed to persecution. He disclaims there having been any remarkable disorders in the colony, the Walker outrage excepted, the full details of which "horrid affair" he had already laid before the king's servants. Disorders and divisions, from the nature of things, could not have been avoided in attempting to establish a civil government under the instructions sent him. Magistrates were to be made and juries to be composed from "four hundred and fifty contemptible traders and sutlers." It was easy to conceive how the narrow ideas and ignorance of such men must offend any soldiers, more especially those of an army who had so long governed them and knew the meanness from which they had been elevated. It would have been unreasonable to suppose that such men would not have been intoxicated with the unexpected power put into their hands and not been eager to show how amply they possessed it. As there were no barracks in the country the quartering of troops furnished perpetual opportunity for displaying their importance and rancour. The Canadian *noblesse* were hated because their birth and behaviour entitled them to respect, and the peasants were abhorred because they were saved from the oppression they were threatened with. This Murray declares was amply proved by the presentments of the grand jury.

Another misfortune was the improper choice and

MURRAY'S REPORT

the number of the civil officers sent over from England which increased the disquietude of the colony. Instead of appointing men of genius and untainted morals, men of the reverse stamp were appointed to the most important offices, under whom it was impossible to give a proper impression of the dignity of government. As an example, the judge selected to conciliate the minds of eighty-five thousand foreigners to the laws and government of Great Britain had been taken from a gaol and was entirely ignorant of the civil law and the language of the country. The attorney-general in the matter of language had been no better qualified. Such offices as secretary of the province, registrar, clerk of the council, commissioner of stores and provost marshal had been given by patent to men of influence in England who let them out to the highest bidders, men ignorant even of the language of the country. No salary being annexed to these places the holders were dependent on fees which Murray was ordered to assess in amount equal to those of the "richest ancient colonies." The rapacity of these men was severely felt by the poor Canadians, but they patiently submitted to it. Though urged to resistance by some of the contumacious traders from New York they cheerfully obeyed the Stamp Act in hopes that their good behaviour would recommend them to the favour and protection of their sovereign.

Murray concludes his report by saying that he glories in having been accused of warmth and firm-

SIR GUY CARLETON

ness in protecting the king's Canadian subjects and of doing the utmost in his power to gain for his royal master the affections of that brave, hardy people whose emigration, if ever it should happen, would be an irreparable loss to the empire and to prevent which he would cheerfully submit to greater calumnies and indignities, if greater could be devised than those he has already undergone.

Murray now disappears from these pages. Whether his language was too warm or not must be inferred from the experiences on which his more distinguished successor is about to enter. As the first governor of Canada the verdict of history is distinctly in Murray's favour. As a brave and faithful soldier his heroic though unsuccessful defence of Minorca a few years later was a fitting climax to his successful defence of Quebec at a much more vital moment.

CHAPTER II

THE NEW GOVERNOR

GUY CARLETON was the third son of Christopher Carleton a landowner near Newry, County Down in Ireland and was born in 1724. The family came originally from Cumberland and were essentially, therefore, members of that Ulster plantation settled by emigrants from Scotland and the English border. The Carletons in short belonged to that virile Scotch-Irish stock which has given Great Britain so many great captains of war and industry, to the United States such a host of hardy settlers and able citizens, and to Canada a proportionately valuable contribution. Both these types of Anglo-Irishmen have in truth produced an extraordinary roll of distinguished men, and I shall hope to show in these pages that Carleton is not unworthy to rank among them.

His father died when he was fourteen and his mother (formerly a Miss Ball, of County Donegal) soon afterwards married the Rev. Thomas Skelton of Newry. To this gentleman's influence and care has been attributed no small share in moulding the qualities that made Carleton what he afterwards became.

On May 21st, 1742, he was commissioned an en-

SIR GUY CARLETON

sign in Lord Rothe's regiment, afterwards the 25th Foot. Promotion at first came slowly and nine years later, at the age of twenty-seven, he was only a lieutenant in the Foot-Guards, while his friend Wolfe, three years his junior, had been a captain at twenty. By 1757, however, Carleton had made up for lost time and was a lieutenant-colonel commanding the 72nd Regiment. Wolfe first mentions him in 1752 as "my friend Carleton" from whom he had just received an English news-budget at Paris, and a few days afterwards speaks of him again, alluding with gratification to his appointment as military preceptor to the young Duke of Richmond on a tour among the fortified towns of the Low Countries. Wolfe it seems could have had the appointment for himself, but confides to his mother that not thinking himself quite equal to it he had immediately recommended Carleton of whom, besides his great personal liking, he had professionally a high opinion. This from the almost hypercritical hero of Quebec is a significant tribute to his friend's qualities both of head and heart.

To Wolfe's busy and facile pen too, we are indebted for the fact that the "patron" at this time of Guy Carleton and his brother, who was also in the army, was William Conolly of Stratton Hall, Staffordshire, M.P. and privy councillor. This gentleman was of powerful Irish connection and died in 1754, an event which Wolfe alludes to as "a deadly blow to the Carletons." Both their fortunes, however,

CARLETON AND WOLFE

survived it bravely. When Wolfe was appointed a brigadier under Amherst for the Louisbourg expedition, both he and his chief were anxious to take Guy Carleton, by this time a lieutenant-colonel, with them; but the king refused and sent him to the British legion serving under Prince Ferdinand in Germany. Wolfe was very wroth. "It is a public loss," he wrote. "The king has refused Carleton leave to go, to my very great grief and disappointment and with circumstances extremely unpleasant to him." Carleton it appears had spoken disparagingly of the Hanoverian troops, a mortal offence in King George's eyes. In the next year when Wolfe was appointed to the chief command against Quebec, occurred the somewhat well-known incident when he sent up Carleton's name to the king as a member of his staff, and His Majesty, still unforgiving, drew his pen through it. Wolfe would not be denied, and Pitt in full sympathy with his disappointment sent the commander-in-chief, Ligonier, back to the presence to press Carleton's appointment, but the king remained firm. So did Wolfe, and begged that it should be represented to His Majesty that a general who was to be held responsible for a difficult undertaking should at least have the choice of his coadjutors. At a third appeal urged in this form the king relented, and Carleton went out as quartermaster-general. We have Wolfe's own words that he relied chiefly on his friend to supply the lack of ability among his engineers.

SIR GUY CARLETON

During the siege Carleton was sent up the river in command of a force to Pointe-aux-Trembles where he landed, searched the country for provisions and brought off some prisoners. Later on, before the final operations, he was entrusted with the difficult task of drawing off the troops from the camp at Montmorency. In the battle on the Plains of Abraham he was on the left of the line and was wounded, but not seriously. Returning to Europe he took part, in 1761, in the attack on Port Andro and was wounded again. In the following year he became a full colonel and at the siege of Havana served under Albemarle with much distinction, being once more wounded in a sortie. We know nothing more of Carleton but these bare facts till he was appointed to succeed Murray at Quebec. To deal impersonally with the incidents in which he figured before he began the work by virtue of which his name lives, would be futile and prodigal of space which should be better employed. Hitherto he had been the resolute and efficient agent of other men's tactics. In future he was to be his own master as well as oftentimes his own agent. Till 1766 and his forty-second year it had been his business to obey. For the rest of his long life when in active service it was his lot to command and nearly always, whether in peace or war, to command under circumstances of exceptional difficulty.

Carleton arrived in Quebec on September 22nd, 1766, and was sworn in the following day. Murray

THE NEW GOVERNOR

retained the governorship-in-chief for about two more years and his successor was in actual fact his deputy.[1] The holding of a colonial governorship in those times had no necessary connection with its duties and responsibilities. Many of these officers in North American provinces were and had been deputies, while the shadowy figures of their titular chiefs have no place in the local story. Colonel Irving had, of course, been merely a temporary administrator during the short interval between Murray and Carleton. The latter received three simultaneous addresses from the council, the magistrates, and the traders of both nationalities, all couched in cordial and respectful language. To these he returned suitable replies, declaring among other things that he intended to make no distinction between classes, but only between the worthy and the unworthy.

I have already described the discontent existing among all parties, and during Irving's brief administration expectancy of changes to come had increased the general anxiety. Carleton wrote home to his government that he was favourably impressed with the good sense of the reception addresses. He notes that these separate addresses were due to the fact of the people, from mutual jealousies, being unable to act together. The effect of the Stamp Act, too, was already visible in Canada, for he writes that there had been some

[1] Carleton was appointed governor, January 12th, 1768.

SIR GUY CARLETON

objections to the addresses on that account and many bloody noses. He found enough friction also in the matter of the Indian trade at the western posts to call for judicial treatment. One of his earliest experiences was characteristic. He had ventured to consult privately two or three of his council on some matter in which they had special experience; whereupon the remainder sent him a remonstrance against so unconstitutional a proceeding. Carleton snubbed them very severely, replying that in any matter where the formal consent of the council was not required, he should consult whom he chose, not merely such members as were best qualified to give advice on the subject in hand but any persons outside whose opinion might be considered of value. " The movers of this protest," he says, " are Mabane, who was a surgeon's mate in the army, Murray, a strolling player, and Mounier, the solitary French-Canadian member, an honest trader who will sign anything his friends ask him to." What made the rebuff more direct was the fact that Colonel Irving had signed the protest, at the same time excusing the governor to his friends on the plea that his action had been merely an accident. Carleton replied that it was nothing of the kind, and that he intended always to consult such men as he could find of good sense, candour and impartial justice, and who preferred their duty to the king and the tranquillity of his subjects to unjustifiable attachments, party zeal and selfish, mercenary laws.

HIS DISINTERESTEDNESS

If strict impartiality was then possible in Quebec those possessing it must have thought that they had a governor after their own heart.[1]

In November the Jesuits, thinking that Murray had gone beyond the king's wishes in refusing their reinstatement, petitioned the Crown, de Glapion, superior in Quebec, forwarding the address through Carleton. It set forth that the order was established in Canada by the benevolence of French kings; that its chief purposes were: firstly, the instruction of Indians in the knowledge of God; and secondly, the education of youth; and that they had been unable since the siege of Quebec to carry on their work from want of teachers and buildings, such of the latter as were left to them being occupied as storehouses or officers' quarters. They prayed that Murray's order against their receiving either European or Canadian students be revoked, and that their buildings be restored with indemnification for damage.

In the same month the new governor gave an unmistakable instance of the singlemindedness and high sense of honour which distinguished him throughout life in relinquishing by proclamation all the fees and perquisites attached to his office. Carleton was not a rich man, and no sort of stigma had ever attached to what were legalized payments. Indeed Murray took some offence, for he regarded Carleton's action as reflecting in some sort on him-

[1] See appendix H.

SIR GUY CARLETON

self, an intention which Sir Guy hastened to repudiate. He informed his government that he thought it unbecoming in the governor of a distant province to receive such emoluments. The province he said had been impoverished by the war, the frauds of Bigot and the retreat of many of the richest families, so that the imposition was burdensome. " There is a certain appearance of dirt, a sort of meanness in exacting fees on every occasion. I think it necessary for the king's service that his representative at least should be thought unsullied." He thought the fees for higher licences should be increased for the good of the people, and he would apply the surplus for the relief of the distressed *noblesse* who had hitherto depended largely on the French Crown.

At this same time too, in Carleton's first autumn, the Walker affair of two years before, which still remained a mystery, broke out again, as a witness had come forward to swear to the persons who had assaulted the much hated magistrate. He was in truth a lame sort of pillar on which to rest a case—a discharged soldier of the 28th Regiment, named M'Govoch. This man lodged information against the following gentlemen for participation in the outrage: Saint Luc de La Corne, a well-known French officer, Captain Disney of the 44th, Captain Campbell of the 27th and Captain Fraser, who, it will be remembered, was the indignant paymaster, and a Mr. Joseph Howard. All these persons were arrested in their beds in Montreal and

THE WALKER INCIDENT AGAIN

taken to Quebec, Walker objecting to their being bailed since he declared that his life would be in danger. Carleton must have been at some disadvantage in dealing with an affair which had been wholly outside his personal knowledge, though there had been much talk about it two years before in London The Walker view of it seemed at that distance the only possible one to take, besides which the plaintiff had friends there to suppress his own extravagances of temper and pretention, and to represent him as a normal sort of person and the victim of unprovoked aggression. Carleton's new chief-justice was Hey, an able and sensible man to judge from his writings, and he was distinctly prejudiced against Walker. Masères, the attorney-general, had an opposite bias, from the fact that as a French Huguenot of a family driven from France in a former generation he was a bitter opponent of everything connected with popery, and in this business a somewhat aggressive Protestant was ranged against soldiers who were at this time in general sympathy with the Canadian *noblesse*, one of whom indeed was actually a prisoner. Masères it may be noted was a fellow of Clare, Cambridge, and had achieved considerable academic distinction. Walker was backed by a strong and trenchant letter from Conway who had been a secretary of state in the preceding March.

The prisoners were now thrown into the common jail, and were refused bail in spite of urgent petitions signed by influential people of all kinds, members of the council, leading French-Canadians, and of course the British officers. They were soon afterwards, however, sent back to Montreal and some improvement in their comfort was eventually made. Walker wished the trial to be deferred, presumably that the prisoners' discomfort might be prolonged. Hey consented, but in such case would admit the prisoners to bail. This action not commending itself to Walker the trial proceeded. On the first case, that of Lieutenant Evans, being thrown out by the grand jury, Walker let loose the vials of his wrath in court, which did not increase the public sympathy for him. Masères prosecuted for the Crown and made some unsuccessful efforts to reconstitute the grand jury upon ancient statutes, which the chief-justice pronounced to be doubtful and odious. In short the grand jury, eight of whom were of the French-Canadian *noblesse*, threw out the bills against all but Disney who was now a major. This officer was tried in March, and after a hearing of eight hours and the examination of many witnesses was "most honourably acquitted" having proved an alibi, the jury taking no more than the time occupied in reading out the notes of the depositions to come to that verdict. M'Govoch, the discharged soldier and chief witness for the prosecution, contradicted himself so deplorably under examination that the grand jury presented him for perjury, and he was sent to prison. There really appears from the voluminous

HIS MISSIONS

correspondence on the subject to have been something like collusion between this man and Walker, or as Hey puts it in a lengthy report, Walker's animus against the military cast had caused him to forget caution in the kind of character whose assistance, as a witness, he called in. One indirect result of the trial was the dismissal by Carleton of Colonel Irving and Mabane from the council.[1] Before the Walker trial they had headed a miscellaneously organized crowd of petitioners on behalf of the prisoners, a proceeding which Carleton objected to in their capacity of councillors. So ended this mysterious and quite remarkable affair. One grudges the time occupied in going through the papers relating to it only to come to the same conclusion as all other chroniclers of the period, *i.e.*, that though there must have been many people at the time who knew or suspected the truth, it is absolutely hidden from any later student of the voluminous literature relating to it. It cannot be ignored, however, in the incidents of Carleton's period since it shook Canada from end to end, and exhibits the curious cleavages that just then existed in Canadian society.

Carleton's first mission, from 1766 to 1778, was to attach the French and save the colony from the tremendous magnetism of the American republic. His second, from 1786 to 1796, was to reconstitute the country when two rival races of about equal

[1] See appendix I.

SIR GUY CARLETON

strength were struggling in unsympathetic and dangerous fashion for mastery, and the seeds of future greatness had actually been sown.

The chief domestic question of the colony continues to be its legal code, or rather lack of one. Against the English criminal law there had never been a murmur save from a few seigniors who thought it over lenient. In the civil code, besides their general aversion to it, the feudal prejudices of all the upper class caused them to cavil at *habitants* being elevated to the dignity of jurymen. It is supposed that these latter took as yet very little interest in the matter, beyond the dull, latent suspicion of change natural to a class politically and intellectually dumb. The discussions and disagreements lay between the few hundred British and French traders and Canadian seigniors, notaries and doctors. It is difficult to say how much of English civil law was forced upon the French-Canadians, but speaking generally the struggle to do so was gradually abandoned, sometimes from weariness, sometimes by special ordinance. One trouble in regard to land laws was that when it suited the interests of a French-Canadian to be guided by English custom he followed it even after its nominal abandonment, and there were often persons who adopted such means only in order to shirk the more beneficent clauses in the French code. Seigniors for instance would make terms more advantageous for themselves than their own laws had allowed, or tenants

THE JUDICIAL SYSTEMS

would build wretched houses on smaller areas than was permitted by Canadian custom. In conveying land also, fines and dues were shirked on the pretext of this otherwise ignored English code.[1]

The French chafed at the delays and the costs of the new courts, their own system having been quicker and cheaper. The grievance was recognized and more frequent sittings were given; French lawyers were permitted to plead and in their own language. The salaries, too, seemed extravagant to the French, accustomed to a perennial scarcity of money. The ordinances regulating the courts having been published in French, the fact that the English language as well as law was generally unintelligible made the hostility to the latter stronger from this very ignorance, while the arrogance of the small English community bred an unceasing dislike of the British law simply because it was British. Carleton himself believed in the English criminal and French civil law in their respective entirety, but he had too much sense to set up his own views on codes and statutes against those of professional jurists. He ordered his attorney-general, Masères, to draw up a report, although it was felt that this honest and able man was hampered by his immovable prejudices. He made four suggestions to Carleton. The first was to draw up an entirely fresh code; though the technical difficulties, Masères declared, were immense, and the erudition required would

[1] See appendix J.

SIR GUY CARLETON

involve the services of the highest lawyers of France. The plan, however, would have the advantage of terminating that constant reference to old French precedents which kept alive the reverence for everything emanating from France. The second plan was that of Carleton's—to retain the French civil law and abolish the criminal code, which included questions by torture, breaking on the wheel, and such like barbarities, and to introduce the *habeas corpus*. The third choice was to make English law universal, retaining only some of the ancient customs which were harmless; and the fourth was practically the same, only stipulating that the reservations in the way of French law should be distinctly tabulated. These last two schemes would have satisfied the English community, but the French feared the lack of finality about any interference with their own civil code, though they might have accepted a new Canadian one if the difficulties of creating it had not been thought by the attorney-general to be insuperable.

The validity of Murray's proclamation of 1762[1] ordaining that English law was to be followed with certain vague reservations, was being questioned on the grounds that it had not the consent of both Houses. In short, something like chaos pervaded the whole legal machinery of Canada at this time, and compromise was made more difficult by the irritation between the French and British parties in the two

[1] See appendix K.

DIVERGENT VIEWS

cities. The British ministry was very anxious to find a *via media*, and in June 1767, Shelburne wrote very strongly to that effect to Carleton, and in December acquaints him that Mr. Maurice Morgan had been ordered to Canada to study the legal situation, with the assistance of the chief-justice of the colony and other "well instructed persons." The upshot of all this was much consultation in 1769 between the legal authorities of the colony, Carleton, and the home government, with a view to some definite codification of Canadian laws. It would weary the reader for little purpose to relate the divergent views of the various prominent persons concerned in these transactions which were ultimately welded into the Quebec Act of 1774, a period we have not yet reached. A letter from Carleton to Shelburne under date November 25th, 1767, partly explains his personal adherence to an undiluted French civil code, and makes it quite evident that he did not anticipate any numerical increase in the British population of the province. Ontario, it must be remembered, was still an unconsidered wilderness and the American revolution, with its resulting flood of United Empire Loyalists, as yet in the lap of the future. At the same time Carleton was prepared to apply his views to a country whose western limits were ill-defined and vast, and which virtually included what is now known as the middle west of the United States, and this must be accounted against him and those who thought with him.

SIR GUY CARLETON

The letter alluded to is written in reply to a notification of the British government that the civil constitution of Quebec was a matter of immediate concern to them, and it gives a brief sketch of the province as seen by Carleton. The town of Quebec, he declares, is the only post in the province with any claim to be called a fortified place, for the flimsy wall about Montreal, even were it not falling to ruins, could only turn musketry. As for Quebec it would be a good camp for ten or twelve battalions. Its front is fortified by a bastioned rampart faced with masonry, built for the most part upon a rock without ditch or outworks; its profile slight for a fortress, though substantial for an encampment; its parapet in very bad order. The flanks and rear in 1759 were closed partly by a thin wall, the rest by great stakes now carried away on rollers. With a number of men sufficient for this post, their flanks and rear might be secured and so guarded as to induce an enemy to form his attack in front; but in proportion as the numbers fall short the danger increases of being stormed with little ceremony, especially when this line is open in many places as at present. Carleton goes on to say that the total number of troops now with him is sixteen hundred and that the king's old subjects, i.e., the British, if collected from the rest of the province into Quebec might amount to four hundred. With two months' hard labour they might then place the town in a proper state of defence and he would then have just about one third of the

THE NOBLESSE OF CANADA

number requisite for defending it. In view of a war with France, Carleton points out that the king's new subjects could put into the field eighteen thousand men well able to carry arms, about half of whom had already served with as much valour, more zeal, and more military knowledge for American purposes than the regular troops of France who acted with them. As the common people are greatly influenced by their seigniors he encloses a list of the *noblesse* of Canada, showing with tolerable exactness their age, rank, and present place of abode, together with such natives of France as had served in the colonial troops so early in life as to give them knowledge of the country. This list mentions over a hundred officers all ready to be sent back in case of war to a country with which they are intimately acquainted, and who may with the assistance of regular troops stir up a people accustomed to pay them implicit obedience. "On the other hand," he continues, "there are only some seventy of these officers in Canada who have been in the French service, but not one of them has been given commissions in King George's service, nor is any substantial inducement held out to them to support the king's government. These gentlemen it must be remembered have lost their employments by becoming his subjects, and as they are not bound by any offices of trust or profit we should only deceive ourselves by supposing they would be active in defence of a people who had deprived them of their honours, pri-

SIR GUY CARLETON

vileges, profits and laws, and in their stead have introduced much expense, chicanery and confusion, with a deluge of new laws unknown and unpublished. While, therefore, matters continue in their present state, the most we can hope for from the gentlemen who remain in the province, is a passive neutrality on all occasions, with a respectful submission to government. This they almost to a man have persevered in since my arrival, notwithstanding that much pains have been taken to engage them in parties by a few whose duty and whose office should have taught them better." The French minister, Carleton continues, seems to have foreseen this disposition and to have done his best to attract them to France where they would be useful in any war with England. All these officers were assigned quarters in Touraine. They received, so long as they remained there, full pay upon a recently increased scale, and this was offered, together with arrears, to any of those remaining in Canada who might choose to return to France.

Having given the disproportionate strength of His Majesty's old and new subjects in Canada, Carleton proceeds to indulge in prophetic utterances. "There is not the least probability" he continues, "that this superiority of numbers will diminish; on the contrary it will increase and strengthen daily. The Europeans who emigrate will never prefer the long inhospitable winter of Canada to the more cheerful climate and more fruitful soil of His Majesty's southern prov-

TRADE AND POPULATION

inces. The few old subjects at present in this province are mostly here by accident, and are either disbanded officers, soldiers, or followers of the army who, not knowing how to dispose of themselves elsewhere, settled where they were left at the reduction, or else they are adventurers in trade, or such as could not remain at home who set out to mend their fortunes at the opening of this new channel for commerce. But experience has taught almost all of them that this trade requires a strict frugality, which they are all strangers to, or to which they will not submit. So that many have left the province and I greatly fear many more, for the same reasons, will follow their example in a few years. But while this severe climate and the poverty of the country discourages all but the natives, its healthfulness is such that these multiply daily, so that barring a catastrophe shocking to think of, this country to the end of time must be peopled by the Canadian race, who already have taken such firm root that any new stock transplanted will be totally and imperceptibly hid amongst them, except in the towns of Quebec and Montreal." Of all the Canada that then existed and that Carleton knew, his forecast was a sufficiently accurate one. This illuminating letter winds up with military suggestions for the defence of Canada, and the building of a proper citadel in Quebec, proposed plans for which Carleton encloses. His list of the Canadian *noblesse* gives one hundred and twenty-six heads of families, or independent

SIR GUY CARLETON

bachelors resident in the colony, three fourths of whom are in the district of Montreal, and seventy-nine resident in France as officers.

Many private individuals among the English population of Canada were in the habit of communicating their views on the state of the colony to the home government, and a favourite burden of their theme was the dark plots they believed the French population to be engaged in for overthrowing British authority and regaining the country for France. Carleton seems to have thought it worth while to allay the anxiety thus created in the minds of the government by one very full letter on this subject which was transmitted in 1768. In this he says that since his arrival he has not been able to discover any signs of such secret assemblies, nor could he believe that the chiefs of their own free notion in time of peace would dare to assemble in any numbers to consult and resolve on a revolt, nor was it credible that any assembly of military men should be so ignorant as to fancy they could defend themselves by only a few fireships against any future attack from Great Britain after the experience of '59. Nevertheless it seemed to Carleton that in spite of their "decent and respectful obedience to the king's government hitherto, there was no doubt of their secret and natural affection for France, an affection that would continue so long as they were excluded from all appointments in the British service and they were certain of being reinstated at

MILITARY SERVICE

least in their former commissions with a return to French dominion; for it was by such employment they chiefly supported themselves and their families."

Considering the vexations in the matter of fees and the frequent litigation that the Canadians had been put to, and that their British rulers had never taken a single step to gain one man in the province by making it his private interest to remain the king's subject, Carleton owns that the fact of his never having discovered any treasonable correspondence was not proof sufficient that none existed; but if so, probably very few were entrusted with the secret. A false report had been sent over secretly to France in the previous year that the king of England intended raising a regiment of his new subjects, and on its being echoed back to Canada most of the seigniors in the province had applied to Carleton to admit them into the king's service, assuring him that they would take every opportunity of testifying their zeal and gratitude for "so great a mark of favour and tenderness extended not only to them but to their posterity." "When I further consider," wrote Carleton, "that the king's dominion here is maintained by a few troops, necessarily dispersed, without a place of security for their magazines, for their arms or themselves, amidst a numerous military people, the gentlemen all officers, poor without hopes that they or their descendants will be admitted into the service of their present sovereign, I can

SIR GUY CARLETON

have no doubt but that France as soon as deter mined to begin a war, will attempt to regain Canada should it be intended only to make a diversion, while it may reasonably be undertaken with little hazard should it fail, and when so much may be gained should it succeed."

Carleton evidently thought it possible, though six years were to pass before the Declaration of Independence, that the American colonies would attempt to support their views by armed force, and thus wrote to Lord Hillsborough. In such case France would probably come to their assistance, when Canada would be the principal scene, so Carleton imagined, of the critical struggle, and Canada in the hands of France would be no longer, as of old, the enemy of the British provinces but their ally and protector. Carleton could not then realize how anxious, and rightly anxious, the Americans would be to give France no excuse for reoccupying her ancient territory. He pointed out the disadvantage Canada as a British province would be under in such an eventuality, unless they did something practical to win the allegiance of the French-Canadians. On the other hand he indicated how ardently Canada might permanently support British interests on the American continent, in view of the fact that she was not united in any common principle with the other provinces in their already budding opposition to the supreme government. Carleton indeed is repeatedly admonishing the home

THE CORRECTION OF ABUSES

government to the effect that one of these alternatives is necessary for the security of the colony in the course of a war which he already foresees—either a great force of troops or some method of attaching the population to the Crown. How true was his foreboding and how consistent his application of the latter principle is a matter of history and common knowledge. In all this secret correspondence both Hillsborough and the king himself cordially approved of Carleton's recommendations and regarded them as "of the utmost use in assisting those plans now under deliberation on the propriety and necessity of extending to that brave and faithful people a reasonable participation in those establishments which are to form the bases of the future government of the province of Quebec." But Hillsborough feared that the clamours and prejudices which attacked every measure, however judicious, would make the question of military service a difficult one, though personally he quite agreed that the experiment should be tried.

Maurice Morgan was all this time investigating the legal difficulties of the colony with the assistance of Masères and others. Carleton viewed with concern the abuses that were inevitable to the situation and set himself to cure some that were not so. Among the last were the scandalous methods pursued by many justices of the peace to excite litigation among the people for the sake of the fees accruing to themselves. Those who prospered in business

SIR GUY CARLETON

could not spare the time to sit in court, while such as "from accidents or ill-judged undertakings became bankrupts sought to repair their broken fortunes at the expense of the people." These precious justices employed bailiffs of doubtful character, disbanded French soldiers or deserters, and virtually entered into collusion with them, dispersing them throughout the parishes armed with blank citations. Their rôle was to promote factious litigation and to catch at every little feud or dissension among the people, and encourage suits in cases which might easily be amicably settled were the parties left to themselves. The unfortunate *habitants* were then mulcted in costs far beyond the value of the often trifling sums they were incited to sue for; with ruin as the result in innumerable cases. Carleton declared "there was not a Protestant butcher or publican that became bankrupt who did not apply to be made a justice. They cantoned themselves upon the country and many of them rode the people with despotic sway, imposed fines which they turned to their own profit, and in a manner regarded themselves as the legislators of the province. Three or four hundred families have been turned out of their houses, land sold for not one eighth of its value, debtors ruined and debts still undischarged, fees absorbing everything." Carleton himself ordered the release of a number of imprisoned debtors whose liabilities averaged about two pounds apiece! In one of the many tours he took through

USELESS LITIGATION

the country the outcry of the people concerning these abuses was general and bitter.

Imprisonment for debt was a new experience to the *habitants*. A respected and venerable French captain of militia wrote a letter to Carleton setting forth the situation in simple but trenchant terms. "Every day may be seen only suit upon suit for nothing; for twenty or thirty score suits are entered which usually amount up to forty, fifty or sixty livres, owing to the multitude of expenses heaped on these poor people by bailiffs appointed by the authority of the justices of the peace. These bailiffs are instigators of unjust suits. They entice the poor people who know nothing of the matter to get suits against each other. These writs the bailiffs carry in blank, which require only the addition of the name of the plaintiff and defendant and the date of appearance. I send one as a curiosity for your Excellency to judge by of it. It often happens that a single person has several citations to answer at different courts on the same day, and this being impossible he is condemned by default. Thereupon the bailiffs seize, carry off and sell everything these poor men may be possessed of. Frequently when these alleged bailiffs go to make a seizure should there be no one in the house and the doors locked they break open the door to get in; and these manifold robberies reduce the poor peasant to the lowest beggary. If the goods seized and carried off are not sufficient to discharge the multitude of costs laid on

SIR GUY CARLETON

for the travelling costs of the bailiffs and otherwise, a warrant of imprisonment is obtained, and thus after having been robbed of all they have and possess in the world, their furniture as well as their cattle, these persons are finally laid hold of as a guarantee, that the tyranny may be complete. I should never finish were I to attempt giving the whole story of the sad situation in which these poor people are placed, who are very tractable and whom I have guided for the space of twenty-five years as captain and very often as judge."

This was no highly coloured picture. The report of the government committee on the administration of justice, prepared for the Crown and issued in September 1769, and approved by Carleton and his council, amply endorses the old French captain's evidence, quoting among other instances one where the expense of collecting a debt of eleven livres amounted to eighty! It is not surprising that the blessings of English civil law as administered by the British community from Quebec and Montreal were not wholly appreciated by the French-Canadians, to the infinite prejudice of many undoubted benefits of British rule. As a remedy to this iniquitous state of things Carleton caused a fresh ordinance to be passed and approved by the king early in 1770, the object of which was to give cheap and honest justice in all such cases. The power of the magistrates in suits affecting personal and real property was withdrawn or curtailed.

A HOUSE OF ASSEMBLY

Something similar to the "Homestead Exemption Act" now in use in the United States was enacted, protecting the peasant against seizure of certain necessaries of life and industry, and no execution was to be issued for sums of less than twelve pounds against land or houses. Proper courts were instituted for all these transactions. The ordinance created a great outcry among British traders and a deputation waited upon Carleton presenting a long table of objections. But Carleton stood firm in the fact that more respectable and industrious peasants had been ruined by this chicanery than there were British residents in the whole of Canada. The outraged magistrates, among whom Carleton admitted were some most worthy men, made a violent struggle for the repeal of the ordinances, and issued handbills calling a meeting of the people to discuss grievances, importuning and even insulting some French-Canadians because they would not join them.

The agitation for a House of Assembly that had been so lively in Murray's time was less pronounced under Carleton, but it never wholly ceased. In 1768 a petition in favour of it was taken round for signature, but the French seigniors, in spite of some plausible modifications of the Protestant monopoly, were wholly against it, while the *habitant* had as yet not the faintest perception of its meaning. Carleton's views on the subject may be inferred from his frequently written opinions of the men who would comprise such a parliament, and need no further

SIR GUY CARLETON

definition. Even if this fraction of the population had been of a good representative type in breeding and education, the absurdity of their attempt to impose their will on the colony would seem obvious enough. Nor again, to take a lower motive, could any colonial governor with ordinary official interest have been anxious to reproduce on Canadian soil the wranglings that distinguished the capital of nearly every American province at that moment. Carleton, however, conscious of his own integrity, his knowledge of men and keen desire to be just and impartial, could scarcely have regarded the agitation of the British handful in Canada for such monopoly without contempt. He was always courteous, however, even to those who he had reason to think ill deserved courtesy, and we find few complaints of the snubs which the hotter-headed Murray administered to his tormentors.

Morgan and Masères sailed for England in 1770, about the same time, with full reports on the state of the province. Both men were to prove useful in drafting the new constitution which was to be considered at some length in London.

CHAPTER III

THE QUEBEC ACT

CARLETON soon after this returned himself to England, but in the meantime we have anticipated somewhat, and must take note of some of the minor incidents and duties that helped to occupy the busy hours of his first four years of office in Canada. His deputy-governorship ended in 1768, when Murray resigned his titular appointment, a detail, however, without significance in our story. The troubles which were seething in the provinces to the south had affected Canada as yet but little. The Stamp Act and all that followed was a trifling matter among the more vital issues which agitated the Canadians. While the New Englanders were concerned with the rights of man and splitting hairs on constitutional questions, they were smuggling rum into Canada and sorely interfering with the revenue on wines and spirits which Carleton was anxious to raise, both on account of his meagre budget and for reasons moral and sanitary. The two chief questions, however, which stood out in Canadian politics, after the more pressing ones relating to legal and military matters, were the Church and the western fur trade with all its Indian complications. Everything concerning the former was under con-

SIR GUY CARLETON

sideration pending the settlement of the affairs of the colony, and in Carleton's opinion it required most delicate handling. The Jesuits had been constantly importuning him for the recovery of their property and influence. The bishop and clergy sent a petition to England in favour of retaining their services for the education of youth and for missions among the Indians, for which last duties they had been accustomed, before the conquest, to receive fourteen thousand livres a year from the king of France. The bishop, Briand, was a loyal and quiet living man, and Carleton writes that far from maintaining any undue state and pretention, as certain persons had reported, he had modest quarters at the seminary at Quebec, even feeding at the common table. He had especially repudiated any pomp and ceremony when he came out, contemporaneously with Carleton, professing only to be an ordainer of priests and wearing a plain black gown, to be exchanged in time, however, for the purple robe and the golden cross—the usual insignia of the Roman Episcopate.

The Indian war in Murray's time had materially upset the western trade. The posts had been reoccupied and secured, but Carleton had constant troubles in dealing with the complaints of the Montreal merchants against the way in which the trade permits and rules were interpreted by the officers of the posts. The French-Canadians in the west were always suspected of intriguing against the British power, while the interests of Canada were materially

REPORT ON MANUFACTURES

opposed to those of New York, Virginia, and Pennsylvania, whose traders were in a sense her rivals. Carleton had applied for leave to return to England on private affairs for a brief period in 1769. The moment, however, not seeming propitious, he had postponed his departure and it was not till August in the following year that he left Canada. He went home nominally for six months but there was much to be done in framing the new constitution. His advice was indispensable and he remained four years. His deputy in Canada was the lieutenant-governor Cramahé, the Swiss officer already frequently mentioned who had done good work as a councillor throughout the administrations of both Murray and Carleton. He had been Murray's secretary and was most highly thought of by that officer, and as we know had been sent on a mission to London to represent the condition of the province to the British government. He had also been governor of Three Rivers, between Quebec and Montreal.

Shortly before leaving his government Carleton sent home a report on the manufactures of the country. We gather from this that flax was generally cultivated, but was mainly utilized by the people for a coarse linsey-woolsey, woven of wool and thread for the clothing of the men. All caps were imported from England. A coarse earthenware was in use and some tanneries were producing an indifferent kind of leather; the best leather being

[1] See appendix L.

imported from the British colonies. The forges at St. Maurice turned out forty thousand weight of bar iron annually. Edge tools and axes of a serviceable kind for both whites and Indians were manufactured. A small business in pearl-ash and potash with a rum distillery complete the list. Carleton says nothing of the timber which must have been an article of trade, masts for the navy being one item of export.

For the next four years Carleton was watching over the interests of the Canadians, while measures, momentous in their consequences to the latter, were being discussed and prepared. The Canadians at home under the sufficiently able direction of Cramahé were awaiting those ordinances which were to decide their future with a patience arising from their confidence in a speedy settlement. There would be little to say of the colony during Carleton's absence, even were the subject quite relevant to the title of this book, except that it pursued a tolerably uneventful life, in spite of the chaotic conditions of its legal machinery. The British party presented another petition for a representative assembly and persuaded a few of their French fellow-subjects to confer with them on the subject, but the presence of eight of them at the conference was the limit of their coöperation. They could not persuade, even had they wished, any more of their people to evince an enthusiasm for a parliament chosen from four hundred British-American Protestants. Ninety-one of the latter, only five of them being freeholders,

PETITION AND COUNTER PETITION

signed the petition, but Cramahé replied that it was too important a matter for a lieutenant-governor to decide. This seems only to have been expected, and another petition, somewhat more cautiously framed as regards the exclusion of Roman Catholics, was sent to the king with one hundred and fifty-eight signatures, mainly British. The French had decided to forward a petition of their own. This, however, bore only about fifty signatures and related mainly to matters legal and lingual, for it is hardly necessary to reiterate that the French-Canadians had little interest in representative government, though the document advanced a claim for civil and military employment. It did, indeed, suggest an assembly, but only on condition of a full representation of the French-Canadians. The desire even for this was expressed in luke-warm fashion, either from the lack of political fervour which distinguished the petitioners at that time, or from a feeling that such a concession was hopeless from a British government. But they evinced no such indifference regarding the prospect of a Protestant parliament, for the seigniors were "utterly unwilling to consent to a House of Assembly from which they should be excluded." They prayed for their own laws, hinting at the financial benefit this would be to the government on account of the feudal dues and profits accruing to it under the old custom. They prayed also for the restoration of Labrador to Canada as well as those portions of the West which

SIR GUY CARLETON

the country had lost since it became a British province.

Carleton on reaching England found that his own views, formed on long experience, were practically identical with those of the home authorities derived from equity and theory. Yorke and de Grey, attorney-general and solicitor-general some years before, had already pronounced in a long and learned report against "new and unnecessary and arbitrary rules (especially as to the titles of land, mode of descent, alienation and settlement) which would tend to confound and subvert rights, instead of supporting them." Now in 1772 Thurlow the attorney-general, and Wedderburne solicitor-general, argued on the same lines, declaring the French-Canadians entitled by the *jus gentium* to their property, as they possessed it upon the treaty of peace, together with all its qualities and incidents by tenure or otherwise. Dr. Marriott, the advocate-general, was of the same opinion, and agreed with the others in thinking it inexpedient under the circumstances to call an assembly. Masères alone was somewhat opposed to Carleton, taking the view that the *habitants* on the whole were in favour of English law, as it gave them relief from the "insolent and capricious treatment of their superiors" (the seigniors). He thought they would have expressed this opinion freely but from the fear that their religion would be endangered.

Masères' strong prejudices as well as his un-

THE QUEBEC ACT

doubted integrity and abilities have been already noticed. He had the honesty, however, to avow in answer to a query of Lord North's, that he did not think certain points of English procedure would be followed even if they were introduced. Chief-Justice Hey and de Lotbinière, a prominent French-Canadian, also rendered assistance with their advice. Four years seems a long period for the consideration, drafting, and passing of the Quebec Act, a measure which Bourinot calls "the charter of the special privileges which the French-Canadians have enjoyed ever since." But it was not till May 17th, 1774, that the Act was introduced into the House of Lords, a procedure which offended some members of the Lower House and gave them an excuse for taking a brief part in the discussion. But few were qualified to share in it, and but a meagre House took the trouble either to listen or to vote. Carleton was of course greatly in evidence throughout the whole of this protracted business and, when the bill came down to the Commons, was called as the leading witness, together with Chief-Justice Hey, Masères, de Lotbinière and Marriott.

The delimitation of Canada was the weakest part of the bill, for it practically followed the old lines of the French claims extending through contentious territory, outraging the geographical susceptibilities, if not the rights, of Virginia and Pennsylvania, and terminating at the Mississippi, while to the northward the Hudson's Bay Company's territory was

SIR GUY CARLETON

the far away limit to this immense region. Canada beyond a doubt in matters of constructive legislation should have been limited to the more immediately occupied regions, terminating, say, at the eastern end of Lake Ontario. The West, virtually untouched as yet but by hunters, traders, and garrisons, should have been retained under temporary administration to await future lines of development.[1] The emigration of the United Empire Loyalists settled this question in a satisfactory but unlooked-for way. As it was, those who were hostile to the retention by the French of their laws and religion had some reason in objecting to their establishment over millions of fertile acres yet untouched.

The Quebec Act, speaking broadly, gave sanction and definition to existing usages rather than to new ones—full freedom of religion to the Roman Catholics together with recognition of the ancient means of collecting dues. In all the branches of civil law the Canadian custom was preserved, while the criminal code of England being more merciful and already popular with the French subjects, was confirmed in perpetual use. An assembly was for the present withheld, the administration to be continued vested in a governor with executive and legislative council to consist of not less than seventeen nor more than twenty-three members.[2]

This was the drift of the Act. The minor clauses,

[1] See appendix M.

[2] See appendix N.

CONTEMPORARY OPINION

conventional or precautionary, are of slight moment here. There was a great deal of opposition. The self-interest of a few in England, the religious prejudices of the many, the wrath of the British-American colonies, were stirred to the depths. The debate on the bill continued through the 6th, 7th, 8th and 10th of June. It was carried in committee by eighty-three to forty and on the third reading was carried by fifty-six to twenty. On June 18th, 1774, it was sent back to the Lords and immediately passed, though opposed by Chatham, by twenty to seven votes.

Some of the comments of members and scraps of the evidence of Carleton and his witnesses merit notice. Among the former Mr. Dunning remarked that he would as soon see the country restored to France at once as that arbitrary government should be set up at the back of the colonies where people going in would pass from liberty to despotism. The liberty-loving Mr. Dunning, however, would have cheerfully consigned the lives and liberties of nearly one hundred thousand old inhabitants to the dominion of a few hundred somewhat ill-qualified strangers. There was much more logic in his suggestion, however foolishly expressed, that the vast wilderness about to be added to Quebec by a British Act of parliament would be claimed on that account by France should a retrocession of Canada ever become a question of policy or necessity, and still more in his criticism of the wide geographical extension of the Act.

SIR GUY CARLETON

Lord North said that a legislature was withheld from the lack of eligible people. Mr. Townshend desired a government for Canada, not a despotism, a government, that is, by a Protestant faction. This gives to us of the twentieth century another curious instance of the mental attitude of the eighteenth century British Protestant. It is only perhaps when quite fresh from an excursion into the century preceding that it is possible to feel such a measure of sympathy with these people as is unquestionably their due. The error of judging them from a modern standpoint is too elementary a one perhaps to call for mention. The French government had shewn itself to be even less liberal in matters of religion than our own worst-seeming bigots proposed to be. The attorney-general, Thurlow, on the other hand, thought it unjust to compel the French to use English laws of property and inheritance. Sergeant Glyn considered the nation bound to conform to the generous measures of the king's proclamation of 1763. Wedderburne, the solicitor-general, opined that to force English law upon the Canadians would prove a curse. Fox objected to the Lords having taken the initiative in introducing the bill and professed a proper horror of popery. Two or three members wasted what was really valuable time as the session was closing in discussing the arrogance of the House of Lords in this matter, and asked the speaker for his opinion, whereat that official snubbed them with heat and

EVIDENCE AND OPINION

decision. Colonel Barré declared it to be preposterous to suppose that the Canadians would fail to recognize the superiority of good and just (i.e., English) laws. Another member on the behalf of Pennsylvania complained that the limits of the new province cut right through their territory, but he was assured by North that vested interests would be protected.

Messrs. Mackworth and Townshend demanded that the written opinions of the Canadians and British law officials should be produced, and found many supporters. It was answered that at so late a period the delay would be fatal, whereupon Burke remarked that the delay of a year would be a less evil than to pass a bill without proper information. It was urged that the verbal information to be given by Carleton and other witnesses would be desultory compared to these opinions. Two witnesses from Canada were examined on behalf of the London merchants who affirmed that Canadians as well as English were anxious for English law and trial by jury. Carleton then gave evidence to the effect that Canadians were willing enough for English criminal law, but in other respects objected to a code of which they were ignorant, embodied in a language they did not understand. They were ready enough for the latter when it happened to favour their particular case. As regards an assembly, the French, said Carleton, felt little interest in it, while the Protestants were neither numerous enough nor

SIR GUY CARLETON

sufficiently eligible. A characteristic incident occurred during the governor's examination when North asked him if he knew aught of a certain Le Brun. "Yes!" said the downright proconsul, "I know him very well. He was a blackguard at Paris and sent as a lawyer to Canada, where he gained an exceedingly bad character in many respects, was taken up and imprisoned for an assault on a young girl eight or nine years old, was fined twenty pounds, but not being able to pay it he was—"

Townshend here interfered and Carleton was asked to withdraw the statement. Then Lord North explained that Le Brun was sent over to represent Canadians in favour of an assembly and English laws, and that it was necessary to know what sort of a man he was. Carleton had probably said enough. Hey differed somewhat from his chief, and thought a blending of the French and English civil code was the best method. Masères spoke in somewhat the same strain. The *habitants* objected to juries on the score of expense which could easily be arranged by a small compensation. Any alteration in the laws of inheritance or land would be offensive to them. They could not, however, object to the *habeas corpus*, while as regards the assembly they had but dim ideas of what it meant. De Lotbinière said that if their land laws remained untouched he thought they would be contented enough with the remainder of the English code. He had never heard the assembly much discussed but thought they

AN APPEAL FROM LONDON

would be satisfied if the *noblesse* were admitted. Marriott, the advocate-general, though his written opinions were clear enough, proved such a sphinx under examination that Colonel Barré declared: "There's no hitting this gentleman."

The corporation of London now appealed to the king to withhold his signature from the bill, professing themselves greatly alarmed for the safety of their Protestant fellow-subjects in the province. That "wonderful effort of human wisdom," trial by jury, not being provided for (in civil cases), they urged that the bill was a breach of the promises made to the British settlers when invited into the province and not in harmony with the promises of His Majesty's declaration of 1763. They deny that any laws or statutes can be ordained for the said province other than those in use in England. King George is reminded of his coronation oath to maintain the Protestant religion, and that his family was called to the throne for that purpose to the exclusion of the Stuart line, that the Roman Catholic religion is known to be idolatrous and bloody, and that the said bill was brought in late in the session when most of the members had retired into the country. It does not seem to have occurred to any of these people that the reconstruction of a community alien in blood and spirit and of ancient origin could not be achieved after the fashion of another Georgia or Virginia, and that no such conditions as now faced the rulers of Canada had been contemplated by those who held these precepts for British people.

In considering this bill it must be remembered that two things had to be taken into account: the troubled state of the American colonies which made the attachment of the French indispensable, and the probability that the country would remain homogeneously French. To judge of this question by English standards is idle. There is a type of mind so wedded to popular shibboleths that it gives but grudging assent to the success of Carleton and to the Quebec Act in saving Canada. The English settlers, mainly traders, had a bad reputatation, and increased slowly, while the French were prolific. The forecast was justified in providing for the attachment of a French province, rather than for a possible inrush of British immigration that before the war did not seem a likely eventuality.

As for the British colonies, the attitude of the recently summoned congress towards the new Act is always one of the most entertaining incidents in American history; for in formulating their grievances against the Crown, the liberal treatment of the French in leaving them their religion had been a burning indictment against king and Commons, and floods of indignation were poured out against the Catholic Church. A famous document declared that the new Act gave legality to a religion which had flooded England with blood, and had spread hypocrisy, murder, persecution, and revolt into all

COLONIAL CRITICISM

parts of the world. This address was circulated throughout the American colonies as a useful stimulant to resistance, and the injury was coupled in Philadelphia with that of the closing of the port of Boston. The reader would not be human who could regard without a smile the endearing address of congress in the autumn of 1774 to the French-Canadians, in which its members recall their joy in 1763, when the King of England granted the Canadians all the rights of Englishmen, in addition to the privileges of their "bloodthirsty, idolatrous, and hypocritical creed," as formerly designated.

The Quebec Act and its indulgences to popish slaves was even now being used as a stick for King George's back in New England, New York, and Philadelphia, by the same men who were shedding documentary tears of a crocodile nature for the woes of the French-Canadians. The latter were treated to a lengthy disquisition, indicating under various heads the ideals without which they could neither be free nor happy. The tenure of land in Canada was a monstrous anachronism, so the Canadians were told, in complete oblivion of the fact that this was a concession from, not an imposition by, "this infamous and tyrannical ministry." They were loaded with sympathy for this criminal withholding of juries, and the misery of existence without them; though this very deprivation was a concession to their own prejudices. They were told in elaborate and bombastic periods

SIR GUY CARLETON

what they ought to do, and what they ought to want, in order to become good Englishmen, and whether they were or not they ought to be profoundly miserable, and that their brethren of the other provinces (who had never before in history had a good word for them), were grievously moved at their degradation. Without an assembly, (of Protestants, of course), they would be slaves. There was no guarantee that even the inquisition might not be set up among them! The addressers knew the liberal spirit of the French-Canadians too well to imagine that religious matters would prejudice them against a hearty amity with themselves. From cajolery the address then proceeded to threats, reminding them of their insignificance, and asked them to choose whether they would be regarded as friends by the rest of the continent or as "inveterate enemies."

This address was translated into French, and circulated among the Canadians, a process made easy by the number of English in Montreal and Quebec who sympathized with the Americans, of whom many were already in the province as political propagandists. The Canadians in short were invited to choose delegates to meet the rest at Philadelphia. The peasantry might be bamboozled with all this, and to a great extent were, but the clergy not so. They had not forgotten the hard words used about them in 1763 and they were aware of the insults heaped on their religion within the last few weeks.

THE SPIDER TO THE FLY

Above all they had every reason to be grateful to the British government, and as many reasons to dislike and distrust the British colonists. The seigniors had almost as good cause to reject these unblushing overtures, and did so to a man, as we shall see. That immortal composition, "Will you walk into my parlour said the spider to the fly," was written for another political occasion, and at another period, but had it been included in the education of the more instructed French-Canadians of that day, it would, no doubt, have leaped to the lips of all of them and been much in vogue.

CHAPTER IV

CARLETON'S MARRIAGE

ALMOST immediately on the passing of the Quebec Act Carleton sailed for Canada and landed on September 18th, 1774. During his long stay in England he had married the Lady Maria Howard, daughter of the Earl of Effingham, who with her two children born of the marriage accompanied her husband across the Atlantic. The lady was less than half Carleton's age, which was now forty-eight. A family tradition attributes the fact of Carleton's remaining so long unmarried to an early disappointment in a love affair with his cousin, Jane Carleton. The circumstances of his marriage were somewhat singular, and were given to me by the present representative of the family. Lord Howard of Effingham, then a widower, was a great personal friend of Carleton's, and of about the same age. On this account and also foreseeing for him a distinguished career, he cordially accepted his overtures for the hand of his eldest daughter, Lady Anne. She and her younger sister, Lady Maria, had seen a great deal of Sir Guy at their father's house, and doubtless regarded him as a benevolent uncle rather than a potential lover. In time, however, they became aware that other schemes were

SIR GUY CARLETON

abroad, and on a certain occasion when Carleton arrived at the house and was closeted with his Lordship it seems to have been pretty well understood what he had come for. The two young ladies were sitting together in another apartment with a relative, a Miss Seymour, and when a message came to Lady Anne that her presence was required by her father its purport seems to have been well known. When this young lady returned to her friends her eyes were red from tears. The others, waiting impatiently for her news, were the more impatient as well as perplexed at her woe-begone appearance. "Your eyes would be red," she replied to their queries, "if you had just had to refuse the best man on earth."

"The more fool you," was the unsympathetic rejoinder of her younger sister, Lady Maria. "I only wish he had given me the chance."

It appears that Lady Anne was already in love with Carleton's nephew, whom she afterwards married and who served under his uncle in Canada.

There the matter rested for some months till Miss Seymour one day confided to Sir Guy what Lord Howard's younger daughter had remarked on hearing of his discomfiture. This so much interested the middle-aged lover, who, no doubt, had recovered from a perhaps not very violent passion, that in due course he presented himself as a suitor for the younger daughter, who proved herself as good as her word. Miss Seymour who lived to old age used

SECOND ARRIVAL IN CANADA

to tell the story to members of the Dorchester family who only passed away in comparatively recent years.

Lady Maria was small and fair, upright and extremely dignified, and was ceremonious to a degree that in her old age almost amounted to eccentricity. She had been brought up and educated at Versailles, which may be held to account for her partiality for the French at Quebec, and may possibly have influenced her husband in the same direction.

Soon after landing Carleton wrote to Dartmouth, now secretary, that he found the king's Canadian subjects impressed with the strongest sense of His Majesty's goodness towards them in the matter of the late bill, and manifesting a strong desire to show themselves not unworthy of the treatment accorded to them. Events to the south, however, which were destined in great measure to upset the governor's sanguine, and justifiably sanguine, expectations, were hurrying forward. For while he was still upon the ocean the first congress had met at Philadelphia and formulated three petitions: one to the king, another to the British public, and that other one to the Canadians already alluded to. Carleton had come back armed with definite machinery for the administration of a province which he had already handled successfully with inefficient weapons. For good or ill the new instrument had been moulded in almost exact accordance with his wishes. But a

SIR GUY CARLETON

war cloud was now rising to the southward which was destined for the moment completely to obscure domestic matters of a peaceful kind. The rôle of wise but beneficent administrator was not yet to be that of Carleton, who was soon to find himself committed to a life and death struggle against desperate odds for the very possession of the colony.

Whatever the wisdom of the Quebec Act, as a matter of domestic policy there is little doubt but that it saved Canada to the British Crown, or rather enabled a resolute commander to perform what at one time seemed a hopeless task. The French population as a whole, it is true, quite failed to justify the reasonable expectations formed of them. But had the Act been so framed that their grievances were real and appealed to their enlightened class, instead of being merely the groundless fears of a deluded peasantry, things would have been much worse even than they were, while a better spirit among the handful of Anglo-American traders would have been of small account amid the clash of arms.

Almost the first letters Carleton received after his return were from General Gage, at Boston, requesting him to despatch there the 10th and 52nd Regiments, a proceeding which left the governor with less than a thousand regulars in the colony. The French subjects, however, took the earliest opportunity of presenting addresses expressing satisfaction with the Act. Even the British of Quebec, in

AGITATION AND INTRIGUE

part at least, followed suit, for partisan feeling was less bitter and pronounced there than in Montreal, whose population, by this time numerically equal to that of the capital, showed little but dissatisfaction. At Montreal meetings were held for the redress of grievances; Walker, smarting with the memory of his injuries, being foremost among the fire-brands, which included one Livingstone, of the famous New York family, who had settled in the neighbourhood as a merchant. Several of these malcontents came to Quebec, greatly to Carleton's disgust, and successfully stimulated the less active discontent of their co-religionists in that city. Letters of sympathy poured in from the colonies, brought in many cases by the hand of political agents who added their insidious eloquence to that of the local orators.[1] Meetings were held after the New England fashion, while missions for fomenting discontent among the *habitants* were privately organized and conducted under the cloak of rural trade. Two clauses of the Quebec Act unfortunately lent themselves readily to misrepresentation; *i.e.*, the legalizing of the tithe which had continued by custom rather than law since the conquest, and the retention of the old French land laws which left to the seigniors such modified control of their estates as they had hitherto enjoyed.

The first could without serious mendacity be pressed home upon the *habitants* as a grievance. As

[1] See appendix O.

to the other matter it was represented that the seigniors had now acquired more than their ancient rights and would revive the *corvées* and other obsolete privileges with more than their former vigour. The agitators multiplied the salaries of the new officials for which the country was to be taxed by ten and sometimes twenty-fold, and went in and out of the thatched and whitewashed houses of the peasantry under the pretense of trade, assuring the people that they would all be miserable slaves liable at any moment to be arrested under *lettres de cachet*, and that their only hope of salvation lay in allowing the American troops a peaceful entry into the country. The *noblesse* on account of their preserved prestige, the notaries who for every reason were attached to the French civil code, and most of the few French *bourgeoisie* were practically secured to the Crown. The clergy were even more attached to it by the late bill, and the priests, one need hardly say, were the most formidable factor whom the emissaries of sedition among their flocks had to encounter. Official Canada with Carleton at its head regarded them as a bulwark of security. It was no fault of theirs that they proved otherwise. The bounds of *habitant* credulity had not yet been fathomed by the new rulers.

By November the "ancient subjects" of Quebec had worked themselves, or been worked up, to the delivery of a petition against the new Act, and throughout the winter the propaganda of sedition

THE FRUITS OF AGITATION

in the country districts was conducted with unabated zeal and remarkable effect. Dark threats were sometimes thrown out by these emissaries of freedom against a rejection of their gospel, and as an alternative to embracing its blessings wholesale an army of fifty thousand men was to enter Canada and with fire and sword lay waste the parishes from Gaspé to Montreal.

The Act was to be put in force on May 1st, 1775. In January Carleton received a despatch enclosing instructions and commissions from Dartmouth, who hoped that a meeting of council might be held before the date of formal inauguration to settle the minor offices, leaving the judicial appointments and ecclesiastical affairs till the arrival of Hey who was coming out, though for a short time only, as chief-justice. Carleton writes to his government that he has grave fears for the effect on the mind of the peasantry caused by sedition-mongers who are moving in such numbers and of set purpose among them. The gentry, he says, are ready enough to serve, but do not relish commanding a militia whose spirit has so obviously changed. As to the peasantry the government had no longer the same hold over them as formerly, the feudal and official influence being greatly weakened. To embody them suddenly and march them off as a militia, even if they would march, would give colour to the stories of impending impression so sedulously circulated by British-American intriguers.

SIR GUY CARLETON

The Act, Carleton intimates, was after all only a foundation for settlement; the whole system of government had to be cast in a new form.

On May 1st, the date of its inauguration, the king's bust in Montreal was daubed black and decorated with a necklace of potatoes, a cross and placard bearing the inscription, "*Voilà le Pape du Canada et le sot Anglais.*" Large sums were offered for the discovery of the culprit. The French upper class were especially indignant, one of them offering a hundred pounds for the arrest of the offender. Personal encounters arising from the incident took place in the streets. It was a strange situation. A clear majority of the British residents—of whom most, it must be remembered, were of American birth—were ripe for revolt, while every Frenchman of the better class was eager to serve the king. The mass of the peasantry was supine, bewildered, suspicious, but so far as one may learn, determined at the moment to stand aloof or to assist the rebels.

During the month of May, 1775, news arrived in Canada that active hostilities had broken out, Ticonderoga and Crown Point, those ancient bases of attack on Canada, having been seized by the rebels, together with the armed craft on Lake Champlain. Carleton in reporting it to the home government had the melancholy consolation of referring to letters written by himself to Gage sometime before, in which he had urged the importance of securing these posts against all risk of surprise.

TICONDEROGA AND CROWN POINT

It was that rude but vigorous Vermonter, Ethan Allen, one need hardly remind the reader, who had accomplished this eminently serviceable but in no way perilous feat. Ticonderoga was garrisoned by an officer and about forty men who were scarcely alive to the serious state of affairs beyond the woods and waters to the southward. It was on the night of May 10th, that Allen with two hundred and fifty men behind him demanded admission to the fort, stating that he had despatches for the commandant. The guard, all unsuspicious, and moreover acquainted with Allen, whose men were invisible, opened the gates, whereat the Vermonters rushed in and secured the soldiers in their beds. After this Crown Point, a few miles away and occupied by a sergeant with half a dozen men, was summoned and had no choice but to surrender. A large supply of cannon and ammunition was here obtained, and the forts were occupied by provincials. The only armed vessel on the lake was next seized and Benedict Arnold, making his first appearance at this early stage of the war with a colonel's commission, sailed the vessel up Lake Champlain with an accompanying flotilla of bateaux to Fort St. Johns on the Richelieu River, twenty miles above its outlet. The object of this visit was the capture of an armed sloop, which Arnold brought away, together with a dozen unsuspecting soldiers who occupied the fort.

Carleton was at Quebec when the news of these

SIR GUY CARLETON

doings arrived at Montreal by the agency of Moses Hazen, who had been a distinguished partisan officer in the French wars and was now farming near St. Johns. The city was stirred to a high pitch of excitement. Colonel Templer of the 26th Regiment, to which the captured detachments of the lake forts belonged, was in command, and at once despatched Major Preston with one hundred and forty men of the same corps to St. Johns which was found deserted. Allen himself had occupied it in the interval, departing only on the approach of the British. But for the warning of a disaffected Montreal merchant, one Bindon, Allen and his men would probably have been cut off. By this same person Allen sent a request for five hundred pounds worth of provisions, ammunition and liquor to those "friendly to the cause" in the city. Bindon, moreover, would have led Preston's detachment into an ambush but for an accident, for which friendly intention the enraged soldiers in Montreal seized and would have hanged the unfortunate man had it not been for the interference of their officers.

Templer now called a general meeting, at which it was decided that volunteers should be raised in companies of thirty, six prominent Canadians undertaking their formation. Fifty French-Canadian youths of family enrolled themselves at once, and marched at Preston's request to St. Johns, which they proceeded to occupy. Carleton, when he received the news which affirmed that there were five

HIS REPORT ON THE SITUATION

hundred provincials on Lake Champlain, and one thousand five hundred on the way there, despatched every soldier from Quebec save a few recruits, sending them mainly to the chief point of danger and attack, St. Johns, a poor ill-defended fort, but in a sense the key of Canada. He himself then hurried to Montreal, and on June 7th did his official duty, and at the same time gave vent to his personal feelings in a letter to Dartmouth. After alluding to the events above narrated, he proceeded to say that although the *noblesse* were full of zeal, neither the peasantry nor Indians would come forward. The consternation was universal; the province was unprepared for attack or defence; and there were not six hundred rank and file along the whole course of the river, nor a single armed ship. The minds of the people were poisoned with lies, and, but for the few regular troops, three hundred rebels might have seized all the provisions and arms in the province and kept post at St Johns. Within the last few days, however, the Canadians and Indians had shown signs of returning to their senses. The gentry and clergy had been very useful, but both had lost much of their influence. He proposed to call out the militia, but doubted if he could succeed in view of the seditious conduct of the British-American people in the province, for the Habeas Corpus Act and the English criminal laws were being used as arms against the State. He expresses in this letter a natural longing at this moment for the powers

SIR GUY CARLETON

possessed in Canada by the old governors, and finally encloses intercepted letters from Allen and Arnold to Walker and Morrison in Montreal and to the Indians at Caughnawaga.

Martial law was now proclaimed and the militia called out, a severe test on the allegiance of the reluctant *habitant* with the memory of the old French levies still tolerably fresh within him. But it was Carleton's only hope, though a slender one enough it may well have seemed, for the peasantry of the district had not responded to the less regular but urgent call of their seigniors and priests, and had sometimes refused with insolence. The proclamation of martial law was fiercely opposed by the British-Canadian Whigs, if I may so style them, with the argument that the Americans intended to let Canada severely alone so long as she remained neutral, but that every attempt to raise the militia would be taken as a threat to invade the northern provinces. This would have been plausible enough but for the fact that the Americans had secured, and were well aware of it, the inefficiency of the Canadian rank and file even as a defensive force and never took them into account at all as potential invaders. Furthermore the decision to invade Canada, arrived at in the summer of 1775, was with a view to prevent the colony from becoming the base of attack for a fresh British army, and the capture of Quebec, coupled with wholesale promises to the Canadian peasantry in their present condition, would have

THE CALL TO ARMS

gone far towards achieving this result. Carleton at any rate had not the slightest doubt of their intentions and in his desperate straits had no time for the sophistries of village lawyers or partisan pamphleteers.

Apart from all other considerations a peremptory call to arms could not have been other than distasteful to a rural people who had experienced more than enough of fighting under their own monarch, when native resentment and race hatred had been a powerful stimulant. As a further deterrent the once hated Bastonnais were stumping through the parishes and protesting that the measure of ease and freedom the *habitant* now enjoyed was slavery compared to the Utopia they were longing to create on the banks of the St. Lawrence. How could the simple Canadian peasant know that the only Utopia comprehended by the Bastonnais was one which meant the probable destruction of all the traditions, prejudices and customs that rightly or wrongly he held dear? It was in vain that the priests thundered from the pulpit, that the seigniors waved their swords and that Bishop Briand invoked their defence of their king and religion through the agency of every parish pulpit. A few meagre companies it is true were scraped together in the rural districts, but even these, for the most part, melted away through individual or wholesale desertion. As a class the *habitants* turned a persistently deaf ear to priests, to seigniors, and to officials. After all, it was a good

SIR GUY CARLETON

deal to ask of a peaceful farmer that he should leave his plough, his family and his home, and offer his breast to bullet and bayonet in a dispute he did not understand and the issue of which he might well believe would not materially affect him. Both sides were foreigners and heretics and it is not difficult to understand the sullen determination of the mass of Canadian peasantry to leave these mad Britons to fight out their incomprehensible quarrel alone.

Carleton was under no delusions, as his frequent letters to Dartmouth at this period bear ample testimony. He had scarcely any troops and very little money and only hoped the *habitants* would prove nothing worse than neutral. The British in Montreal, as a body, refused point blank to serve. Hey, however, who had accompanied Carleton thither, harangued them in such scathing fashion that many were shamed into the king's service while a few were always staunch. Guy Johnson too, nephew of the redoubtable Sir William, arrived from the Mohawk country about this time with three hundred of the Six Nation Indians. The Caughnawagas in similar strength had also been attached, and a grand council was held at which their services were accepted on the condition that they were not to fire till first fired upon. The chief value of the Indians was for scouting purposes, and upon this service they were soon despatched with orders to watch the Americans at Ticonderoga.

In mid-July having done all that was humanly

A PERILOUS POSITION

possible in Montreal and leaving Colonel Prescott in command, Carleton returned to Quebec. The Act had come into legal force on the first of May, but practically nothing had been yet done to get it into working order.

The notary Badeaux, who has written an account of the invasion, tells us that at Three Rivers the governor was entertained by Tonnancour, a wealthy Canadian trader, money-lender, landowner and militia colonel. Perceiving an armed Canadian promenading outside the window, Carleton inquired the cause and was told it was a guard of honour, whereupon he at once went out to the man and gave him a guinea as the first armed Canadian he had seen in the district. Tonnancour's son, it may be noted, raised a company in the locality and was very active in the British service. The same diarist tells us that most of the parishes in the Richelieu country showed a marked sympathy with the rebels. Some of them supplied a few men to the militia, while from others not a single combatant could be secured.

The feelings of Carleton as he sailed down the St. Lawrence to Quebec for the purpose of formally inaugurating a policy of which he had formed such high hopes may well claim our sympathy. The very people in whose interests he had so strenuously exerted himself had now turned upon him, in a negative sense at least, and in some districts in an active one, and had succumbed to the crafty

SIR GUY CARLETON

intrigue of those who had treated them with traditional contempt and to protect them against whom he had laboured amid much opposition. That this was mainly due to their unexampled credulity made the situation if anything perhaps more galling; for with such people the secret agitator is at a marked advantage over the highly placed proconsul, with whom truth and honour count for something, and with Carleton they counted for much.

On his arrival at Quebec Carleton encloses to the home government among other documents a fresh American address of sympathy to the Canadians, commencing with characteristic bombast: "The parent of the universe hath divided this earth among the children of men;" also a copy of a scrap of paper thrust under the doors of the *habitants* throughout the country,

> "Honi soit qui mal y pense
> À lui qui ne suivra le bon chemin.
> "Baston."

In truth a somewhat melancholy gathering must have been this opening of the first legislative council under the new Act on August 17th, 1775, with so obvious a possibility of its being the last.

Twenty-two members, including Cramahé as lieutenant-governor, met their chief on this depressing occasion. Eight of them were French-Canadians, for the oath of supremacy had been remitted in favour of an oath to which Roman Catholics could conscientiously subscribe. The oath of allegiance to

ALARMING NEWS

the king was followed by a clause renouncing all "equivocable mental evasion or secret reservation." Hey, as before mentioned, was chief-justice and among the other councillors were Saint Luc de La Corne, de Contrecœur, Hugh Finlay, Drummond, Dr. Mabane, Pownall, Allsopp and John Fraser. But a very few days, however, were permitted to the peaceful labours of the council, for with the opening of September imminent dangers from outside banished all thought of internal legislation; news arriving that the rebels, this time in much greater force, had crossed the border and were again on the Richelieu. Carleton at once hurried back to Montreal leaving Quebec of necessity as bare of troops as ever; but Quebec for the moment was regarded as secure from immediate danger. Instructions came from London too, about this time, which must have provoked the much harassed governor to a bitter smile. His Majesty, he was informed, relied on the zeal of his new Canadian subjects, and Carleton was authorized to raise a force of six thousand men, either to coöperate with Gage or to act independently, whichever course should seem advisable. Arms and money for half the number were already upon the sea. Whether it was a consolation to Carleton to learn that the court of Russia had evinced a practical sympathy for His Majesty's troubles in America, is problematical; but it was better hearing that a corps of twenty thousand infantry had been applied for, and that it was hoped to despatch a considerable number

SIR GUY CARLETON

of them to Canada in the spring, for Carleton held that Canada offered the best vantage ground for overawing the provinces,—an opinion which the designs of congress amply confirmed.

The king and his government had all this time a pathetic, if most natural, reliance on their much indulged Canadian subjects. As they had not even yet realized the temper or attitude of their own people in North America the *habitant* may well have remained an inscrutable item in their imperial survey. Carleton had also secret intelligence emanating from Governor Tryon of New York that three thousand troops from the middle and southern colonies, to be joined by as many more from New England, were to muster at Ticonderoga. He accordingly sent an urgent application to Gage for a couple of regiments. The despatch arrived a few hours after Gage had sailed for England, but Sir William Howe, now filling his place, promptly ordered a battalion and two transports to Quebec. Graves was then in command of the fleet and appears to have been, in spirit at least, a survivor of the ante-Chatham period when the chief object of the two services was to thwart each other to the utmost of their power, for he refused the ships, under the plea that an October voyage to Quebec was too difficult and dangerous. This was altogether too much even for Howe, not himself distinguished for prompt action in this lamentable struggle. But he was powerless, and could only vent his indig-

A FORLORN PROSPECT

nation in a letter to Carleton and wish him well out of his scrape.

Carleton, though he saw nothing before him but ruin, had at least not lost the spirit which had early marked him out as one of " Pitt's young men." He had now some seven hundred troops of all ranks at Fort St. Johns under Preston, including five hundred of the 7th and 26th Regiments, one hundred and twenty Canadian volunteers, mostly French gentlemen, and a few artillerymen. There were eighty regulars too at Chambly under Major Stopford, while besides the handful at Montreal there were one hundred men of the Royal Emigrants, largely recruited from the Highland soldiers who had settled after the peace on the northern frontier of New York and at Murray Bay on the lower St. Lawrence, and became afterwards the 84th Regiment. They were raised and commanded by McLean, an able and zealous officer who did yeoman's service throughout this whole campaign.

CHAPTER V

MONTGOMERY AND ARNOLD

IT is generally conceded that the hand of congress had been somewhat forced by Ethan Allen and Arnold in their prompt seizure, during the spring of 1775, of Ticonderoga and Crown Point. The inspiration at least had in this case been local rather than federal, and the exploit, which was creditable in a tactical rather than heroic sense, was at the time not admitted as having been authorized. Strong professions of reluctance to harass Canada were expressed at headquarters for some weeks afterwards, and we must remember that warlike acts during this whole summer were regarded, officially at any rate, as only a means to an advantageous reconciliation with the mother country. As the summer advanced, however, these views entirely changed for the excellent strategical reason already referred to, and others of common knowledge.

It was now regarded by Washington as of high importance that Canada should be occupied, an achievement which must have seemed at that time an extremely simple one. Carleton they all knew had to be reckoned with, and no one underrated him. His past record was familiar in America and his name spelled respect. But Carleton was no

SIR GUY CARLETON

magician; yet if he was not a Wolfe he was at least a Montcalm; for the rest the province lay bare and open save for seven or eight hundred regular troops, a few British Loyalists, and a handful of Canadian gentry. Ample evidence had been secured from innumerable and reliable sources that the peasantry would remain neutral at the best, and that they would furnish food and valuable transport assistance to the Americans even if they did not take up arms.

Congress, as Carleton had been rightly informed, had now seriously undertaken the invasion of Canada, though even Carleton was unaware that at the very moment he reached Montreal, Benedict Arnold with eleven hundred picked men was starting for the mouth of the Kennebec with Quebec itself as the objective point. It was enough for the present to know that fifteen hundred provincials were gathered on Lake Champlain awaiting reinforcements. Of this force Schuyler had taken command, the father-in-law of Alexander Hamilton and a member of that famous Albany family whose loyalty and liberal hospitality had been a useful and picturesque feature in the old French wars. Temporary business of a diplomatic nature with the Indians, followed by an attack of illness, removed Schuyler from this scene of operations and Richard Montgomery, of immortal but partly fortuitous fame, succeeded to his command.

Montgomery was the son of a country gentleman

GENERAL MONTGOMERY

and M.P. in Donegal. He was educated at Trinity College, Dublin, and at eighteen gazetted to the 17th Foot. He fought at Louisbourg and in those subsequent operations under Amherst and Haviland which completed the conquest of Canada. Later on as a captain he served at Havana and elsewhere in the West Indies. After the peace he sold his commission, through pique it is said at being passed over, and repaired to New York, where he bought a property at Kingsbridge and married a daughter of Judge Robert Livingstone whose family was perhaps the most conspicuous among the British community of the Anglo-Dutch province. The Livingstones were the leading partisans of congress, as the de Lancys were of the Crown. One or two of their name had settled near Montreal and were active among the Canadian malcontents, and Montgomery no doubt fell under their influence. He had, moreover, all those advantages of stature, good looks and an engaging manner which, added to other qualities, make for success. He was sent to the provincial congress, and being known as a gallant and experienced soldier was at once employed in that capacity.

He was now a brigadier, having succeeded Schuyler with whom he had gone as second in command. Schuyler, during the brief period of his command, had already demonstrated against Fort St. Johns, received its fire, fought a skirmish in the woods with Carleton's Indians and stationed a force

SIR GUY CARLETON

at Ile-aux-Noix with a view to preventing some armed vessels recently built by the British at St. Johns from ascending to the lake. Montgomery before leaving Crown Point had despatched Ethan Allen with four score Indians to the Richelieu and the St. Lawrence to cement the friendliness of the *habitants* and feel the country. But on meeting with a small body of provincials under Brown near Sorel, and fired perhaps with the memory of his bloodless capture of Ticonderoga, Allen proposed to the other nothing less than the capture of Montreal. Brown agreed, but seems to have thought better of it and deserted his friend at the critical moment. When the latter appeared with one hundred and fifty men on the south shore of the river opposite Longueuil he found much good-will among the natives. The party, however, was soon discovered, the alarm was given, and Carleton promptly called in all the ladders outside the town, a precaution which was met in so hostile a spirit as to show the temper of the local peasantry. Allen then sent a messenger to Walker, who was residing six leagues away, in the full hope that he would raise his friends in force, but that gentleman was too wise to stir.

On September 24th, 1775, Allen transported his men across the river in canoes and occupied some barns and houses at Long Point, a league from the city, upon which Carleton sent Major Carden with thirty men of the 26th Regiment and two hundred and fifty militia to dislodge him. This operation

ETHAN ALLEN'S CAPTURE

took just half an hour. Allen and thirty-five of his men were surrounded and captured and the rest driven off, though it cost the life of Carden, a gallant officer, and Mr. Patterson, the only killed on the British side. Of the others five were killed and five wounded. The prisoners were put in irons and sent to Quebec on the schooner *Gaspé*, whence they were shipped to England. Here they were confined in the high perched castle of Pendennis so familiar now-a-days to all visitors to Falmouth in Cornwall. This foolish attempt of a handful of riflemen to take even a poorly defended city of eight thousand souls is somewhat characteristic of the heady Vermonter. It is suggested by one historian that, annoyed at being sent out of the way when the siege of St. Johns was impending, he took this alternative of seeking notoriety, with the hope of assistance from the disaffected inhabitants, and furthermore that Montgomery regarded his somewhat raw and egotistical ardour as unlikely to prove a wholly unmixed blessing in a siege operation. Allen's mishap had some effect on the Canadians and brought a few more militia into the town. With the news of the fall of Fort Chambly, however, which arrived soon afterwards, they lost even this small measure of zeal, and Carleton writes that his Indians were as easily depressed as his handful of better disposed militia. More than one seignior who had collected a small company of men, and was marching to the front, was insulted and compelled by force to disband them.

Compromising letters to Walker fell, at this moment, into Carleton's hands and he sent a file of men to his house at L'Assomption with orders to arrest him. Walker and his household, however, opened fire on the soldiers from the windows, wounding the officer in command, whereupon the house was set on fire and the owner with his wife dragged out of the windows and carried to Montreal where the former was locked up. Montgomery who seems to have been fond of delivering bombastic compositions at his opponents now despatched one to Carleton upbraiding him for putting Allen and his followers in irons. For this stringent measure the governor thus justified himself in his next despatch to England: "We have neither prisons to hold nor troops to guard them, so that they have been treated with as much humanity as our own safety would permit. I shall not answer Montgomery, not choosing to enter into communication with rebels."

During these events Montgomery himself had not been idle at St. Johns, before which post he had sat down on September 18th. The fort was some twenty miles from the foot of Lake Champlain at the head of the first rapids of the Richelieu, but had no natural advantages of defence. Schuyler had in the meantime contrived the defection of the Caughnawaga Indians. So Preston, now shut up in the fort, was without their badly needed assistance as letter-

THE FALL OF CHAMBLY

carriers and scouts. A persistent artillery duel continued into October without results, and Preston had by that time some reason for confidence, since like all sieges in the Canadian woods remote from a base of supplies, the near approach of winter was the dread of the one side and the hope of the other. To Preston of course it spelled the latter, so he put his little garrison on half rations and awaited the coming of his frigid ally with something approaching confidence. But now tidings of such a nature reached him that hope died in his breast, for Chambly had fallen. If St. Johns was the key of Canada, so Chambly was the key of St. Johns and was considered quite secure. It stood on the banks of the Richelieu some fourteen miles below, and was a strong stone fort with bastions. It was held by Major Stopford, a son of Lord Courtown, with over eighty men and was proof against anything but the heaviest cannon. It was well provisioned too, and well supplied with guns and ammunition, but Stopford had tamely surrendered after a thirty-six hour siege maintained by a small force and one, some say two, fieldpieces. He had not even preserved sufficient wits to throw his stores and powder into the river which almost lapped the walls. All these and several guns and mortars were now transferred to the camp of Montgomery, who stood greatly in need of them, and Preston's position behind such poor defences became untenable. There appear to have been no extenuating circumstances attached to this more than "regrettable incident," which directly caused the temporary fall of Canada and all the misery thereby entailed. If ever an English officer deserved to be shot one might well think it was Stopford; but he was a peer's son, and there is no evidence that he was even censured. In days when a high-born officer cashiered for cowardice in the field could afterwards become the first minister of the Crown, anything was possible.

Carleton was known to be making every effort to raise the siege of St. Johns, but he had sent nearly all his available men to his subordinates at the front, and when news came to Preston that his efforts to reach him had failed, the latter, after some haggling over terms, was compelled to surrender from shortness of food and ammunition. Montgomery's unhappy turn of manner in this affair broke out in the articles of capitulation, which Preston was otherwise prepared to accept, concluding as they did with "regrets that so much bravery, etc., had not been shewn in a better cause." As a king's officer Preston insisted that this superfluous "improvement of the occasion" should be expunged, vowing that he and his men would rather die at their post than subscribe to a document bearing such an offensive sentiment. On November 2nd the garrison marched out with the honours of war six hundred and eighty-eight strong including eighty wounded, and were sent prisoners to New Jersey, several of the Canadian *noblesse* being among them.

REASONS FOR FAILURE

On learning the critical situation of St. Johns, Carleton had made an attempt to cross the St. Lawrence at Longueuil with a view to marching to Sorel and thence up the Richelieu with one hundred and fifty regulars and a mob of doubtful militia. But the provincial troops were now swarming in the country and the governor found the south shore lined by a strong force of sharpshooters under Allen's friend and colleague, Seth Warner. An attempt to land such troops as his in the face of their deadly fire proved hopeless, and Carleton now despaired of Montreal, as well he may have. Writing to Dartmouth on November 5th he gives some of the reasons for his failure. The construction of a sufficient number of new vessels to dispute the passage of Lake Champlain had failed for want of artificers. The entrenched camps to be formed near Chambly and St. Johns were rendered impossible by the corruption and stupid baseness of the peasantry, and thus St. Johns, which for two months was left to its own strength, was forced to capitulate. The Indians had left. The militia from the parishes had deserted and the good subjects were frightened at the rebels in arms without and the traitors within. Montreal must be given up as soon as attacked. The common people would not act and there were no means to defend the place, while Arnold was marching on Quebec which stood unprepared. As a matter of fact Arnold had practically arrived there on the very date of this letter.

SIR GUY CARLETON

Carleton now only awaited a fair wind to attempt the convoy of his small force from Montreal to Quebec, the route by land being blocked on the south shore by Montgomery, and on the north shore above Quebec by Arnold's men. Of the latter, while Carleton is spiking his guns and preparing to leave Montreal to its fate, something must now be said.

Benedict Arnold, of sinister but famous name, first appears in history with Ethan Allen's surprise of the Champlain forts in the spring of 1775. He was then thirty four, a native of Norwich, Connecticut, and of respectable family, though his father, a merchant sailing his own ships, had before his death fallen into poverty and bad habits. Arnold's great-grandfather, however, had been lieutenant-governor of Rhode Island, and the young Benedict had received a fair education, and married into a respectable family of New Haven, Connecticut, where he now resided. Carleton alludes to him casually as a "horse jockey," not quite a fair description of a man who carried on a West India business which happened to include the shipping of horses, but the sociology of New England would hardly be a strong point with a British aristocrat and governor at Quebec. Arnold's business seems to have included also occasional trips to Montreal and Quebec, which proved doubtless of much subsequent service to him. He was not regarded as over scrupulous, but he was popular and high-

BENEDICT ARNOLD'S ADVANCEMENT

spirited, a good horseman and a dead shot. He was captain of one of the companies of "Governor's Guards," the crack militia corps of Connecticut. After the Lexington affair he assembled his company, and, re-inforced by a number of Yale students, broke into the New Haven powder magazine, and marched to Cambridge fully armed and equipped. Here he so impressed the Massachusetts committee that they gave him the commission of colonel, and accepted his suggestion of seizing Ticonderoga, empowering him to raise men in their province. While attempting this he found that Allen had not only anticipated his scheme, but already had the men for carrying it out, so Arnold had no choice but to join him as a volunteer. These two heady persons clashed considerably after the capture of the forts, Arnold with his colonel's commission refusing to take orders from the Vermonter. After the affair of the forts, Arnold had proceeded to St Johns and brought away an armed sloop.

The Massachusetts committee seem to have viewed the strenuous methods of their nominee with only a qualified approval, at which the latter took offence, declined further service, and went straight to Washington's quarters at Cambridge. That sound judge of men quickly recognized Arnold's value, and when the invasion of Canada was projected appointed him commander of the less important but more hazardous of the two expeditions designed for the service. The main at-

SIR GUY CARLETON

tack by the natural and historic route as we have seen was confided to Schuyler and Montgomery, so Arnold was entrusted with the far more perilous task of leading a force to Quebec through the rugged north-eastern wilderness which is now Maine, and thence down the valley of the Chaudière. Arnold may possibly have had a share in suggesting it, but Washington already possessed a copy of a survey made some years before by Montresor, a British officer who had traversed the same line. Eleven hundred of the eighteen thousand men gathered before Boston were selected, and are described as "the flower of the colonial youth." Three companies were hardy Scotch-Irish riflemen and Indian fighters from the mountain frontiers of Pennsylvania and Virginia, among whom were the celebrated partisan leaders, Morgan and Hendricks. Among the rank and file were many bearing names notable in New England annals, Bigelow, Thayer, Hubbard, Colbourn, and Aaron Burr, the future vice-president, but better known to history as the slayer of Alexander Hamilton. A sixth of the force is described as "Irish emigrants," which at that time usually meant the Scottish Presbyterian colonists from Ulster. On September 18th, 1775, Arnold and his men sailed from Newburyport for the mouth of the Kennebec, and up that river to Fort Western, the present Augusta and the head of deep navigation, where two hundred bateaux had been hastily constructed.

ARNOLD'S MARCH

On the twenty-fifth they began their march of three hundred miles through what was then, for the most part, an uninhabited and shaggy wilderness, pushing or dragging the heavy bateaux laden with supplies and ammunition, against swift, and as they advanced, often shallow and rocky currents. Half the distance, broadly speaking, was up the Kennebec River, the other half along Lake Megantic and down the Chaudière. About midway was the long relief of the "Dead River," overhung by the mountain watershed which parted the streams, and at the same time Canada, from the New England provinces. One advantage of this secluded route was the reasonable prospect it offered of taking Quebec by surprise in its undefended state. The route had been used occasionally by small war parties of Indians or Rangers, but the "blaze" on the line of the portages, one of which was twelve miles long, was in many cases no longer distinguishable.

This march of Arnold's has been traditionally regarded as a great achievement of courage and endurance. More than one historian on the British side, however, has been inclined to make light of it, but hardly I think with justice, while within recent years an American author has devoted much industry to illuminating the truth of the business by a number of the private journals and letters of various members of the force; men for the most part by no means unaccustomed to backwoods travel, peril and exposure. In face of such evidence there can be little doubt that the suffering and hardship endured by men who refused to flinch under it and turn back, has justified the panegyrics posterity has bestowed on the exploit. If it had been ultimately successful; had the force actually surprised and seized Quebec as it nearly did, this would have been beyond a doubt the great episode of the Revolutionary War, with Arnold for its hero.

They were just a month in traversing the wilderness between the last settlements on the Kennebec and the first clearings on the Chaudière. An unusually cold spell, and a freshet of almost unparalleled violence, transformed an enterprise of ordinary hardihood and bearable fatigue into one of peril, semi-starvation and complete exhaustion. The tangled swamps were flooded, the bateaux destroyed, and the provisions, of which the wilderness furnished none, washed away or spoiled. Before crossing the divide, half the force at the decision of their officers refused to proceed in the face of what seemed to them certain starvation. Colonel Enos, the chief officer responsible for this decision, was afterwards court-martialed and honourably acquitted. The more stubborn half followed Arnold over the barrier, even carrying several of the bateaux on their galled shoulders over the wooded and rocky ridges from whose northern slopes the fountain waters of the Chaudière, still in flood, carried them

IN SIGHT OF QUEBEC

down to the bosom of Lake Megantic. Food had now completely given out. A dog was eaten greedily; leggings and moccasins were eagerly chewed, and fifty or sixty men died in their tracks. Arnold on a rickety raft with four men sped down the unfamiliar waters at a headlong pace, regardless of dangers escaped more than once by a hair's breadth, till he reached the first fringe of Canadian settlement. Here by good luck he found sympathy and provisions, and what was more vital, assistance in conveying them through the woods on the backs of horses to his starving men. The rest of the route presented by comparison few difficulties, and Arnold who had behaved throughout with that characteristic resolution no one has ever denied him, eventually brought his men safely to the neighbourhood of Point Lévis on November 8th. Over fifty had died on the road from various causes. Between six and seven hundred remained, of whom a sixth were prostrate. Their leader now went forward to Point Lévis to reconnoitre the situation, and found that every boat and canoe had been withdrawn to the north shore only a few hours previously, for Cramahé in command at Quebec had received notice of the approach of the Americans through a fortunately intercepted letter that Arnold had entrusted to an Indian for delivery to Washington.

Arnold now held a council of war on the expediency of making an attempt on Quebec as soon as practicable. Only one voice was raised against it, so efforts were at once made to collect canoes higher up the river and construct scaling ladders, in both of which enterprises the *habitants* showed themselves both willing and useful. The presence of the invaders was now sufficiently apparent to the garrison. The frigate *Lizard* and the war-sloop *Hunter* lying in the basin opened fire on them whenever they showed themselves, and sent forward a boat to reconnoitre, from which the Americans captured a midshipman who stoutly refused to give them any information, and seems on that account to have won their respect. Arnold wrote on November 8th to Montgomery congratulating him on the St. Johns affair and at the same time informing him that forty Indians had joined his own force, that the Canadians were friendly and that he would attack Quebec if there was the slightest prospect of success. In any case he would meet Montgomery in his advance through Canada, and Quebec short of provisions (so Arnold thought) and ill-defended (which was true) must inevitably fall.

After a few days devoted to the recuperation of his men, to the collection of canoes and the construction of ladders, Arnold crossed the river in the small hours of November 13th with most of his force, and, undiscovered by the British, landed at Wolfe's Cove. During the day they demonstrated in front of the city walls, giving three loud hurrahs, so one of the garrison tells us, and were answered

DISSENSION WITHIN QUEBEC

with defiant cheers and a salute of cannon balls. Proceeding across the ridge they took up their quarters about the General Hospital and in a country house of Major Caldwell's near the St. Charles River. Arnold now sent a summons to surrender to Cramahé presenting the usual mixture of cant, bombast, threats, and bad taste so characteristic of the effusions of this generation of American commanders. Cramahé would not even receive it. Arnold says he fired on his white flag, but Cramahé declared that this was a fable for use in the American press. After a day or two of inactivity, relieved by trifling incidents or demonstrations of mutual defiance, Arnold and his officers concluded that the city was invulnerable to their ill-equipped efforts and for better security marched their troops to Pointe-aux-Trembles, some twenty miles up the river, there to await Montgomery.

Within the city there was justifiable anxiety. "Montgomery's success" writes an inhabitant "had induced many to show their sentiments and indeed to act as though no opposition might be shown the rebel forces. The Republican method of calling town meetings was adopted and in these noisy assemblies the mask was thrown off, and there one could perceive who were and who were not for the government." Some of the malcontents we are told had articles of capitulation already drafted for the Americans, but even thus early a majority of the militia both English and French behaved very well and mounted guard regularly. Besides these volunteers there were sixty or seventy of the 7th, nearly all in short of that famous regiment who were not prisoners in the colonies. Allen McLean, a tower of strength, arrived on November 13th from Sorel with his hundred Royal Emigrants, while ninety recruits for the same corps had just landed in Newfoundland under Campbell and Malcolm Fraser. These with a few artillerymen and artificers made up the total of the regular force. A council of war had been held in which it was arranged that the two warships now in the harbour should remain for the winter, and the crews with their guns, under Captain Henderson, assist in the defence of the city. On the nineteenth, "to the unspeakable joy of the garrison," who feared with good reason he might have been cut off, Carleton reached the city in safety to assume the command and create an atmosphere of confidence and hope.

Carleton and his handful of combatants did not leave Montreal till November 10th, when Montgomery was actually within a league or two of the city. Many of the loyal inhabitants accompanied him to the wharf, and the scene of his departure is described as a melancholy and pathetic one. Prescott and the effective garrison, numbering one hundred and thirty men and officers, embarked with him in a flotilla of eleven craft and the wind held fair till they reached Sorel, where the provincials under Easton had erected batteries to dispute his passage.

CARLETON'S ESCAPE TO QUEBEC

At this critical spot, as ill-luck would have it, the wind veered to the east and the situation became a precarious one. Easton demanded their surrender, and a council being held at which the urgency of Carleton's escape and presence at Quebec was insisted upon. Captain Belette, commanding one of the armed vessels, pledged himself to face the enemy's boats long enough for the governor to get away. Another skipper, Bouchette, who for his rapid journeys had earned the sobriquet of *La Tourtre*, or the "wild pigeon," guaranteed to get the governor clear of the enemy and out of harm's way.

So on the night of the tenth Carleton put himself in the hands of this loyal and enterprising Frenchman who ably fulfilled his promise. They started with muffled oars and through the narrow passage of Ile-du-Pas the crew paddled the boat with the palms of their hands. Lake St. Peter they traversed swiftly and safely and arrived in due course at Three Rivers, where Carleton was informed, though falsely, that there were six hundred congress troops marching along the north shore towards Quebec, and more truly that there was a strong force already close to the city. On resuming his journey he exchanged his faithful pilot's boat for the armed sloop *Fell* under Captain Napier, and arrived, as we have seen, to the great joy of the Quebeckers on the nineteenth. In the meantime Prescott and his men had been captured by the provincials, and their ships proved of the utmost service in helping to convey Montgomery and his force down the river to Quebec, the capture of which city may well at this moment have seemed to the rebel general and his friends almost an accomplished fact. Carleton declared that everything possible under the circumstances had been done by Cramahé and his officers, with one mental reservation. This last he soon gave expression to by issuing orders that every man who was not prepared to take his part in the defence of the city must leave it within four days, a measure which caused a wholesale exodus of the timorous, the lukewarm and the disloyal, and went far in depriving the enemy of their channels of information.

After this purging, Quebec under the stimulating influence of Carleton prepared to face the fourth and last siege in her history. The militia before this ordinance had included, we are assured by one defender, numbers of "rank rebels," while Cramahé himself wrote Dartmouth that he feared these traitors within more than the enemy without. The British muster roll had shown about five hundred men, and was reduced by Carleton's edict to about three hundred and thirty. The French on the other hand were increased by it from four hundred and eighty to five hundred and thirty-three. Besides the *Lizard* and *Hunter* a dozen or more merchant ships had been detained, and their seamen and officers, together with the blue jackets and a few mariners, introduced a further force of four hundred men into

MONTGOMERY'S PLANS

the garrison. The number of souls within the town during the siege is estimated at five thousand. Colonel Caldwell, a retired officer of the army resident in Quebec, commanded the British militia, while Colonel Voyer led the French. The latter may be further credited with a company of students and other less active volunteers, who guarded prisoners and performed similar useful duties. The complete roster of French combatants during the siege shows seven hundred and ten names, that of the British unfortunately is not extant.

There were provisions in the town for eight months, but firewood, a vital need, was scarce, and the country was already covered with a foot of snow. There was nothing to fear as yet, however, from the water-front, as it was now full of floating ice, Carleton well knew that so long as he held Quebec Canada was not lost, so also did Montgomery. "I need not tell you," he wrote to Robert Livingstone, his father-in-law, then attending congress, "that till Quebec is taken Canada is unconquered. There are three alternatives, siege, investment or storm. The first is impossible from the difficulty of making trenches in a Canadian winter and the impossibility of living in them if we could." As to mining he was informed that the soil did not admit of it, and lastly his artillery would be useless for breaking such walls. As for investment he had not enough men to prevent a garrison in a familiar country from getting food and firewood and he complains that a lack of specie sadly limits the number of Canadians willing to enlist, for congress paper had already begun to stink in their nostrils. There were, however, fewer objections to storming. If his force was small Carleton's was not great, the length of his enemy's works which in other respects favoured him, would prove to his disadvantage and assist Montgomery who could select his point in secret, while the constant strain of expectation on so mixed a garrison would breed weakness and discontent among them.

Thus Montgomery summed up his chances in a frame of mind already much less sanguine than that in which he left Montreal. From the first, therefore, he practically decided on the bold venture leading which in person he so bravely fell. Openly at least Montgomery was sanguine enough, and his boast that he would eat his Christmas dinner in Quebec or hell is a familiar tradition, if not scientific history. One may suspect that the alternative was supplied by his enemies.

We are not concerned here with Montgomery's brief occupation of Montreal nor yet with his journey down the St. Lawrence, both of which were uneventful. The greater part of his army had been left under Wooster at Montreal and in various ports to the south of the river, and it does not seem that when he joined Arnold at Pointe-aux-Trembles their united forces amounted to much more than a thousand men, exclusive of some Canadian militia,

THE DEFENCES OF THE CITY

though British accounts both modern and contemporary have always rated it as larger. His own troops were nothing like so good as Arnold's men whose physique and discipline he regarded with admiration and surprise. Nor were the defences of the city "ruinous" as Arnold had somewhat prematurely described them, but were in a good state thanks to Cramahé's forethought and to an efficient engineer, namely, James Thompson who was alive half a century later to tell stories of that famous winter, and has moreover left a journal that throws much light on the siege. The stone walls and bastions and deep trenches which formed the normal defences of the city on the landward side were now well furnished with guns. The interval between the rocky breast of Cape Diamond and the St. Lawrence was heavily stockaded to protect the passage into the Lower Town at this narrow gap, while similar barricades were erected at the further opening on the banks of the St. Charles.

With regard to the Lower Town it should be generally noted that in those days the tide rose and fell over a considerable area where are now wharves and streets. The familiar spot at the south-west, however, where Montgomery fell has not materially altered, but the point of the most formidable attack by Arnold's division, the Sault-au-Matelot, has been greatly changed by artificial reclamation from the waters of the river. In those days the narrow artery from St. Roch to the Lower Town

SIR GUY CARLETON

by the waterside was only a footway, and had even to cross the projecting spur of rock which gives its name to the spot. Here the narrow neck was guarded by a strong barrier defended by cannon, and at the further end of the street which began here and led to Mountain Street, the only approach to the Upper Town, was a second barrier similarly defended. This stood at the present junction of St. James and Sous-le-Cap Streets where, as at Près de Ville, a tablet has recently been erected in commemoration of the defenders. This barrier and Montgomery's point of attack at the extreme western end of Champlain Street were the only spots where the assailants could enter the city save by scaling the walls. How the desperate attempt was made and frustrated will be related presently.

Montgomery who had taken up his quarters at Holland House, some two miles from the city, prefaced more active measures by two characteristic missives, one to Carleton and another to the inhabitants. In the first he accused his opponent of ill-treating himself and of cruelty to his prisoners, but his own humanity, he said, moved him to give Carleton the opportunity of saving himself and others from the destruction which hung over them. He informed him that he was well acquainted with his situation, "a great extent of works in their nature incapable of defence manned by a motley crew of sailors, the greatest part our friends, or of citizens

A CHARACTERISTIC LETTER

who wish to see us within their walls, and a few of the worst troops who ever styled themselves soldiers," and descanted further on the impossibility of relief, the want of necessities in the event of a simple blockade, and the absurdity of resistance. He was himself, he declared, at the head of troops accustomed to success, confident in the righteousness of their cause and so incensed at Carleton's inhumanity that he could with difficulty restrain them. More follows in a style which suggests the Buffalo militia of thirty years later, and when read by the side of Montgomery's letter to his father-in-law presents a quite remarkable specimen not only of unadulterated bluff, but of futile bad taste as addressed to a distinguished and able servant of the Crown. He winds up by warning Carleton against destroying stores, public or private: " If you do," concludes this inflated document, " there will be no mercy shown."

Montgomery, rightly assuming from former experiences that no letter from him would be received in the ordinary way, sent this one by an old woman, and Carleton appears to have seen it, doubtless to his great entertainment. Several copies of a further address to the inhabitants were shot over the walls by arrows, and their contents were not calculated to conciliate the eight hundred volunteers in arms representing the male portion of the civil inhabitants, whom he styles " a wretched garrison defending wretched works." He draws a lurid picture of " a

SIR GUY CARLETON

city in flames, carnage, confusion, plunder, all caused by a general courting ruin to avoid his shame." This one-sided correspondence took place on December 6th and 7th, the days following his arrival. The city was now cut off from the outer world. Many of Carleton's Canadian militia had been caught outside the walls at St. Roch, and had been, willingly or unwillingly, disarmed by Jeremiah Duggan, a hairdresser from Quebec, who with a following of French-Canadians was an active and useful partisan of Montgomery's. The latter's artillery in the meantime had been hauled up from the river to the Plains of Abraham and a battery of five twelve-pounders was opened half a mile from the St. John's Gate, to be quickly demolished, however, by the superior guns of the city. Another battery of mortars, more securely placed in St. Roch, behind protecting buildings, though only two hundred yards from the walls, threw shells into the city; but they were small and did little damage. "Even the women," says a diarist, "came to laugh at them."

The situation of the besiegers was not an enviable one, for winter had now set in with rigour. Though the provincials were largely clad in British uniforms captured at St. Johns and Chambly they had no winter clothing, and what was still more serious smallpox had broken out among the *habitants* and soon began to exact its toll of victims in the American camp. The garrison from the very first behaved

AN ATTACK EXPECTED

admirably and under the cheery firmness and the confidence of Carleton kept their ordinary watches, and responded to the not infrequent summons of night alarms with spirit and alacrity. In these three weeks of interval pending Montgomery's attack there was little actual conflict. Carleton's gunners made effective practice on all attempts of the besiegers to get their light guns into advantageous position, though the St. Roch mortars continued, it is true, to throw showers of almost harmless shells into the city. Arnold was driven from his headquarters in St. Roch which were riddled with shot, and Montgomery's horse was killed by a cannon ball while the owner was seated in his cariole. The Alleghany riflemen, however, from various shelters outside the walls and from the cupola above the intendant's palace carried on a deadly fire, picking off almost every man who showed his head above the ramparts.

On December 22nd, Colonel Caldwell's servant, bearing the significant name of Wolf, arrived in the city. He had been taken prisoner in trying to save something from the wreck of his master's country house which Arnold had burnt, and in company with a deserter had succeeded in making his escape. They reported that Montgomery intended to attempt the city on the next night, and a thousand men were kept under arms in consequence. They were right, for another deserter was hauled over the walls the next day who confirmed the report but gave Wolf's

SIR GUY CARLETON

escape as the reason for postponement, and declared that it had been arranged for that very night unless his own flight to the enemy should again alter Montgomery's plans. As a matter of fact the latter had called a council of war, of which the majority were for storming the town as soon as a daily expected supply of bayonets, axes and hand grenades had arrived. The general himself was for delay till a further attempt to open a breach in the walls with artillery had been made; but the others were so eager for immediate action that he finally gave way. The first design was to assault the walls at four different points between Cape Diamond and Palace Gate, three of these movements, however, to be feints, the one at Cape Diamond alone to be pressed home. Aaron Burr, Montgomery's aide was very forward in the affair and was actually assigned fifty picked men to be drilled in the practice of scaling ladders.

At this moment, however, Antell and Price, disaffected Montrealers, and the former Montgomery's engineer, arrived and insisted that the Lower Town was the right point for attack and would be less dangerous. As a military move it was the most rash, for even the capture of the Lower would leave the assailants at the mercy of the Upper Town. But the Montrealers' minds ran strongly on politics and they had persuaded themselves that the inhabitants would then compel Carleton to surrender in order to avoid the destruction of their property and warehouses. But the stormy weather acted as a deterrent from

MONTGOMERY LOSES HOPE

day to day, while Montgomery's confidence, though not his courage, was oozing away. Arnold had so alienated some of his officers that they refused to serve under him till urgently appealed to by their general. Smallpox too was increasing and some of the New England troops whose period of service terminated on December 31st, vowed they would not stay a day beyond that date. The intense cold and frequent frostbites cooled the ardour of the majority, only warmed from time to time by occasional sallies from the city for wood, and in the case of the riflemen by their congenial occupation of "sniping."

The twenty-third passed uneventfully, for the reasons already given, and so did Christmas Day, Montgomery eating his substitute for turkey neither in Quebec nor in the other place, but in Holland House and in desponding mood. He writes from there of the factions against Arnold, blaming the latter not at all but complaining that he himself has no money, paper being valueless, and Price who had been an invaluable friend to the cause having exhausted his own means of supply. He would resign if it came to a mere blockade but would make a desperate effort first. The spirit of the potential slaves in Quebec and the agility of the contemptuous Carleton in escaping his clutches, galled him sorely. The promise of becoming a successful and living hero had lately seemed so fair, and now the presentiment was dark upon him that he could only be one, unsuccessful and possibly dead. Carleton, during these anxious days, each one of which was expected to end in a night assault, remained cool, vigilant and wary. His bearing, says an eye-witness, carried no trace of anxiety though he slept in his clothes at the Récollets'. Every man of the garrison had his post and when off duty lay by his arms. The once apathetic French and the erst grumbling British militia now vied with each other in alertness and eagerly waited for the attack.

A change of weather, which deserters had spoken of as the signal for action, came on the twenty-eighth. But that night passed quietly, as did the next after a day of "serene sunshine," and again to the vigilant and shivering sentries on the walls there came no sign out of the darkness below. On the thirty-first the thermometer fell again, but the feeling in the city was strong that the moment was come. The intuition was correct, for about four o'clock on the last morning of the year, Captain Malcolm Fraser of the Royal Emigrants, who was in command of the main guard, and indeed of all the sentries on the walls, saw strange signal fires and the flash as of lanterns or torches at various points from the St. Charles to the St. Lawrence, while almost immediately two rockets shot up into the sky from beyond Cape Diamond. The alarm was now raised, and in a brief time all doubt was ended by the opening of a sharp fire against the walls to the south of the St. Louis Gate and towards Cape Diamond. Drums beat and bells rang

THE ATTACK

wildly out into the now stormy night and in less than three minutes, says one account, every man in the garrison was under arms at his post, even old men of seventy going forward to oppose the rebels.

The plan of attack had in the meantime been altered. Montgomery was moving quietly along the narrow strand of the St. Lawrence from Wolfe's Cove, heading for the barrier which defended the western end of the Lower Town beneath Cape Diamond. Arnold with a larger body was to pass from St. Roch beneath the Palace Gate and attack the similarly defended barrier already spoken of at Sault-au-Matelot. The rockets were a signal to Arnold that Montgomery was on the march. In the event of success, which achieved in one quarter would have materially favoured it in the other, the two forces were to combine in an assault, if such seemed feasible, on the Upper Town. The firing heard at the walls in front had been that of Montgomery's Canadians led by Livingstone and some provincials under Brown, and was intended as a diversion to distract the garrison. It was pitch dark, and a biting wind laden with fine snow blew from the north-east directly in the face of Montgomery's long extended column, and indeed it considerably deadened both sounds and signals during that first period of excitement.

In almost the last letter of his life Montgomery had alluded to Wolfe's achievement as a series of

SIR GUY CARLETON

lucky hits. He himself may well have seemed to be asking a good deal of the fickle goddess on this somewhat desperate venture as he led his men along the narrow strand between the gloomy cliffs and the frozen river. Deep drifts of snow and slabs of ice forced up by the tide on to the narrow way seemed to have further impeded the toilsome progress of the column from Wolfe's Cove, where it had descended to the shore. As Montgomery and his leading file arrived within fifty yards of the barrier the men who were standing behind it with lighted fuses say that they could just perceive them pausing for a moment as if in uncertainty. Then one of their number sprang forward, —Montgomery, no doubt, who according to an American diarist cried out, "Come on, brave boys, Quebec is ours!" A small group followed him. At this moment the battery was fired, and a hail of grapeshot swept every one of these dimly visible assailants off their feet. Further discharges with a sharp musket fire sent the main and invisible part of the columns flying back into the darkness and out of action, so far as that memorable night and day were concerned. "The rest is silence," save that the groans of dying men were heard by those within the barrier. All that was to be seen outside it on the following day by Carleton's search party was one stark hand above the snow, which falling steadily for many hours had covered a dozen frozen corpses. The hand was Montgomery's.

CHAPTER VI

LAST DAYS OF THE SIEGE

THE little battery of four guns at Près de Ville had been thus admirably and effectively handled by Captain Barnsfare with an artillery sergeant and fifteen sailors. In the blockhouse above were thirty-five French-Canadians, whose bullets followed the flying enemy into the darkness. Strange to say, however, an extraordinary panic succeeded this doughty deed, apparently caused by an old woman, who cried out that the rebels had forced the Sault-au-Matelot, and were upon them in the rear. One might be permitted to wonder if this was the same old woman who had taken Montgomery's insulting missive to Carleton, and had been drummed out of the town for her pains, and thus sought revenge. If so she had it, for according to one account, men actually tumbled over each other in their superfluous terror.

Arnold's column, too, though in far different fashion, had by this time already failed in its attempt. How this came about must now be told. Whether Arnold saw the warning rockets seems uncertain, but at any rate he started about four o'clock on the morning of December 31st to pick his way through St. Roch in the direction of

SIR GUY CARLETON

the barricade of the Sault-au-Matelot, which was his goal. He was followed by six hundred men, headed by the redoubtable Morgan and his Virginia mountaineers. Small hope of surprise could have lingered among his calculations by the time he was under the Palace Gate, for the bells of the city were by then clanging wildly, and the sound of heavy firing from the feigned attack upon the western walls beat up, though in muffled fashion, against the storm. As he reached the narrow strip between the tide of the St. Charles, then nearly at flood, and the steeps above, his column was fired upon by pickets above the Palace Gate and the Hôtel Dieu. His men, encumbered with scaling ladders, were exposed to view by fire balls thrown from the buildings above, while he himself was soon afterwards hit in the leg and put hopelessly out of action. Morgan now took the command, though not strictly entitled to it, and attacking the first barrier with some of his mountaineers and other ardent spirits, eventually carried it, though the time and energy expended in the proceeding is a matter of much disagreement among even contemporary chroniclers.

However that may be, the Americans poured over the first barrier in spite of the gun and the guard, and found themselves in a street some two hundred yards long lined by houses, at the further end of which was a second barrier protected by cannon. There would seem to have been some pause here, and anxious thoughts were cast in the

THE REPULSE

direction of Montgomery, who in the event of success should then have been within the city. But of him nothing had yet been heard. Carleton had now learnt that the first barricade had been fired, (Americans say by a surprise of the guard who were drinking and in ignorance of the situation), and he despatched Captain Laws with seventy men by Palace Gate to take Arnold in the rear. In the meantime Caldwell, who seems to have moved rapidly from point to point and grasped the situation, leaving his own militia to their obviously easy task on the western walls, led a mixed party that he had collected down to the Lower Town and to the back of the second barrier, where he joined Nairne and Dambourges, who with Voyer and his French-Canadians were there holding the enemy in check.

Around this inner barrier which overlooked the Americans now swarming in Sault-au-Matelot Street and protected the approach to the Upper Town, a great deal of confused and severe fighting took place before the besiegers were finally overcome. The latter were inevitably crowded in the narrow street, and suffered much from the raking of the battery at the end and the fire from some houses which had been occupied by the defenders. The barrier itself seems never to have been in danger. One ladder was placed against it, but was dragged over the walls by a French-Canadian militiaman amid a hail of American bullets. Some of the houses, however, were forced by the Ameri-

SIR GUY CARLETON

cans, only to be recaptured at the point of the bayonet by the British. The various accounts of this hour or two of not continuous but often fierce fighting give what each man heard and saw in the blinding snow and darkness, illuminated only by the flashing of guns and hand grenades. The confusion was added to by the British uniforms worn by most of the Americans, for a paper inscribed, "Liberty or death" pinned in their hats was a futile distinction in such a mêlée. But the Americans, being mostly in the open street, suffered out of all proportion to their opponents. Morgan and many others behaved with infinite gallantry, the former killing Captain Anderson, the only officer who fell on his side. The hopelessness of the effort, however, at length became evident, and a retreat was attempted.

In the meantime Laws, who had been sent out with two guns by Carleton to take Arnold's men in the rear, accompanied by McDougall and Fraser with some of the Royal Emigrants, and by Captain Hamilton, of the *Lizard*, with blue jackets, became engaged in St. Roch with a belated company of Arnold's under Dearborn, which had just crossed from their quarters beyond the St. Charles. After some desultory fighting among the houses, the provincials were captured or routed, and, furthermore, the rebel battery in St. Roch was taken and its guns carried off Laws and his friends, now heading for the Sault-au Malelot, took Morgan's already

THE LOSSES

shattered force in the rear, and completed their discomfiture. Many of the Americans escaped over the ice of the St. Charles, a perilous venture for strangers in the dark. The greater part, however, laid down their arms. The number of unwounded prisoners was about three hundred and ninety, of wounded forty-four. The killed were returned at thirty-two, but from the number of bodies found afterwards in the snow and recovered in the spring when it melted, and from the estimates of Americans present, the number must have been much greater. McLean, who as second in command should be something of an authority, states, in a private letter, that they buried in all two hundred and twenty. The British loss was given as one officer and five privates killed, and a few wounded. Possibly it was about double that, but in any case quite trifling. Carleton in a letter to Howe says that between six and seven hundred were killed, wounded or captured. The prisoners were paraded before Carleton in the Upper Town, and after a good breakfast the officers were quartered in the Seminary, and the men in the Récollets'.

Carleton was now urged by some of his officers to order a sortie on the presumably demoralized, and certainly diminished, besiegers. But he was too old and cool a soldier to take any risks with his heterogeneous and small force, and with but little chance of any solid advantage. His business was to hold the city till the spring, not to indulge in futile,

SIR GUY CARLETON

even if victorious, skirmishes on the Plains of Abraham or in the suburbs. He might yet want every man he had, for there was nothing but the winter to prevent reinforcements of the enemy from entering Canada. It was not known yet that Montgomery was dead. But on a scouting party's being sent through the barrier at the Près de Ville they collected after a considerable search thirteen bodies all buried, as has been stated, in the newly fallen snow, Montgomery's hand and forearm alone protruding from it. One man only, a sergeant, still breathed and uttered a few words, but quickly died. There was no certainty about Montgomery's corpse till it was brought into the town and identified by some of the prisoners. Carleton, with the humanity that never forsook him, sent out search parties to the scene of Arnold's march and attack at the Sault-au-Matelot, who brought in many wounded, including some officers. He caused Montgomery to be quietly buried in a hollow under the St. Louis bastion, attending the funeral himself with some half dozen others.

Wooster, hitherto in command at Montreal, now came up to replace Montgomery, for Arnold's wound kept him out of the field till April, when in a pet at some fancied slight from his commander he got himself transferred to Montreal. But their two enterprising commanders removed and their numbers reduced to about eight hundred men including Livingstone's rebel Canadians who were not very

AN ESTIMATE OF CARLETON

formidable and whose numbers seem vague and fluctuating, the besiegers were no longer, for the present, a cause of serious anxiety to Carleton. He had ample provisions and could now obtain firewood with less risk than before; above all his garrison were thoroughly pleased with themselves and with him. Whatever complacency he may himself have felt he relaxed nothing of his precautions, and resolutely refused all proposals of his subordinates to adventures in the open field. A smaller man would have given way before their importunities. His inspiring demeanour is thus described: " General Carleton wore still the same countenance; his looks were watched and they gave courage to many; there was no despondency in his features. He will find a numerous band to follow him in every danger. He is known, and that knowledge gave courage and strength to the garrison."

We must not linger here over the minor doings which mostly filled the four following months till the arrival of ships and troops from England put a prompt end to the siege. The day-to-day journals continue the story in minute detail[1] and would be interesting enough to quote from if this volume were a record of the campaign and not a life of one of the chief actors in it.

It was creditable to the spirit of the besiegers

[1] There are six different journals extant concerning this siege of Quebec besides an orderly book, the work of several persons concerned in the campaign. Though some are fuller than others they all agree in substance, and call for no elaboration or notice in these pages.

that they held to their posts. The expected reinforcements came in but slowly, the rigours of a Canadian winter proving not only a deterrent to the new provincial troops, but to the equally crude machinery that was to supply them with the necessaries of war and existence. The besiegers, however, persevered. Batteries were opened to be quickly dismounted by Carleton's guns, save one at Point Lévis, which proved too remote or too feeble to do much harm either to town or shipping. The prisoners in the city made one or two fruitless attempts to escape, though they confessed to receiving the best treatment that circumstances afforded. Later on they were removed to the ships. Ninety-four, of British birth mostly, had voluntarily enlisted in the garrison corps, but when a dozen or two had deserted, Carleton confined the rest on the ships in the harbour.

Rumours of all kinds were constantly brought into the city by deserters, among others that large forces were preparing for a descent on Canada in the spring, a statement that the evacuation of Boston by Howe made readily credible. But Carleton had reason to hope that an army from England had already sailed for the St. Lawrence, though he knew nothing for certain, and a sole dependence on the good intentions of a British ministry of that day might well whiten the hair of a remotely placed official. By early April, 1776, reinforcements had brought the besieging force up to two thousand men

A COMMISSION FROM CONGRESS

including invalids, and with some heavier guns they hoped to breach the walls. But the walls mocked their batteries for the brief period before the defenders' fire put them out of action. The *habitants*, too, had become restive under the continuous demands for provisions and labour in return for worthless paper money and were changing their attitude, while the Americans irritated by the cold, privation and defeat, were no longer always able to maintain a philanthropic and brotherly mien towards the peasantry. No thought of another attempt to storm the city was entertained by Wooster, and indeed improved defences both in the way of timbers and batteries, together with a united and confident garrison, put it out of the question. The last diversion of all was on May 3rd after the ice had broken, when a fireship was sent up the harbour from the Point of Orleans and caused some brief anxiety, but ultimately drifted out of harm's way.

Arnold, in the meantime, slighted as he thought himself by Wooster, had repaired to Montreal cured of his wound, just in time to meet a commission sent from congress with full powers to look into the military situation of Canada and probe if possible the depths of the *habitant's* mind. No less a person than Dr. Franklin headed it, while Carrol of Carrolton, and his brother, a Roman Catholic priest, afterwards the first archbishop of the United States, for politic reasons went with him. There was much sociability

SIR GUY CARLETON

at Montreal during the visit, the irrepressible firebrand Walker and his wife doing the honours, and giving the visitors no doubt their interpretation of the French-Canadian attitude and of British tyranny. It may be interesting to note that when the astute Franklin had done with the Walkers, which was not till he had reached Albany on his way home, he made a little entry in his journal which may be read to-day, to the effect that in whatever place this worthy couple might set up house he opined that it would soon become too hot to hold them. The parenthesis may be pardoned as justifying the strong language used about this notorious couple in the despatches of Carleton and Murray, and accounting for the extraordinary resentment they had aroused in the breasts of light-hearted captains and subalterns, British and French.

Franklin's commission, however, at the end of April reported the military case of Canada as hopeless, though occupied at the moment by four thousand American troops; but these were unpaid, ill-fed, and badly commanded. Wooster came in for scathing criticism, in which we may detect a trace of Arnold's influence. Wooster was recalled and Thomas, of Bunker Hill notoriety, despatched to his command. The accomplished Maryland priest had not moved the apathy of the *habitants* nor touched the loyalty of the clergy. The commission expressed infinite sympathy with the treatment of the inhabitants by the congress troops, which seems unfair,

A SORTIE ORDERED

while the creditable perseverance and undoubted courage of the besiegers of Quebec met with scant recognition at the hands of these critical civilians. The summing up, however, of their report was in effect that the capture of Canada was hopeless, and that it would be well for congress to confine itself to protecting the lake route to the Hudson against incursions from that inhospitable country.

But we must now return to Carleton whose deliverance and moment of action had at last come. Early in the morning of May 6th, 1776, every citizen still in bed in Quebec rose to join the crowds that were already thronging the ramparts. A sail was in sight, and Carleton soon knew that Dartmouth— by this time, however, superseded,—had not failed him. The sail proved to be that of the British frigate *Surprise* to be followed quickly by the *Isis* and a war-sloop. They brought welcome reinforcements, and the still better news that a fleet and armament were upon the sea. For the moment there were infantry and marines enough for the occasion. These were soon landed, and Carleton now felt justified in indulging the long restrained ardour of his faithful garrison. "The drums beat to arms," says a joyous diarist, "and it was ordered that all volunteers in the English and French militia should join the sailors and troops to march out and attack the rebels. Every man almost in both corps was forward to offer his service."

Carleton placed himself at the head of eight

hundred men, and the column marched at twelve o'clock, with McLean, whose conduct in the siege had been above praise, second in command, and Caldwell, who was sent to England a day or two later with the joyful tidings, at the head of his British militia. The little army extending itself across the plain made a noble appearance. General Thomas was now in command of the enemy *vice* the disgraced Wooster, but he had made no preparations, and a general stampede at once ensued. Nine hundred Pennsylvanians took ambush for a brief period in the woods, but they soon joined their flying countrymen. "They left cannon, muskets, ammunition, and even clothes," to quote again from the diary. " We found the roads strewed with rifles and ammunition, while clothes, bread and pork all lay in heaps in the highway with howitzers and fieldpieces. So great was their panic that they left behind them many papers of consequence to those who wrote them, and to whom they were writ. Look which way soever, one could see men flying and carts driving away with all possible speed."

The small force of provincials who throughout the spring had occupied Point Lévis and protected the battery there, on seeing the plight of their friends on the north shore of the river had nothing for it but to make their escape as best they could through the woods. A few days later Carleton, with the humanity that always distinguished him, ordered all his militia officers to institute a diligent search

CARLETON'S HUMANITY

of the surrounding country for such American fugitives as might be in distress through hunger or sickness. These were to be afforded all necessary relief, and to be brought to the General Hospital. This was made known by proclamation together with the promise that as soon as their health was restored they should have full liberty to return to their respective provinces.[1]

In the meantime the frigates had sailed up the river to seize the enemy's craft; the General Hospital and suburbs had been re-occupied, and by night (May 6th, 1776) all was over. The Americans had vanished, and peace once more brooded over the faithful city.

[1] Carleton's liberal attitude toward the Americans was well revealed in the following letter to Howe, August 8th, 1776. (B. 39, p. 93).

"I have sent the rebel prisoners taken in this province (except such as have chosen to remain here . . .) to New York, that they may from thence return to their respective homes; in hopes that the confinement they have undergone may have brought them to a sense of their past crimes and that this proof given to the rebels still in arms, that the way to mercy is not yet shut against them, the contrary being inculcated by their chiefs, and those who have interest in fomenting the disorders of the country, may tend to work a favourable change in their minds and contribute to restore the peace of America.

"It appears that this Congress is intent only upon exciting the people of America to acts of blood, and industrious even with every falsehood best calculated for their purpose, to divert them from all hopes of reconciliation: probably the sending back their prisoners, notwithstanding this, loaded with every favour which was in my power to confer upon them, will be such testimonies to the thinking people among them, of the humanity and forbearance with which His Majesty's just resentment towards his revolted subjects is tempered as may serve effectually to counteract the dangerous designs of those desperate people whose fatal ascendency over them has already conducted them to the brink of ruin."

CHAPTER VII

THE EVACUATION OF CANADA

THE only criticism to be made upon the American retreat from Quebec is the ill-regulated fashion and undignified despatch with which it was executed, and the loss of material thereby involved. The surviving troops of Arnold and Montgomery had at least deserved well of congress, which had made great and not unsuccessful efforts throughout the winter and spring to reinforce them, as the figures already quoted will have shown. It was beyond doubt of great importance to the revolutionary leaders that Canada should be regarded in the colony as a virtually annexed province for as long as possible, even if the authorities knew its retention was impossible. Three Rivers, under the command of Livingstone, had been the dépôt whence the constantly arriving men and supplies had been forwarded to Quebec, while guns had been cast at the well-known forges in its neighbourhood. The main body of fugitives passed quickly through, leaving only a small force there for a brief period, and hurried onward to Sorel where General Thomas had decided to make his chief stand against Carleton.

In this very month of May, too, Arnold who had

SIR GUY CARLETON

from one to two thousand men with him in Montreal was threatened from the west by a small British force under Captain Forster. This officer, with a small detachment of forty men of the 8th Regiment and a dozen volunteers from the remote garrison of Detroit was stationed at Oswegatchie (Ogdensburg), some fifty miles up the river. On hearing of the raising, or prospective raising, of the siege of Quebec before British reinforcements, he judged that a demonstration before Montreal might possibly attach sufficient Loyalists and repentant malcontents to his side to enable him to secure the city. So feeling his way thither with his own little company and two hundred Indians he found Major Butterfield entrenched at the Cedars with four hundred men and some guns barring his way. With the further help of a local Canadian seignior, de Senneville, and a score or two of followers, Forster compelled the surrender of the post with its garrison. A considerable number of Canadians having joined him, he crossed the western mouth of the Ottawa to the Island of Montreal and marched towards the city.

Arnold, however, was on the alert with one thousand five hundred men at Lachine, and Forster, whose venture was more spirited and useful than vital to British interests, had no choice but to recross the water to Vaudreuil. He had scarcely landed when Arnold arrived on the hither shore at Ste. Anne, near which there stood and still stands in ruin the old fortified château of Senneville or Boisbriant From these posts he advanced in bateaux over the league of water to Vaudreuil, where Forster with his cannon gave his boats such a warm reception that he was forced to retire. The fortnight's campaign, including some skirmishes unrecorded here, resulted in Forster's giving up four hundred and thirty prisoners for a like number to be exchanged later by congress, a compact which was scandalously broken on a plea of Indian outrage which was proved to the hilt to be a web of fiction. Forster then retired to Oswegatchie, and Arnold burnt the château, which, erected about the year 1700, still displays its ruins picturesquely set at the point of a country-house garden which fringes the shore of the Lake of Two Mountains. It is in part roof high, flanked by the remains of its once fortified courtyard, and overhung by forest trees, and presents the most suggestive relic of remote frontier warfare, so far as I know, in all Canada or in the United States, while just above it on a ridge stands a restored stone tower even older than the château.

But we must return to Carleton, who in spite of that calm demeanour which was at once the envy and the solace of those who shared his dangers, must have been happy enough in his past success and present relief from so long and arduous a strain. After completing all arrangements for the governance of the city, and among other precautions having

SIR GUY CARLETON

ordered that none of the disloyal who had left it at the beginning of the siege should return without a permit, he started up the river with the 29th and 47th Regiments, leaving the trusty McLean to receive the still larger reinforcements already ascending to Quebec. At the same time the garrison was paraded, and the volunteers dismissed to their civic duties with the thanks they so thoroughly deserved. The immediate rendezvous of the troops was to be at Three Rivers. The transports could not actually reach that point on account of adverse winds, but Carleton saw them to within a short march of it and then turned back, leaving Fraser in command to complete the occupation and await the rest of the force. The Americans were at Sorel, with a reputed four thousand to five thousand men on the spot or within call. Carleton was back at Quebec in time to receive Burgoyne with the main army on June 1st. In their apparently overwhelming strength these gay soldiers little foreboded the catastrophe that was to overtake them within less than eighteen months.

The harbour was now alive with transports, and the Château St. Louis was gay with the resplendent uniforms of British and German officers, for the king's birthday, June 4th, which fell on an auspicious day for Canada, was observed with fitting ceremony. The 21st, 24th, 29th, 31st, 34th, 53rd, and 63rd Regiments of the line were all here, together with four batteries of artillery. Of Bruns-

THOMPSON ATTACKS FRASER

wickers there were three infantry regiments, including one of grenadiers, three of dismounted dragoons and a regiment of Hessians, all under the command of Baron Riedesel. The latter, an admirable and tried soldier, was soon to be joined by his courageous wife, who faced the later perils of Burgoyne's campaign, and has left one of the most interesting records of it. On June 5th, Carleton despatched Riedesel to Three Rivers by way of the north shore with a force of English and German troops, a few Canadian volunteers and three hundred Indians. Fraser by this time was waiting at Three Rivers with some of his men in the town and some in transports just below it. Sullivan who was in chief command of the Americans at Sorel saw his opportunity (though, indeed, success would have led to little), and despatched General Thompson with about two thousand men to attack Fraser, and if possible to surprise him. The thirty-five miles he traversed were mainly represented by the length of Lake St. Peter, a broad and shallow expansion of the St. Lawrence. Thompson crossed it near the upper end, and marched down its northern shore. He was happily espied by a Canadian militia captain, and according to another account he was conducted circuitously by an unfriendly Canadian guide.

In any case Fraser was warned in time, and threw out the 26th which repulsed Thompson's attack, while other troops came up to complete his discom-

SIR GUY CARLETON

fiture. Thompson lost a good many men in killed and wounded, and in his escape might have been most severely handled if not actually cut off, but Carleton, in spite of his deliberate refusal to recognize the status of American officers, was strongly imbued with the humane and conciliatory view of the struggle, and seems on this account to have been anxious to drive the rebels out of Canada with as little bloodshed and suffering to individuals as possible. That he maintained this attitude and retained at the same time the confidence of his officers, is a significant tribute to his character. The next morning, leaving a garrison at Three Rivers, the troops sailed for Sorel, which was found deserted. Fraser in the meantime had been sent with a force up the north shore of the St. Lawrence with a view to crossing it higher up, while Burgoyne with the troops at Sorel was despatched up the Richelieu to recover Chambly and St. Johns, as soon as Fraser should have joined him. Burgoyne marched on June 15th, and found Chambly, the scene of Stopford's disgraceful surrender seven months previously, already abandoned by the enemy. Pushing on twelve miles further to St. Johns, where Preston had honourably failed, he found this fort also deserted. The Americans had, in fact, travelled at a headlong pace and in great disorder. They were only a few hours ahead of Burgoyne, but when his scouts reached the head of Lake Champlain there was nothing whatever to be seen of them, and the

THE EVACUATION

evacuation of Canada was complete. General Phillips and Riedesel in the meantime had sailed with a third division up the St. Lawrence towards Montreal till the wind failed them, when they marched to Laprairie and thence across to the Richelieu, joining Burgoyne at St. Johns. Arnold and the men left with him at Montreal had a narrow escape, which is described at some length in the memoirs of his aide-de-camp, Wilkinson, the future somewhat well-known general. The near approach of the British seems to have come as a surprise to this usually alert individual, but he showed his best qualities in getting his troops across the river with much despatch and, by a forced march, reaching St. Johns before Sullivan, and his worst qualities, according to Wilkinson, by carrying off some military supplies and selling them for his own benefit in New York.

So far Carleton's operations had been carried out with complete success and unlooked for rapidity, but now they came to a sudden stop. Canada was saved, and as it proved, for all time. But the aggressive movement into the colonies and the occupation of Crown Point and Ticonderoga, for which immediate object the army had been sent from England, presented difficulties insuperable for the moment. The only route for a large force southward to the Hudson and into the colonies was down the waters of Lake Champlain. But every boat and craft had been either carried off or destroyed by the invaders who were now entrenched at Crown Point and Ticonderoga with a large flotilla of boats, armed and otherwise. Nor was there at that time any road through the dense forests that flourished everywhere to the very verge of the water, bristling on the rocky bluffs and mantling still more thickly on the swampy, low grounds. Carleton's object then was to occupy the above-named forts, not only for the further security of Canada but as a base of such operations against the adjoining colonies as might afterwards appear advisable. No distinct plan at this time seems to have been evolved. The feeling was strong in England that the mere display of so great a force would probably end the war. Indeed the persistent refusal of the British government and people at large to realize the true nature of the American revolt is one of the strangest features of that epoch. Unfortunately for Carleton, as we shall see, and still more so for the success of the king's northern army, the most inefficient minister that has perhaps ever served the nation in this particular capacity, had during the summer succeeded Dartmouth.

Germain, who as Lord George Sackville commanding the British cavalry at Minden had gained unenviable fame for his persistent refusal to charge at the critical moment, was now the fountain of honour and authority at a still more critical one in the nation's history. Unlike so many officers of his day he had never seen America; nor did he show

AN INEFFICIENT MINISTER

any measure of anxiety to make up for this disadvantage by acquainting himself with the peculiar difficulties that country offered to military movements. He was haughty, narrow-minded, mean and revengeful to a degree, and "as bellicose in council" said a noted wag, "as pacific in the field." But he had been a good friend to Wolfe as colonel of his regiment, though rarely favouring it, as Wolfe's private letters show, with his august presence. He had an old grudge against Carleton for rejecting one of his favourites and no one believed his protestations to the contrary. Finally, he was self-willed in proportion to his ignorance and to his utter unfitness to direct a campaign upon American soil, but unfortunately he had both the confidence and the ear of the king.

Matters, however, went smoothly at first as there was no great occasion for friction. Carleton had urged the inclusion among the supplies sent with the troops to Quebec of a large number of boats in sections for immediate use on Lake Champlain. A few only of these were forwarded, followed later by others. So while the tedious business of building a fleet on Lake Champlain was in progress, for which purpose in the confused state of the country skilled men were extremely scarce, Carleton set to work to reduce into something approaching order the chaos into which Canada had fallen.

It is not worth while to dwell at length on the reaction which had taken place in the political sympathies, if so definite a word may be used, of the Canadian peasantry. That they were heartily tired of the American occupation is no particular discredit to the provincial troops themselves, who, compelled by necessity and irritated by failure, had not often been more severe with them than the urgency of the case required. But this was quite enough for the simple *habitant* who had so readily believed the wondrous stories by which his neutrality or assistance had been invoked and secured.

The exhaustion of the invader's silver money had been the first shock in the process of disillusionment, while the soon-proven worthlessness of paper money, to say nothing of the occasional exercise of the hated *corvées*, finished the business. Districts had differed much in the measure of their admiration for their deliverers, but as scarcely any gave willing, and very few even grudging, assistance to Carleton, the other side of the question does not call for elaboration. Incidentally it may be noted that the parishes south of the river in the Richelieu county, the richest in Lower Canada, were the most active in the American interest. The priests, some of whom had been badly treated by the invaders, soon had their flocks in hand again though the seigniors never recovered their former influence, as was perhaps natural enough.

Carleton moved about the country with much energy and despatch, now at Chambly and St. Johns, where the improvement of the defences as well as

THE BEGINNING OF FRICTION

shipbuilding was proceeding apace, now at Montreal receiving deputations of Indians and enduring those tedious and fantastic ceremonies indispensable to any appeal for their assistance. The Iroquois, those ancient allies, once more swore devotion to their Hanoverian father and his deputy; but the western Indians, who also presented themselves and were equally forward, were accepted by Carleton only as benevolent neutrals. He also granted to Sir John Johnson, loyal son of a famous father, the commission to raise a battalion of Loyalists in his country which was conspicuous afterwards as the King's Royal Regiment of New York. Early in August the governor and commander-in-chief was back at Quebec issuing commissions of the peace, re-opening courts of justice and filling up the vacancies in the legislative council. He received in due course complimentary letters from Germain expressing a high sense of his services, and in one of them the first hint is thrown out of detaching Burgoyne, though under Carleton's orders, to co-operate with Howe. On September 28th we find Carleton stung into retort by a complaint from Germain that he had not sent home with his other despatches his plans for driving out the rebels in the past spring. The general replies "with ironical brevity" that the object at the time of writing was the expulsion of the rebels from Canada, which was accomplished long before any instructions could possibly have had time to reach him.

SIR GUY CARLETON

Burgoyne, Phillips, and Riedesel had come out as major-generals and there were four brigadiers, Fraser, Nesbitt, Powell and Gordon. A painful incident in July was the shooting and killing of the latter from an ambush as he was riding home unarmed from a social visit in the neighbourhood of Chambly far within Canadian territory. The perpetrator was a Connecticut lieutenant, Whitcomb, and Canadians said that the object was the general's watch and sword. Unfortunately his superiors did not thus regard it, for he was soon afterwards advanced two steps in rank, to the indignation of the British and of some even of his own people.

CHAPTER VIII

ADVANCE INTO THE ENEMY'S COUNTRY

THROUGH most of August and the whole of September, 1776, Carleton was among his troops and shipbuilders. The former were cantoned at various points down the Richelieu from St. Johns and also along the overland route from there to Laprairie, while barracks and redoubts were being constructed at Ile-aux-Noix, fifteen miles above St. Johns, and not far from the foot of the lake, the island being intended to serve as a dépôt for supplies during the campaign in prospect. It was not till October 5th that the newly constructed fleet sailed lakewards from St. Johns. All the troops, except the few left in the Canadian garrisons, were now gathered at various points in or near Point au Fer. Few readers will need to be reminded that Lake Champlain is a narrow sheet of water from five to fifteen miles in breadth and stretching a length of some ninety miles due southward from Point au Fer to Crown Point and thence in a greatly contracted channel to Ticonderoga. Here was a portage of nearly two miles at a considerable elevation above the shallow connecting river to the spot whence the navigable but narrow Lake George reached southwards again to

SIR GUY CARLETON

the ten-mile road which tapped the Hudson. On the tenth, the improvised British fleet swept proudly out past the Ile la Mothe before a fresh north wind, Carleton having hoisted his flag, if the expression be permissible of a general, on a modest schooner carrying twelve six-pounders. Like the sea-going warriors of earlier days, however, he carried a master mariner with him, in the person of Lieutenant Dacre, while Captain Pringle of the navy had charge of the navigation of the whole flotilla. The latter, besides Carleton's own ship named after himself, consisted of the *Inflexible* carrying nearly thirty guns, the greater part twelve-pounders, the *Lady Maria* of fourteen six-pounders, six twelve-pounders, and two howitzers, besides a gondola with six nine-pounders. There were also twenty gunboats thirty feet by fifteen, carrying each a brass piece of from nine to twenty-four pounds and four long-boats with a gun apiece serving as armed tenders. With the fleet went a cloud of smaller boats carrying troops, baggage, provisions and stores. The ships were manned by six hundred seamen from the men-of-war and transports at Quebec, while the guns were handled by detachments of artillery.

This unconventional armament now sailed out to wrest from the Americans the naval supremacy of that mimic ocean, which was, nevertheless, of such supreme importance in these eighteenth century wars. On the next day, October 11th, a ship from the fleet of the enemy was espied making

THE ESCAPE OF ARNOLD

for the island of Valcour, just off the modern Plattsburgh, but fearful of being intercepted her crew raced her hurriedly on to that island and were taken off under the fire of Carleton's guns by the Americans, whose fleet now discovered itself in the narrow strait between the island and the mainland. The squadron numbered only fifteen armed craft of divers sorts, but was about the same in weight of guns as the other and was under the command of Arnold. The north wind and the chase of the stranded ship had carried Carleton's larger vessels so far past the strait where Arnold's ships lay, that they were unable to beat back in time to prove of service. Carleton himself, however, got in with his gunboats and a brisk cannonade was maintained on both sides for some two hours. The Americans were now in a trap from which it was thought that they could not escape in the night. But as no supports came up, and as his ships and gunboats lacked ammunition, Carleton sheered off, and the gunboats anchored in a line across the mouth of Cumberland Bay into which Arnold had retired.

In spite of the chain of British gunboats and the fall of the wind, the resourceful Arnold slipped by them in the night with muffled oars, and before his enemies were any the wiser was out of sight and heading for Crown Point. Arnold puts his losses in killed and wounded at sixty besides two ships, while others were badly damaged. This feat of getting a battered and ill-built flotilla through the British sentry boats undiscovered was but another instance of Arnold's resourcefulness and dash. But the escape was merely for the moment, for the breeze held fair for the next day and when it dropped in the night the rowboats towed the sloops and schooners. Carleton caught him on the following morning a few miles short of Crown Point.

The fight was soon over. The *Washington*, commanded by General Waterbury, was quickly overpowered. Arnold's flagship, the *Congress*, which took the first fire, was so maltreated that he ran her on shore together with as many of the others as Carleton's guns and the hurry of the moment permitted, and set fire to them all. Two or three gondolas, however, were captured, while only a schooner, sloop and galley got away in safety. Though swept off the lake, yet by burning his ships so promptly, Arnold diminished by so much the value of the victory. Most of his exploits, however, seem in a measure dimmed by some rumour calculated to discredit them. There is a story here, for which Riedesel is the authority, that he left his wounded men in the burning ships, their cries being audible to the British on the lake.

Carleton reports ten vessels burned besides those captured. Arnold in the meantime hurried on to Crown Point and set fire to every building there that would burn, and thence proceeded to Ticonderoga ten miles beyond. There seems to have been no

AN IMPORTANT DECISION

British loss in this second action. Carleton took on with him to Crown Point the American wounded as well as about a hundred prisoners. The former with his customary humanity he caused to be well cared for ; the latter he discharged on parole.

The lake now cleared of every hostile vessel and the British fronts advanced to Crown Point, the vital question arose whether the original scheme of the summer should be carried out at this late date. Crown Point was the obvious base for an attack on Ticonderoga ; but the latter was a strong fortress, in good repair, occupied by Gates with a large force, well furnished and accessible to reinforcements and fresh supplies by the Lake George route at its rear. It would almost certainly be a long siege, and Carleton at Crown Point would be a hundred miles from his nearest base of supplies. There were only five or six weeks remaining before the iron hand of winter would seal up the lake, and for much of the interval its surface would be swept by gales of force sufficient to baffle or hamper navigation. The task of supplying a large force by rough trails through the dense snow-laden woods would be a Herculean labour, even if it were worth the effort, above all in the teeth of the scouting parties which the Americans, so efficient in this business, were sure to send out. Carleton, however, took a survey of the fortress from the water, a proceeding that only confirmed his resolution to postpone all further action till the following spring, when with full possession of Lake

SIR GUY CARLETON

Champlain there would be few obstacles to immediate success.

It goes without saying that there were ardent souls present who saw before them only a fortress which might possibly be captured, and in any case would provide that honourable form of entertainment for which they wore a uniform. But Carleton knew the northern winter and also the high qualities of some of the congress troops, and he may well have hesitated to stultify this experience by attempting an exploit which, even if quickly successful, would leave him in a situation laborious to maintain and of doubtful utility. For putting aside these grave difficulties and granting that the fort were immediately captured and that he could sit down within it in strength and supply his garrison with ease, a wild country would still lie between his army and the settled districts to the south and east of it. Against these he could not operate during the winter, as Germain sapiently suggested, without bivouacking his troops in the open, and to submit European troops, or indeed any troops but perhaps an odd party of hardened Rangers, to such a course was to subject them to certain death. Indeed the notion was too absurd for comment by any person of North American experience. Burgoyne was taken into Carleton's council and fully agreed with him, so far as his opinion could be worth anything in a situation physically outside his knowledge. A letter, however, from General Phillips to Burgoyne seems to point

RETIRES TO CANADA

to the fact that both, though soldiers of too much experience to think it likely that Ticonderoga could be captured then, were dissatisfied that nothing in the way of more active demonstration had been undertaken.

Phillips was discontented because a force was not left to winter at Crown Point, a seemingly purposeless proceeding. Phillips was a good officer but may have been somewhat *difficile*. We get a glimpse of him, through Baroness Riedesel's journal, grumbling at his friend and chief Burgoyne in the same way and possibly with better reason. But Carleton's action in this matter was the cause of discontent to many, which may be accounted for by the fact that there were several hundred officers in the country who had never known a Canadian winter, nor as yet been subjected to serious trials of any kind in the North American wilderness. Carleton's decision, however sound, was fraught with ominous significance, for it was the cause of his supersession by Burgoyne, and Burgoyne's promotion led to a great and historical disaster.

So Carleton and his army at the beginning of November retired to Canada into winter quarters; the former to his official post at Quebec and to those civic duties which the faithful Cramahé had been discharging with his accustomed efficiency.

In the meantime the year's operations to the southward may be briefly summarized as follows: Howe, by orders from home, had abandoned Boston in

SIR GUY CARLETON

March as not worth the sacrifice which its retention would entail. Carrying his army by sea he arrived before New York towards the end of June, being there joined by reinforcements which gave him in all over twelve thousand men. By September Washington, who covered and held this city, was after numerous actions compelled to evacuate it and occupy the forts without. Driven in time from these he crossed the Hudson in November and retreated through the Jerseys to Philadelphia followed by Howe in a fashion so futile and ineffective as to have furnished a wealth of ridicule for the historian. The latter now retired to New York and to a long season of social festivities, leaving New Jersey occupied by his scattered detachments. Though in overwhelming force, most of Howe's posts were recaptured by Washington, and one or two severe defeats, accompanied by surrenders, were inflicted while the English general busied himself in providing entertainment for the garrison and citizens of New York. With a force increased to twenty-five thousand men he allowed the spirits of the congress party, now at zero, to rise rapidly during the winter before the cheering spectacle of his own apathy and the masterly strokes of Washington with his comparative handful of ill-clad and ill-fed men. The Loyalists suffered in proportion, and valuable allies were gradually reduced to rebel sympathizers or to ruin. Such in brief outline was the state of affairs while Carleton's army in Canada

AN OPINION OF THE CANADIANS

was preparing for a campaign in support, as it turned out, of this hopeless general, and while the dismissal of the best available commander was being decided upon by an incapable minister.

There is no occasion to particularize the manner in which Carleton distributed his army this winter. St. Johns and other forts on the Richelieu and at the foot of the lake were all occupied. Some troops wintered along the south shore of the St. Lawrence, while Montreal, Three Rivers and Quebec had each its garrison. Many of the soldiers were quartered among the *habitants*, who seem to have quite recovered from their republican leanings and to have received the soldiers in friendly fashion. Carleton, however, could not overcome his soreness at their recent defection.[1] "There is nothing to fear from the Canadians," he writes to Germain, "so long as things are in a state of prosperity; nothing to hope from them when in distress. There are some of them who are guided by sentiments of honour, the multitude is influenced by hope of gain, or fear of punishment."

The merits and demerits of the Quebec Act ceased for the time to concern men's minds. They were all full of the part they had just played in stirring scenes and might yet have again to play. The peasantry had had enough of politics; money was flowing into the country; markets were brisk. Gaiety on a scale that even the old French régime

[1] See appendix P.

SIR GUY CARLETON

had never known was stimulated in Quebec and Montreal by the presence in the colony of several hundred officers, relieved for the time from the tension of war or the possibility of attack. Lady Maria Carleton with her children, now increased to three, had returned and proved a sprightly and popular young hostess at the Château St. Louis. On the last night of 1776, the anniversary of Montgomery's attack, Baron Riedesel tells us that the governor gave a dinner of sixty covers, which was followed by a public fête and a grand ball, where all social Quebec danced out the old year which had broken on them in so dramatic and different a fashion. In the morning of the same day the archbishop celebrated a grand mass in the cathedral, and those citizens who had shown sympathy with the rebels had to do penance in public. The Church which had suffered a serious fright breathed again. The seigniors, whose sustained rights, like those of the Church, had been so successfully twisted into a goad for the fears of the peasantry by the enemies of government, within and without, were more than satisfied. They were a recognized element now in the governor's council and the question of an elective assembly, even an Anglo-French one, had few charms for men who cared nothing for popular government, and, as a matter of fact, rather shrank from the notion of sitting in so mixed an assembly. Indeed if they had a grievance, it was the minor one of being liable to serve on the new juries in criminal

PLANS FOR NEW CAMPAIGN

cases and sitting with butchers or peasants.

Preparations for the coming campaign, however, proceeded as steadily as the season permitted. Carleton had sketched out a plan and sent it by Burgoyne, who went home before Christmas for the good of his health and better service of his country, as he puts it with unconscious irony in a letter to Germain written soon after landing. Another reason for his return was the illness of his wife, to whom he was deeply attached. Finally, Carleton wished him to go so that the plans for the coming season's operations might be thoroughly discussed in London; for, as we have said, Burgoyne took with him Carleton's plans for the campaign, which he himself had willingly subscribed to and indeed actually urged upon Germain, though without avail. It has been mentioned that Germain's malevolence towards Carleton arose from the latter's attitude towards a protégé of his in the matter of a staff appointment.[1] Carleton had refused to turn out a good public servant, merely to make way for a new arrival without any better claim whatsoever than Germain's personal countenance.

Carleton was now to reap the fruits of this. It was not till May, 1777, that he received the letter confining his authority to the limits of Canada, and notifying him of the fact that Burgoyne was to command in the coming campaign. If Germain before deciding on this course had already been in

[1] See appendix Q.

SIR GUY CARLETON

receipt of Carleton's reply to one or two of his own futile despatches, his action would be more excusable. But there is documentary evidence that he wished him out of the way long before Carleton had expressed the opinion, in as forcible English as official etiquette admitted, that he thought the minister not only an ignoramus and a fool but a wholly mischievous person. Carleton's notice of removal from all command in the coming campaign had been forwarded as early as the preceding August, but the letter had been entrusted to a ship that had failed to make Quebec and was returned to Germain's hand. This was now enclosed with another that filled Carleton with righteous indignation, and left him with no option as to his procedure. This last communication was dated March 26th and was received in the middle of May. The news of the defeat and surrender at Trenton of eight hundred Hessians had reached England, and upon the top of the belated enclosure of August 22nd Germain heaps the preposterous insinuation that Carleton's decision against a winter occupation of Ticonderoga had released enough of its garrison to give material aid to Washington in achieving this bold stroke against the Hessians. Putting aside the fact that three hundred miles intervened between the Delaware and Lake Champlain, Germain by inference admits that nearly thirty thousand highly disciplined troops are insufficient for his other general to protect the environments of New York from

AN IRONICAL REPLY

a quarter of the number of ill-provided and ill-fed provincial militia.

On May 20th Carleton sat down and wrote his reply, which is a lengthy and pungent one. He regrets that Germain's first letter of August 22nd, 1776, had not reached him by November 20th as it might have done, but he had been in no way inconvenienced by the lack of instructions from home at that period, as he imputed their absence to the rather widespread opinion that any officer entrusted with the supreme command ought, from his situation, to be a better judge of what was most expedient than a great general at three thousand miles distance! The irony in this phrase seems somewhat thinly disguised. Carleton then alludes to the well-known events of the winter of 1775-6, which had made any preparations for navigating Lake Champlain notoriously impossible, but reminds Germain that he had constantly urged in the spring the forwarding to Burgoyne's army of a good supply of boats in sections and of artificers. Very few either of the first or second had been sent, and many even of these arrrived too late. Seeing the disregard paid to these pressing matters, Carleton did his Lordship the credit to suppose that his measures in North America had been taken " with such great wisdom that the rebels must immediately be compelled to lay down their arms and implore the king's mercy without our assistance." The order contained in the August letter—which as Carleton points out might

165

SIR GUY CARLETON

have reached him in November—for occupying the forts and thence despatching all his force not needed for the protection of Canada to operate to the north of Howe in support of him, as a vague midwinter expedition is exposed in its naked absurdity. Carleton then proceeds to rub in the elementary truth that an army cannot conduct an active campaign in that country during the winter season, and he descends to Germain's level of intelligence by describing many homely truths and elementary facts which that exalted personage had been either unable or unwilling to master.

It is not the ignorance of a private gentleman of that day concerning North American physical conditions which startles us—that would be nothing—but the sublime effrontery of a man entrusted by the king with the conduct of a great war still cultivating this complacent and deplorable indifference after months of office. Carleton explains, with a forbearance not always so evident, that the soldiers composing this suggested midwinter expedition, assuming that they were ably led and well provisioned, which last would be impossible, assuming also that the enemy was considerate enough not to harass them before they got in touch with Howe, which again was quite unlikely, would nevertheless have all perished from cold alone. Indeed to have attempted the investment of Ticonderoga in November, would have been, writes Carleton, a risky and laborious business even had its

AN IMPLIED CENSURE

capture then been of great practical utility. "I regard it as a particular blessing that your Lordship's despatch did not arrive in due time," he adds. With regard to any assistance rendered to Washington by troops set free from Ticonderoga, Carleton does not seem to think it worthy of argument, but with justifiable sarcasm calls the attention of Germain to the numerical strength of Howe's army, which, with ordinary precautions, could have easily prevented such a disaster as Trenton "though all the rebels from Ticonderoga had reinforced Mr. Washington's army."

As regards the immediate future, he notes that General Burgoyne is to have the command of almost the whole army of Canada for an attack on the famous fortress and subsequent movements, whereas he himself is ordered to remain at Quebec throughout a season of the year when no legislative duties require his presence, and a lieutenant-governor of tried worth and experience is always in residence. The censure that this change of plan implies seems to Carleton as unmistakable as it is unjust, and he proceeds at some length and in trenchant and lucid fashion to summarize the events of the last eighteen months: the critical situations he has emerged from with success, and the difficulties that he has overcome with scant means, though cut off from all the world. With regard to the obstacles inevitable to a large force moving up or down the Champlain route, he suggests an object lesson to Germain in

SIR GUY CARLETON

the failure of Amherst in 1759 to relieve Wolfe by this channel when motives for haste were of extreme urgency, when opposition was ineffective, and an officer of high repute was in command backed by a powerful force and a sympathetic countryside, which now was hostile.

"But I," writes Carleton, referring to the previous year (1776), "pent up in this town till May in a province mostly disaffected and over-run by rebels, when troops arrived a numerous army to expel, who in their retreat burned or destroyed all that might be of use to us. Arrived at the end of those navigable waters, not a boat, not a stick, neither materials nor workmen, neither stores nor covering nor axemen! All must be sought for amidst confusion and the distracted state of an exhausted province. Yet a greater marine force was built and equipped, a greater marine force defeated, than had ever appeared on that lake before. Two brigades were taken across and remained at Crown Point till November 2nd, for the sole purpose of drawing off the attention of the rebels from Mr. Howe, and to facilitate his victories; nature had then put an end to ours. His winter quarters, I confess, I never thought of covering. I never could imagine why, if an army to the southward found it necessary to finish their campaign and to go into winter quarters, your Lordship could possibly expect troops so far north to continue their operations lest Mr. Howe should be disturbed during the winter! If that great army near the sea-

TENDERS RESIGNATION

coast had their quarters insulted, what could your Lordship expect to be the fate of a small corps detached into the heart of the rebel country in that season? For these things I am so severely censured by your Lordship, and this is the first reason assigned why the command of the troops is taken from me and given to Lieutenant-General Burgoyne."

A week later, on May 27th, Carleton wrote again sending in his resignation. "Finding I can no longer be of use to the king's service on this continent, either in a civil or military capacity, under your Lordship's administration, on the contrary, apprehending that I may occasion no small detriment to it, for all the marks of your Lordship's displeasure affect, not me, but the king's service and the tranquillity of his people, I therefore flatter myself I shall obtain his royal permission to return home this fall, the more so that from your first entrance into office you began to prepare the minds of all men for this event, wisely foreseeing that under your Lordship's administration it must certainly come to pass, and for my own part I do not think it just that the private enmity of the king's servants should add to the disturbances of his reign. For these reasons I shall embark with great satisfaction, still entertaining the ardent wish that after my departure you may adopt measures tending to promote the safety and tranquillity of this unfortunate province, at least that the dignity of the Crown may not appear beneath your Lordship's concern."

SIR GUY CARLETON

This outspoken arraignment of Germain's attitude towards him was almost Carleton's last word on the subject in his despatches which continue for another year. For though his method of tendering his resignation to Germain left no opening, even though the desire had been there for combating it, arrangements for filling his place could not readily be made. Of Germain it is related in Lord Edmund Fitzmaurice's *Life of Shelburne* that a contemporary statesman remarked: "He endured every species of indignity from Sir Guy Carleton in particular and other officers with whom he was obliged to correspond. There was a general diffidence as to his honour and a general disrespect for his person." Regarding Germain's rancour towards Carleton, a year previously the king himself wrote to Lord North: "That there is great prejudice, perhaps not unaccompanied with rancour, in a certain breast [Germain's] against Governor Carleton is so manifest to whosoever has heard the subject mentioned that it would be idle to say any more than that it is a fact."[1]

---

[1] Like most other soldiers of the day, Carleton despised Germain. In their official correspondence, Carleton took little pains to conceal this feeling, while Germain was much more restrained. By the tone of some of his letters, Carleton would seem to have courted recall. This is borne out by a passage in his brother's letter to Shelburne, June 13th, 1777—"his correspondence with *Cain* will not dispose the latter to continue him in his government." (Shel. Mss. 213, p. 97. See also appendix "T").

CHAPTER IX

CARLETON SUPERSEDED BY BURGOYNE

CARLETON remained in office another year, and continued his administration with unabated zeal. But he was very sore and could not resist a dig at Germain from time to time in his official correspondence. Burgoyne arrived in Canada almost simultaneously with Germain's letter to Carleton. There is no reason whatever to suspect him of disloyalty to his former chief; on the contrary he had faithfully presented Carleton's plans for the coming campaign to Germain in London, and had made his own recommendations freely and more or less on the same lines. But Germain had another plan, and Burgoyne seems to have accepted it uncritically and without reserve. Carleton's scheme, agreed to by Burgoyne it will be remembered, was to occupy Ticonderoga as a base, and then to act to the southward or more particularly against Connecticut and Massachusetts as it should seem good, having always in view the distance from Howe's army and the very difficult nature of the intervening country.

Germain's plan was excellent in theory, namely, to join hands with Howe and hold the natural artery formed by the Hudson and the lakes, which

SIR GUY CARLETON

is a straight line from New York to Canada. Burgoyne was to push or fight his way to Albany, and Howe was to send a force up the Hudson to meet him. This would have cut off the New England colonies from the rest of the country, and the bare idea of it thoroughly alarmed Washington, though his fears may have been modified by his growing acquaintance with Howe. Germain, for whom physical geography had little meaning, had not taken any account of the difficulties of the route to Albany, which were not insurmountable, and Burgoyne could not help him. But unfortunately he omitted to take Howe, the other partner in the scheme, into his confidence, and that supine, but, in this case, blameless commander, knew nothing whatever about it. As we all know, he was waging independent war to the south of New York when Burgoyne was struggling to his fate at Saratoga; indeed Howe was actually sailing off to Philadelphia at the moment that Germain's victim was surrendering his army as prisoners of war. The explanation of this would be well nigh incredible had it not been given by the minister's own secretary. The despatch containing Howe's instructions lay awaiting Germain's signature, and the latter, omitting this formality in his hurry to get into the country, forgot it on his return.[1] A second expedition was also planned by Germain, to follow the

[1] See appendix R.

FORT STANWIX

old alternative route from Canada to the Hudson by way of Lake Ontario and the Mohawk valley; in other words the two sides of the triangle of which the direct Champlain route from Montreal to Albany formed the base. Colonel St. Leger was in charge of this expedition with some six hundred men, German chasseurs and Johnson's New York Loyalists mainly, with a force of Indians. He was to join Burgoyne on the Hudson after forcing Fort Stanwix, which lay high up the Mohawk not far from Lake Oneida, and was now held by seven hundred congress troops under Ganesvort.

After a month's march St. Leger got within touch of the fort on March 3rd, 1777, and while engaged in some necessary road cutting heard of a reinforcement of eight hundred militiamen marching to reinforce the garrison. Sending out Sir John Johnson with all his Indians and eight hundred soldiers, they intercepted the colonials, and by means of an ambush killed or wounded just half their number. This, however, was the only success. The fort was impregnable to St. Leger's light guns, and while engaged in futile attempts upon it news came that Arnold with two thousand men was ascending the Mohawk. At this the Indians who had lost heavily in the skirmish above mentioned, known as the battle of Oriskany, could not be induced to stay even by such eloquent partisans as Johnson, Butler, and Claus. Upon this St. Leger had no choice but to retreat, which he did in safety, leaving, however,

SIR GUY CARLETON

his tents, guns, and stores. Though a brave man he seems to have had no particular qualities of leadership. Letters both from Butler and himself to Carleton on August 11th and 15th, make a good deal of the fight at Oriskany, and state that St. Leger on his own responsibility assumed the title of brigadier. The next letter sets out the hopelessness of taking Fort Stanwix, and there is nothing more till he reports himself at Montreal with most of his men but without his effects.

This failure in a minor degree encouraged the armies of congress. Carleton does not appear to have rated St. Leger highly. During the first three weeks of June the troops for Burgoyne were collected at the foot of Lake Champlain, while the 29th, 31st, and 34th Regiments, together with part of the 11th and some Germans, were left with Carleton for the defence of Canada. Carleton himself was there to see the last of them and make such final arrangements with Burgoyne as his command in Canada made necessary. There was no friction whatever between the two leaders. Burgoyne declared subsequently in parliament that if Carleton had been making preparations for an enterprise of his own he could not have given himself more assiduously to the task. Riedesel has left in writing his regrets that his former chief was not to be in command. Many must have agreed with him, though Burgoyne's personal charm must have helped, no doubt, to give a cheerful feeling to all around him.

BURGOYNE

Confidence was hardly required; every one, all such at least as were fresh from Europe, looked forward to a mere promenade, so great was thought to be the demoralization of the congress party and so strong the Loyalist element waiting to declare itself.

Burgoyne was a man of good birth. His father, a dashing captain in the army and second son of Sir John Burgoyne, had run through his own small and his wife's considerable fortune, and died on the King's Bench. Young Burgoyne went from Westminster School into a cavalry regiment, and by versatile talents, aided by good looks and a winning manner, he rose rapidly both in military and social life. At thirty-three he was a brigadier, commanding a mixed British and Portuguese legion, and, besides other achievements, covered himself with glory by the capture of Valentia sword in hand at the head of his men. He entered parliament in time to receive as a member the thanks of the House to himself and his corps for their brilliant services under Count La Lippe. He furthered his fortunes by a runaway love match with a daughter of the house of Derby, whose father forgave them and took him into favour. Though with some weakness for bombast he was an able speaker and a formidable opponent of Clive and the East India Company in the House of Commons. He was a dramatist and versifier of considerable reputation, his plays being acted at the theatres, and his poems very much the vogue in society. To soldiering, however, he was most at-

SIR GUY CARLETON

tached, and made a quite exhaustive study of the chief European armies, which he committed to writing, and supplied Chatham with considerable information on the subject. At the outbreak of the American troubles Burgoyne's sympathies were mixed, but he had no scruple about using force. He himself, however, shrank from employment in America, merely from a soldier's dislike to being ordered on service against armed civilians. Before sailing for Boston as junior major-general in February, 1775, he made a long speech in the House of Commons in which he denied having sought employment in this war, but having been selected for service by the king felt bound to accept it.

In short Burgoyne was a man of deserved reputation as well as of engaging personality, brave, honourable, and quite equal to responsible command in any continental army of the day. He was, perhaps, a little vain, and from lack of special experience not quite suited to this particular campaign, while the further fact that a general who undoubtedly was qualified for the task had just been removed from command, adds another mite of bad luck to the load which Burgoyne's reputation had to bear.

It was in truth a splendid force of some seven thousand men that had marched or sailed with Burgoyne; not all, however, were well suited to backwoods warfare, particularly some of the German regiments whose men wore enormous thigh boots and gigantic hats, and carried sabres of mediæval

THE QUESTION OF RELIEFS

calibre, which three items alone weighed more than the whole equipment of a British linesman. But all at least were disciplined and brave, while the artillery was powerful and the transport ample. The composition of the force hardly concerns us, as we must resist any temptation to follow its gradually declining fortunes to the catastrophe of four months later and two hundred miles away that in effect decided the fate of North America and influenced the history of the world.

The leave-taking of the officers serving with Carleton seems, from some of their accounts, to have been an unusually warm one, and when he turned his back on the expedition that he ought to have led, and his face northwards, he had nothing to reproach himself with if he had much to regret. Removed from all touch with the stirring scenes to the southward, Carleton still had his hands full of details throughout the summer and autumn. Burgoyne, though in direct communication with Germain, made from time to time demands on Canada for detachments of men or animals. Carleton in his position had no authority for granting these reliefs, and was always pleased to remind Germain of that fact, though he forwarded them whenever possible. Carleton had been strongly against calling out too many militiamen, as the peasantry were still in a condition of uncertainty and suspicion. A dread of the old French military compulsion, awakened by agitators and quickened

SIR GUY CARLETON

by the attempted musters of 1775, was still great within them.

For a further replenishing of Burgoyne's force after the latter had occupied and garrisoned Ticonderoga, in July, 1777, Carleton had been compelled to sanction a *corvée*, though with great reluctance, the *habitants* being just now in his opinion "more worthy of compassion than blame." His forebodings were right, for the few hundred militia that were raised with difficulty for Burgoyne deserted in troops as his prospects of success declined. Carleton's frequent warnings as to the temper of the Canadian militia had fallen on deaf ears, and the British government persisted in the delusion that as many thousand as were required could be raised by the simple method of proclamation. The Indians of whom many hundred started with Burgoyne were worse than useless, for with at least as much reason as the French militia they fell away before the impending disaster even more readily. Moreover, their employment, heralded by a somewhat injudicious and bombastic speech of Burgoyne's, gave a handle to the enemies of the government on both sides of the Atlantic that proved of inestimable value, and with more logic alarmed the potential Loyalists dwelling within the sphere of operation for the safety of their homes and families. It did not matter that the other party had enlisted their assistance when possible, as in the case of Arnold and Montgomery, and that in every North American

POWELL AT TICONDEROGA

war they had been a recognized and normal factor in the game, nor again that their interests were as much involved as those of the European races. Whether justly, or unjustly, their enrolment now could be represented with ease and plausibility as a heinous crime. Here, as elsewhere in this war, they were virtually useless, save as scouts, while the occasional outrages inseparable from their employment were trumpeted throughout the world.

Carleton had much correspondence just now with Hamilton and the officers holding the far western posts at Niagara and Detroit, for the distant turmoil of the war and the overtures of the agents of congress in those parts were bringing out the western Indians and forcing them to take a hand with whichever side made them the highest bid. By September sinister messages were coming to Carleton from Powell, who was commanding the force left at Ticonderoga, for a great part of his garrison was sick, the lines of communication with Burgoyne, now on the Hudson, were broken, and continuous attacks were being inflicted on his own post by Seth Warner, who had twice summoned him to surrender. Four companies of the 53rd had also been cut off and captured.

St. Leger had now returned from his repulse at Fort Stanwix on the Mohawk, and Carleton sent him on immediately to Ticonderoga, though as he says with a side thrust at Germain "without any power to do so." And so the summer and early

SIR GUY CARLETON

autumn passed away. Domestic concerns were at a lull pending greater events, and the machinery of government was mainly occupied with military affairs. The news from Burgoyne grew worse and worse, till on October 11th Powell heard he had been defeated and was retreating. He then wrote urgently to Carleton, pointing out the hopeless condition of the fortress in event of a disaster to the southward, and begging instructions. Carleton replied he had no authority over him whatever, but if he had, seeing his own ignorance of Burgoyne's situation or intentions, he should leave the matter to Powell's own judgment, only reminding him that he should either work on the fortifications at once or abandon the spot before it was too late.

On October 20th the news of the surrender at Saratoga reached Powell, and three weeks later he was at St. Johns with his force and stores intact. Before abandoning the fortress every wooden building and defence was destroyed, and the brief but famous story of Carillon, as the French called it, was finished. Its walls and bastions sank into decay, though happily their fragments still survive among the trim scenes of modern life as the most suggestive object, perhaps, next to Quebec itself, in all these northern provinces of ancient and pregnant strife. Carleton would have been more than human had he not felt a qualm or two of bitter satisfaction at the retribution which Germain's flouting of himself had brought upon that fatuous

BURGOYNE'S RASHNESS

minister. But though opposition orators in parliament might openly rejoice at the humiliation of their country, Carleton was the last man to breathe one word of ill-placed censure on his supplanter, the lesser sinner, nay, rather the victim of this disastrous blunder, nor is there the least note of triumph in his laconic business-like despatches to Germain.

Almost every one who has dealt with, and probably every one who has studied, this period has indulged his readers or himself in some measure of speculation as to what might have resulted if the cool-headed Carleton with his intimate experience of local warfare and local conditions and topography, his wise caution and self-abnegation in critical moments, had been in Burgoyne's place, and above all had planned the campaign. Burgoyne was infinitely more sinned against than sinning, but he was without American experience and detailed heavily-accoutred Germans, under officers who could not speak English, on difficult enterprises into remote forests where local knowledge and agility were the chief requisites. He perhaps thought more of his own reputation than of his country's when prudence should have warned him to retreat before it was too late. He refused to turn back when such a movement was still possible and many brave officers urged it as the wisest course, and when he did retrace his steps his movements were so dilatory as to ensure disaster. He had wasted time in the advance, he

SIR GUY CARLETON

wasted more in his brief attempt to retreat, which was much worse, and his march was accompanied by a touch of personal frivolity and untimely luxury at his own headquarters which seemed to some of those about him to strike a jarring note at this moment of impending ruin.

Burgoyne, however, made a good case for himself, insisting that his instructions were explicit to march on Albany. Not only that, but he pictured Howe as advancing to meet him and felt that his own retreat might mean Howe's ruin; strict obedience to orders and chivalrous thought for a brother general were in fact his guiding motives. If Carleton had followed his own scheme none of these risks would have been run; even if he had followed Germain's will-o'-the-wisp one cannot imagine that he would have maintained so blind a faith in the Howe myth without some sign, or in any case that he would have allowed himself to be entrapped. Carleton had neither the contempt for the colonial troops, nor the exaggerated belief in effective Loyalist aid which the king, Germain, Burgoyne, and even Phillips were possessed of. These are, however, futile speculations. Perhaps Burgoyne's presence and Germain's fatuity were a wise dispensation of Providence in arranging the world's future. Carleton's interference might perhaps have left worse legacies for after generations. But in judging of current events so philosophical an attitude would be misplaced, and we must regard them from the

HALDIMAND NOMINATED

point of view of a British soldier of the time performing his duty to his king and country.

Carleton was now weary of his anomalous position. No fitting successor had as yet been found, till in October the news arrived that Haldimand had been nominated. It appears that the new governor when he reached London from Switzerland, his native country, heard much talk of Germain's unjust and foolish treatment of Carleton and requested that his own appointment should be cancelled. This was not accepted and Haldimand sailed in October, 1777, but baffled by contrary winds, was driven back into port and had to remain in England till the following season. There was, therefore, no choice for Carleton but to remain.

The legislative council had not met since its first session in 1775 had been dissolved by the alarms of war. The Quebec Act had not yet been put in operation and the courts of justice placed upon a proper footing. In 1775 Carleton had been compelled to nominate the judges himself, for the country had been left to chaos. No one certainly was calculated to make a better choice. He had appointed or maintained in their appointments, Mabane, Dunn, and Panet as the three judges at Quebec, while Fraser, Marteilhe, and de Rouville held like positions at Montreal.

A clause in the Quebec Act had annulled all appointments held prior to it, but Carleton regarded this as a mere form, though a useful in-

SIR GUY CARLETON

strument for evicting any public servants who had failed in capacity, or in their duties. The home government, however, looked upon it as an admirable opportunity for foisting protégés on the Canadian establishment, and this division of opinion gave rise to a correspondence between Carleton and Germain as acrid as their letters on matters military and almost as entertaining. "I should have reproached myself with an abuse of power and trust if under the sanction of that clause I had turned out any of the king's inferior servants who had executed the duties of their offices with integrity and honour." "Two judges at Montreal," Carleton goes on to say, "have been turned out by his Lordship's nominees,[1] Livius and Owen." Alluding to the former he continues: "'Tis unfortunate that your Lordship should find it necessary for the king's service to send a person to administer justice to the people when he understands neither their laws, manners, customs, nor their language, and that he must turn out of his place a gentleman who has held it with reputation for many years, well allied in the province and who had suffered considerably for his attachment to his duty both as a magistrate and a loyal subject." Carleton's judgment in this case is singularly endorsed by the fact that the ill-used gentleman went back to England and in no long time became master of the rolls and Sir William Grant. Livius, his supplanter,

[1] See appendix S.

PLAIN SPEAKING

as a German-Portuguese with a legal experience gained in New England, was not a happy appointment, though he was quite clever enough to make a good deal of disturbance about his fees and give Carleton great trouble, "greedy of power, more greedy of gain, imperious and impetuous in his temper, but learned in the ways and eloquence of the New England provinces, valuing himself greatly on his knowledge of how to manage governors."

Carleton, unlike Burgoyne, professed no exceptional powers of composition, but it must be admitted that he was roused at times by the performances of the colonial office into bits of English that it is a positive pleasure to transcribe. Plagued by the continual appearance of these placemen, generally the representatives of backstair influence, sometimes the inferior deputies of inferior men at home with political influence who took the lion's share of the salary, Carleton wrote at another time to Germain his dread lest the country "should produce what may be found in others; characters regardless of the public tranquillity but zealous to pay court to a powerful minister and, provided they can flatter themselves with a prospect of obtaining by this protection advantages under the Crown, are unconcerned should the means of obtaining them prove ruinous to the king's service." This, too, is plain speaking, but Germain was getting used to it by now and was to hear still worse things when Burgoyne, and more particularly Burgoyne's

SIR GUY CARLETON

friends, spoke their minds in parliament at a later date. Monk, the solicitor-general in Nova Scotia, was among those nominated, to the exclusion of a well tried and deserving person. Monk, however, was in himself a fitting appointment, but Carleton objected to an equally efficient native of the province being passed by.[1] Monk never forgot the quite just objections of Carleton. Carleton's attitude in all these matters is the more worthy of confidence from the fact that he himself had nothing to gain in the way of favour or support. He considered that he had done with Canada and was only acting in the best interests of the country and of the successor for whose advent he anxiously awaited. All this was the more irritating, as the clause in the Quebec Act annulling all present offices had been introduced with Carleton's approval for the express purpose of eliminating unworthy officers nominated by the pernicious system in vogue. Carleton's retention of efficient servants was in keeping with the spirit in which he intended the Act to be applied. Germain's interpretation of it, on the other hand, was for the perpetuating of those very abuses.[2]

A militia bill was passed which made every able-bodied man liable to be called out in defence of his country. This the *habitants* regarded with great dislike. It was ordained, moreover, that those

[1] William Grant, whom Monk replaced, was not a native of Canada. He resided there for only two years, 1775–1777.

[2] See appendix T.

DREAD OF INVASION

not included in musters should perform the agricultural duties of those who were. After Burgoyne's surrender there was another invasion scare, as well there may have been. There were nearly four thousand regulars in the colony, but the Americans by now were in considerable part no longer raw militia, but hardened and experienced soldiers. The Canadian militia numbered on paper some eighteen thousand men. In the autumn of 1777, Carleton called out one-third of the force from the Three Rivers and Montreal districts under those zealous officers de Tonnancour, de Longueuil, and de Lanaudière. The muster was successful, but the immediate alarm of invasion passed away and the men were disbanded. Some half a dozen persons, too, were arrested this year for treasonable practices, and Livius who was sore at the strict limitation of legal fees which Carleton had managed to secure in the interests of a poor community, used some of these arrests as a means of airing his importance and retaliating on the government. Carleton had also nominated a few members of the council as a committee to work in immediate accord with himself during the period of strain and crisis represented by the years 1776 and 1777. It was a time of urgent peril calling for instant action. Many of his council were in the field, and some were prisoners in the States. Livius was not included, very naturally, seeing that he was a German-Portuguese who had recently come from New England as one of Ger-

SIR GUY CARLETON

main's placemen. There was a kind of opening in the armour of the peace constitution of Canada for a pettifogging lawyer to assail, and Livius gave a good deal of trouble by carrying the matter to the privy council. After Carleton had arrived in England the matter was brought to a head when the council deprived Livius of his office.[1]

[1] Livius was not "sore at the strict limitation of legal fees which Carleton had secured." When using "some of these arrests as a means of airing his importance," Livius found Carleton in agreement, for he was right. When Carleton nominated "a few members of the council as a committee to work in immediate accord with himself," he was contravening his instructions and evading the check which the home government had intended to place upon the actions of the governor by saddling him with a council. Livius was not "one of Germain's placemen." Dartmouth appointed him to the bench, and though Germain promoted him to the chief justiceship that was only the fulfillment of Dartmouth's promise. Livius was not removed "after Carleton had arrived in England," nor was his removal the work of the council. Carleton himself did it, and the incident reflects no credit upon him.

Towards the close of 1777, Livius approached him privately and remonstrated with him regarding his "privy council" referred to above and his refusal to present the royal instructions which directed the adjustment of the constitution to meet the just desires of the English mercantile minority. As this failed to move the governor, Livius waited till he could act more effectively. In April, 1778, he raised both points in the legislative council. His motion calling upon the governor to produce his instructions was defeated by a straight party vote between the "French party" and the English party. His motion pointing out the illegality of the privy council was not allowed to face this test, for the council was summarily dissolved by Carleton. Six days elapsed before Carleton dismissed Livius, and from their intercourse during that interval the latter gathered that the former's "offence at these motions had blown over." Carleton undoubtedly desired to remove Livius from the council, but there was a difficulty in the way. The chief justice was *ex officio* a member of the council, and Carleton could find no flaw in his administration of justice. On April 30th, however, Livius upset a popular judgment against a most

HALDIMAND ARRIVES

Carleton's kindheartedness towards the American militiamen that fell into his hands is a matter of history. Here is an address he made to his prisoners at Quebec when he sent them home, which may be accepted as typical if not accurate to the letter: "My lads, why did you come to disturb an honest man in his government that never did you any harm in his life? I never invaded your property nor sent a single soldier to distress you. Come, my boys, you are in a very painful situation and not able to go home with any comfort. I must provide you with shoes, stockings and good warm waistcoats. I must give you some good victuals to carry you home. Take care, my lads, that you do not come here again, lest I should not treat you so kindly." In his last letter to Germain he told him that if the character of

unpopular man. Though Livius was right, Carleton seems to have jumped to the conclusion that he had found the much desired flaw. He dismissed him immediately, but almost as immediately he discovered his mistake.

Livius at once appealed to the home government and the latter regarded Carleton's drastic action as a very grave matter. There was a thorough investigation by the board of trade and the privy council, but Carleton shunned it in spite of repeated invitations to appear. In his written charges, which were far from honest, he criticised only the councillor and not the chief justice at all—though it was the chief justice whom he had dismissed. The result of the investigation was decisive. Carleton was condemned not only for his dismissal of Livius but also for the course of action which had brought them into conflict, and new instructions were dispatched to Haldimand to prevent him continuing in that course. Livius was reinstated and ordered back to his post. ("Canadian Historical Review," vol. 5, p. 196, A. L. Burt, ("The Tragedy of Chief Justice Livius").

SIR GUY CARLETON

the men sent to Canada were of no consideration to his Lordship, the tranquillity of the people, and the security of so important a province, the dignity and the dominion of the Crown, he hoped, at least, would appear worthy of some attention. "I have long and impatiently looked out for the arrival of a successor. Happy at last to learn his near approach, that into hands less obnoxious to your Lordship I may resign the important commands with which I have been honoured. Thus, for the king's service, as willingly I lay them down as for his service I took them up —the most essential and in truth the only service in my power to render your Lordship's administration." These are Carleton's last words in closing this chapter of his history, and not unworthy ones.

Haldimand, Carleton's long-looked-for successor, arrived in Quebec on June 26th, 1778. Carleton returned to England on the same vessel after more than eleven years of service, and nearly eight of actual residence. He was the only British general who recrossed the Atlantic during this episode wearing the laurels of victory, and of all generals his task had been the hardest. He little thought then, that ten years later he would be called once more to the thorny seat of which he had now grown weary.

CHAPTER X

PREPARATIONS FOR PEACE

THE surrender of Cornwallis at Yorktown in October, 1781, proved to be the last military operation of any moment in the War of Independence. The thoughts of almost all Englishmen were now from different motives turned towards peace, those of the Tories slowly and reluctantly, those of the Whigs with a sense of relief in which an inevitable measure of humiliation was tempered by the sordid satisfaction of a party triumph. For then as to-day in England colonial problems, fraught with fateful issues and understood not at all save by a mere handful of Englishmen, were used as weapons of party strife and handled in debate with a complacent and conspicuous ignorance.

Parliament met two days after the tidings reached England. After a long series of fierce attacks and a gradually dwindling majority Lord North's government, in spite of its changing policy, succumbed upon March 20th, 1782. Further misfortunes had contributed to this. St. Eustatius, St. Kitts, Nevis and Montserrat, and worse than all Minorca, had surrendered one after the other to the French and Spaniards. The greater West Indian Islands were in imminent danger. The serious straits to which

SIR GUY CARLETON

Washington's army in the north and Greene's in the south were respectively reduced were not realized in England, and perhaps fortunately so, since further bloodshed at this date could only have produced further calamities. Even prior to North's fall Shelburne, as secretary of state, had despatched Richard Oswald, a well informed and very diplomatic merchant, to sound Dr. Franklin at Paris with a view to terms. A week later Rockingham had formed a new cabinet with Fox and Shelburne as secretaries of state. Oswald was sent back to Paris and to Franklin, accompanied this time by Thomas Grenville, who was to treat with Vergennes for a peace with France on separate lines. This created some feeling between the French and Americans, and may therefore be set down to the credit account of British diplomacy. Germain was the only member of North's government who had resolutely set his face against concessions. So, bellicose as ever in council, he was transferred to the Upper House where open protest was made against the admission of a man who had been cashiered for cowardice in the field.

Clinton was now returning from his command at New York wearied by five years of work, worry, and disappointment, and Carleton was to go out and reign in his stead though with much wider powers; for it was now the season of propitiation, the promoting of peace, and the carrying out of such treaties as it was hoped would shortly be executed. By far the

CARLETON'S RETURN

most formidable item in a sufficiently complicated programme was that of the Loyalists, the colonists who had fought for the Crown, and the great number of non-combatants, incapacitated by sex or age from bearing arms but who had passively espoused the same failing cause. For these and other critical operations it was essential to send out a man of high integrity, of stainless honour, of wide experience, a man trusted by both parties and in both countries, and for once there was no hesitation and no cavilling at the choice. Once again Carleton set out to face a situation bristling with difficulties and to be the judge and arbiter of conflicting interests under the guns of a powerful and not yet conciliated foe.

He had spent three quiet years mainly on the estate he had bought in Hampshire, and now sailed for New York in the beginning of April, 1782. Deliberations of a tentative but hopeful nature were proceeding in Paris and the suspension of serious operations in America though mutually observed was quite informal. His commission was dated April 4th. "His Majesty's affairs," so run the instructions, "are so situated that further deliberations give way to the necessity of instant decision, and whatever inconveniences may arise we are satisfied will be compensated by the presence of a commander-in-chief of whose discretion, conduct and ability His Majesty has long entertained the highest opinion." Carleton was invested with extraordinary powers. He was a commissioner entrusted

SIR GUY CARLETON

with carrying out the conditions of peace when these should be formulated and signed. He was also "general and commander-in-chief of all His Majesty's forces within the colonies lying in the Atlantic Ocean, from Nova Scotia to the Floridas, and inclusive of Newfoundland and Canada should they be attacked."

His naval coadjutor, with whom it may be at once stated he worked in perfect harmony, was the Honourable Robert Digby, "Admiral and Commander-in-chief of His Majesty's ships and vessels employed in North America." It was left to Carleton's discretion, in case of attack by the Franco-American army, whether to fight or to make terms for withdrawal. The great importance of extricating the troops for His Majesty's service elsewhere, if compatible with honour, was duly insisted upon. Not often we fancy has a British commander been despatched on a mission at once so critical and painful in the execution and yet so barren of prospective glory. The Loyalist refugees were earnestly recommended by the king to Carleton's "tenderest and most honourable care," as well they may have been, and we may readily guess that a general who had earned such a reputation for humanity towards vanquished foes was not likely to fail in his duty towards gallant friends in their hour of trial and distress. The safe withdrawal of so large a body of troops was indeed of much consequence, for though peace was probable with the Americans it was less

A WISER GOVERNMENT

so with France, while Holland and Spain had yet to be reckoned with, the latter no mean antagonist in her still familiar and convenient battleground of the West Indies. "It was impossible to judge," wrote Rockingham's government to Carleton with a sane discrimination, rare indeed then and not universal now, "of the precise situation at so great a distance." In this case, at any rate, even though driven to it by despair, the British government may be credited with sending out the ablest and most experienced man at their disposal. It is also to their credit that they loyally maintained, though shaky and shifting among themselves, their admirable resolves. "The resources of your mind," wrote these now thoroughly sobered statesmen, "in the most perplexing and critical situations have been already tried and proved successful. At this perilous moment they give hope to the nation and entitle you to a most honourable support from His Majesty's ministers of which we are authorized to give you the fullest assurance."

Carleton arrived in New York on May 9th, 1782, and received the usual addresses of welcome and confidence, genuine enough no doubt in his case. The first despatches which reached him from England were full of fears for the safety of Halifax in view of French fleets supposed to be prowling on the Atlantic coast, and announced the deflection to Nova Scotian waters of Hessian recruits destined for New York. But the next told a different story, for while Carleton was on the ocean Rodney's great

SIR GUY CARLETON

victory in the West Indies had altered the situation, and dismantled French battleships were making their way to Boston for repairs leaving other less fortunate consorts at the bottom of the sea.

Carleton had found the troops of his command occupying the city of New York, and the immediately adjacent districts within definite lines. Within the latter too, besides the provincial Loyalist regiments and that part of the civil population who adhered actively or passively to the Crown, were a great number of refugees from all parts of the northern and middle colonies, dependent for the most part on money and supplies provided by the British government.

Up the Hudson and in touch with his outposts lay Washington with the northern army and its French contingents. The entire open country was controlled by congress, its officials and its laws. Those who had befriended the Crown throughout the whole or part of the seven years of war had been either driven to one or other of the seaports held by the British or led the lives of pariahs as they clung desperately to the wreck of their property, hoping vainly for some turn of fortune. Of the large number of Americans in the rural districts, who, to use a homely modern idiom, "sat upon the fence" with judgment during the war and descended at the right moment on the right side, history can never take count. Military statistics give room for some approximate inference by the simple process of sub-

DISTRIBUTION OF FORCES

traction. The results arrived at seem in keeping with ordinary human nature and the sparsely settled condition of so vast a country.

Moreover, unlike most revolutions, this one had not been provoked by cruelty, suffering or oppression in the ordinary sense of the word. Such terms would be ridiculously inapplicable. The "chains and slavery" of Patrick Henry, "whose efficacy" said his rivals "was wholly seated in his tongue" were metaphorical. Nor was it wholly a war, as some would have it, of principles and ideals. There were substantial grievances, commercial mainly, and chiefly felt and resented by the propertied classes, a strong element of whom led the common people by whirlwinds of fiery and skilful eloquence.

Leslie at Charleston in South Carolina with Greene and the army of the South watching him, occupied a very similar position to that of Carleton in New York. Savannah, in Georgia, a province both new and weak and still subsidized by Great Britain, was occupied by a smaller force. The evacuation of both these places had been decided upon. St. Augustine again in East Florida was occupied by a British force, but was scarcely threatened, and indeed had become a resort of refugee settlers with loyal views till it passed to Spain at the peace and necessitated a second flitting.

All these posts and districts were under the command of Carleton, who was almost immediately confronted with an awkward incident, a legacy from Clinton's government, though no fault of his nor indeed of anybody but the obscure persons concerned in the outrage. For it so happened that a few weeks previously a Loyalist named Philip White of New Jersey had met a violent death at the hands of the rival party. This so enraged the Tories that, acting under the instructions of the associated board of Loyalists presided over, strangely enough, by Dr. Franklin's son, Captain Lippincott of the New Jersey corps captured and hanged one Joshua Huddy, a captain in the congress militia. They left him suspended to a tree with this inscription pinned on his breast: "We are determined to hang man for man while there is a refugee existing. Up goes Huddy for Philip White." This raised a storm among the Americans and in congress, and peremptory demands were made for the punishment of Lippincott. Neither Clinton nor Carleton, who found the dispute raging, attempted to extenuate so irregular a proceeding, whatever the crime that provoked it. Lippincott was tried by the highest jurists in New York, who found themselves powerless to convict him for sufficient but technical reasons irrelevant here. Washington now demanded that Lippincott should be handed over to him, and, being very rightly refused, caused lots to be drawn among the British officers on parole in Pennsylvania, which resulted in young Asgill, a lieutenant of nineteen in the Guards, being placed in arrest as a victim for retaliation. This unfortunate young man lay virtually under sentence

THE ASGILL CASE

of death for six months. It was another case of André, with the same intercessions from powerful quarters more painfully protracted though more happily terminated. It was, however, a civil case for congress, not, as the other, a military affair for Washington. Carleton, of course, sent the earliest remonstrances both to Washington, who truly replied that he was powerless, and to congress, who would be satisfied with nothing but the blood of either Lippincott or Asgill. The latter was well connected. His mother wrote pathetic and beseeching letters to many quarters, which may be read in the State papers to-day. In despair she wrote to the French minister Vergennes at Paris, and not only enlisted his active sympathy but that of the king and queen of France, who were melted, it is said, to tears. But congress cared nothing for kings and queens. Vergennes now tried more practical arguments, and pointed out to congress that Asgill was in effect as much the prisoner of the King of France as he was theirs, seeing that His Majesty's arms had contributed so greatly to the victory of Yorktown where he was captured. This was unanswerable, or at least savoured of a demand, and congress with a bad grace, for Washington had long since wavered, gave way. The same dilatoriness, however, distinguished their completion of this small matter as had driven Washington again and again to despair in greater ones, and it was October before the youth who had borne himself bravely, "a credit to the British army" as his colonel writes to Carleton, was actually released.

For a long time, even after Rodney's victory, Carleton and Digby felt much anxiety on the seaward side from some combination of uninjured or refitted French squadrons. Inland a curious, unofficial and even precarious armed neutrality held the two opposing armies. Carleton had been instructed among other things to make known to congress and the American people generally the pacific sentiments of the British government and House of Commons, to acquaint them with everything which could tend towards reviving old affections and extinguishing late jealousies, and to inform them that "the most liberal sentiments had taken root in the nation, and that the narrow policy of monopoly was totally extinguished, that a bill would pass the House after the holidays, the consequence of which would be a fresh commission to treat upon the most liberal terms of mutual advantage, and to propose an immediate cessation of hostilities." This must have been a slightly humiliating task even to a broad-minded man like Carleton, who had always deplored this war though he had done such yeoman service in it. His private opinions he might well have expressed, but to be the mouthpiece of a sovereign and government who had suddenly executed such a *volte-face* was another matter. However, he went through it with a good grace, and wrote admirable letters in the strain suggested, both to Washington and to

BRITISH PRISONERS

congress, who replied without enthusiasm but with suitable courtesy. It is interesting to note that Carleton's presence created some alarm among American extremists who feared that the memory of his lenient treatment of their released prisoners and his conciliatory tact might prove to their disadvantage in making terms. But though the sword was virtually sheathed by tacit consent, even Carleton could do nothing to diminish the gulf that had now yawned so wide between the two parties. Polite letters by the score, in connection with ordinary business matters, passed between the British commander on the one hand, and Washington, Livingstone, as president of congress, and Lincoln, as custodian of the British prisoners, on the other. But the noble sentiments and general expressions of goodwill expressed by one and all were almost invariably qualified by some reference to regrettable incidents by subordinates calling for prompt indemnification.

There were now two large bodies of British prisoners in America, besides several smaller bands captured on less notable occasions. The former consisted of the "convention prisoners" surrendered by Burgoyne at Saratoga, and those more recently taken with Cornwallis at Yorktown. Exchanges had slightly diminished the rolls of all, but there were still six or seven thousand prisoners chiefly in Pennsylvania, Maryland and Virginia. These, in connection with their exchanges, treatment and complaints, occasioned a vast deal of correspondence to

SIR GUY CARLETON

Carleton, who made frequent protests on their behalf to congress and elsewhere. A steady stream of Loyalist refugees kept pouring into the British lines—sometimes widows and children of deceased Tories, sometimes men, the victims of an ever growing ferocity that was by no means always confined to the patriot side. The department of claims and succour was under the immediate management of Colonel Morris, a member of the council of New York and one of Braddock's aides-de-camp at the slaughter on the Monongahela seven years previously. This gentleman is also distinguished as the successful wooer of Mary Phillips, who had previously inflamed the heart but not reciprocated the feelings of Morris's fellow aide-de-camp, George Washington. Mary Phillips was a considerable heiress, sister-in-law of Beverley Robinson, of familiar name in Canada, and her property was the only woman's estate formally confiscated. Twenty regiments of Loyalists at different points were in Carleton's command. There were three battalions of de Lancy's brigade under Turnbull, three more of Jersey volunteers under Skinner, Pennsylvania Loyalists under Allen, and Marylanders under Chalmers, the Loyal Americans under Beverley Robinson, who also commanded a corps of guides and pioneers, while Fanning, of South Carolina, commanded the King's American Regiment, the Queen's Rangers raised and led by Simcoe and Tarleton's noted British legion. The last three were afterwards placed on the

ASKS FOR RECALL

British establishment. The pay rolls of all these corps may still be read in the State papers for Carleton's period, thanks to his indefatigable secretary, Maurice Morgan, who has contributed to the shelves of the Royal Institution nearly forty stout volumes filled with the MSS. correspondence and accounts for the years 1782 and 1783.

Halifax was regarded throughout this first summer as the likeliest point of attack in Carleton's command, but the thoughts of the king's government turned now to recapturing the lost West India Islands, as well as to annexing those that had not been theirs to lose, and they were eager to get troops to those points from the American garrisons. In August Carleton heard that complete independence was to be ceded by the coming treaty, and he promptly requested to be recalled. It is worth noting that while the king and his ministers had blustered and vowed they would die rather than concede anything till the Americans were overcome, Carleton, whose views had been far more conciliatory while a hope remained of retaining the colonies, had firmly drawn the line at independence. His ambition had been to win back the colonists by every concession short of actual separation, and now his hopes were dissipated. He had no wish to stay longer in America. He had counted on his position there as a possible means of yet saving the situation from this uttermost calamity, and the chance apparently was not in his eyes a desperate one.

SIR GUY CARLETON

Now, in the first blush of his disappointment, there seemed no more use for him. But it was not to be. Communications were tedious in those days. It was not easy to find a qualified successor, and it ended, as we all know, by Carleton being the last British commander to leave the American shore. He had been busy as usual with his own secret service, collecting by means of trusted agents the private opinions of prominent Americans throughout the colonies. A vast amount of interesting matter thus collected remains among his papers. To quote an example at haphazard—one member of congress wished to know whether, if relations were resumed on the principle of no taxation or customs regulations, the British government would put the American army on the British establishment!

Carleton through all this period had at least money and supplies. There was no question of half rations nor of deferred pay for his troops or his refugees. Washington's army on the other hand had no pay and was ill supplied, while Greene's troops who were watching Leslie in the south were, according to their general, nearly naked. In August the evacuation of Savannah was accomplished, in July that of Charleston was achieved without mishap, though there had been great irritation and some outpost fighting between the troops of Leslie and Greene. War in the Carolinas, where the Loyalist party was especially strong, had been proportionately ferocious. Leslie, however, got his people away

ROUTINE WORK

to the number of fifteen thousand, of whom about half were refugees. They filled sixty ships,—joyful soldiers sick of unsuccessful partisan warfare, and bound for other scenes and honourable service; despondent refugees ruined mostly and bound, some for England, others for a fresh start in life in the West Indies; negroes careless and excited, no doubt, some free, some accompanying their masters, some taken by self-constituted masters to be sold by auction in the West Indies and to raise future troubles between Carleton and congress.

In the autumn Carleton was ordered to Barbadoes and active West Indian enterprises, and then immediately counter-ordered. He had an enormous amount of miscellaneous as well as routine work on his hands, as his surviving papers show. Leslie's Hessians, eleven hundred strong, and seven hundred Loyalist soldiers, the remnant of seven regiments, now joined his garrison from Charleston. Occasional incidents due to the mutual hatred of provincial Whigs and Tories in or about the lines, once or twice threatened to bring Washington down upon him, while the chance of a French attack by sea seems never to have been quite absent, for Digby was weak in ships. But Carleton was at least not worried by the home government. "All we can do," wrote Townshend, "is to indicate objects and choose a fit man like yourself to carry them out." When the news of the proposed concession of complete independence reached New York

SIR GUY CARLETON

the Loyalists were seized with despair and consternation. Petitions streamed in on Carleton. "If we have to encounter," ran one of them, "this inexpressible misfortune, we beg consideration for our lives, fortunes and property, and not by mere terms of treaty." These men knew the relentless spirit of their foes better than the British government. So by this time did Carleton, who replied that it was impossible not to sympathize with their fears, and that he would lay their urgent addresses with all speed before the king.

As the prospect of peace grew stronger and nearer there was much correspondence between Carleton and Washington, the former, with characteristic warmth, urging consideration towards the Loyalist, the latter replying in civil but entirely non-committal fashion. An intercepted letter from Adams expressed the sentiment that all Tories ought to be hanged. Another from Washington suggested that suicide was their only course. Such ebullitions of feeling give some idea of the situation. To the home government Carleton writes that some, no doubt, will try to make terms with the Americans, but others seem ready to submit to any extremity rather than to their foes. He is trying, he continues, to turn their thoughts towards other colonies, for this was already regarded as the inevitable solution of the problem, and Carleton had been for some time in active correspondence with Governor Parr and others in Nova Scotia regarding lands and

A COMMISSION APPOINTED

places for settlement. Haldimand wrote to Carleton that he was exchanging his prisoners with Vermont on easy terms, in view of the wavering sympathies of that martial and heady little province. The *amour propre* of this staunch and trustworthy old gentleman had taken alarm at some report that Carleton was coming to Canada, which meant the writer's temporary subordination, in which case he would certainly go home at once. Carleton soothed his fears by replying that he had not quitted that government with any thoughts of ever returning to it; an eminently unprophetic utterance!

In the meantime congress, ever bellicose and by this time somewhat decadent, had received the proposed terms of peace with a bad grace. They wanted to know the exact nature and extent of the independence proposed, and passed a resolution to the several states not to remit their exertions for carrying on the war with vigour. They could not be persuaded, however, to pay up the arrears due to the officers and men who had conducted it to the present successful stage. Still they went so far as to order Washington to appoint a commission for the exchange of prisoners. Carleton was at a loss to know whether all this meant that he was to be attacked; but in any case he appointed General Campbell and Mr. Elliott to meet Washington's commissioners and proposed to that general a definite agreement for the suspension of hostilities. Washington replied that Indian raids—alluding to

SIR GUY CARLETON

the ever lively Johnsons on the Mohawk—and marine attacks that in a small way on remoter shores were not infrequent, must in that case be also stopped, which was only reasonable. Generals Heath and Knox were nominated as Washington's commissioners in the matter of cartels, and the four met at Tappan, between the lines. The meeting ended in speedy and farcical fashion, for the Americans opened the ceremony by presenting a big bill for the keep of the British and German prisoners. Campbell and Elliott were amazed. The negotiators were evidently at cross-purposes so all four returned to their respective quarters, the British rather sore at having, as they thought, been brought on a fool's errand, the Americans on the plea that the others were invested with no power to treat.

Carleton had now with him nearly eight thousand Germans, five thousand British regulars, and some seventeen hundred provincials. Nine thousand of the regulars were quartered at McGowan's Pass and about a thousand at Kingsbridge, Paulus Hook, Staten Island and Long Island respectively. The provincials were stationed within the city for obvious prudential reasons. The British regiments were the 7th, 22nd, 37th, 38th, 42nd, 48th, 54th, 57th and some artillery. The German prisoners captured with Burgoyne and stationed mostly in Pennsylvania were also a constant source of trouble to Carleton, though not through any fault of their own, poor fellows. But with the Americans food

THE PLIGHT OF THE GERMANS

was unquestionably scarce, and the prisoners suffered in consequence. The Germans could not be exchanged and some of the understrappers in the congress service had notions far removed from equity or military custom. Some of them certainly displayed a talent for mean and petty oppression and exaction that surely surpassed the low average of the Jacks-in-office of that day in most countries. The poor Germans, often doubtless for lack of other quarters, were confined sometimes in wretched gaols, sometimes in other squalid buildings, and their complaints were met even by superior officers with the retort that the British government was responsible because it would not pay for their keep! All such expenses may well be lumped in a general money compensation to the victor in a long war at a treaty of peace, but I know of no other case where an army still in the field was expected to liquidate the board bill of their comrades in captivity by quarterly remittances. At this distance of time, when all concerned have long been dust, and the Americans have earned a reputation for unexampled hospitality, we may be permitted to enjoy a little the humour of the situation.

The Germans were told, however, that they might liquidate their maintenance account and at the same time secure their liberty by a payment of eighty dollars. As few of them had eighty pence the proposition offered small consolation. It proved, however, only a forerunner to a more practical suggestion;

SIR GUY CARLETON

for plenty of farmers it seems were willing to pay the bonus in return for a three years' indenture of the liberated soldier and his services. An alternative proposition was also pressed upon them with all the eloquence of a rival scheme, the recruiting sergeants being empowered to offer them their liberty and a bounty besides on enlistment in the service of congress. From our modern point of view it seems quite curious how few of these poor men took advantage of either, and with what indignation the great majority repudiated both offers. These German mercenaries are often written of to-day and were then, among the Americans, usually regarded as oppressed peasants, torn unwillingly from their homes by petty princes who fattened on the proceeds of their nefarious bargain with the British government. Much of this arises and arose from ignorance of the military conditions and customs of Europe in that day—an irrelevant subject here. But one gets from the attitude assumed and the answers given by these much pitied mercenaries, a curious glimpse of how strong among them was the pride of military caste. Some of the meetings between groups of these people and the American officials were vividly described by one or other of their number and forwarded by way of protest to Carleton, and may still be read among his papers. They scorned the notion of doing menial work as an indentured servant or "slave" to an American farmer. The recruiting sergeants quite approved of this and

LOYALTY

applauded the repugnance shown by men who followed "the glorious trade of war" to becoming "the slaves of farmers"—for this is how these unblushing republicans actually put it. But when the latter came forward with their bounty, less no doubt their own commission, and an offer to pursue the paths of glory in the continental line, these simple people found their duty to their own prince and oath of allegiance to King George an insuperable obstacle. "Though we are treated not like prisoners of war but like wretches fallen into the hands of barbarians," writes one of them, after they had been addressed on the subject of the above proposal, "we replied that every word was thunder in our ears and were struck dumb with such barbarous proposals." Such warmth of language to the modern Anglo-Saxon would appear quite overstrained, while to prisoners in durance vile the offers might seem tempting enough, and the transfer of allegiance at that moment may well have seemed a mere trifle to an American. But neither they at that time nor we at this can put ourselves in the place of a Hessian corporal of the eighteenth century with feudal superstitions, homesickness, and domestic affections tugging at his heart strings. The great number of private men, corporals, and sergeants counting fifteen and twenty years service strikes one as remarkable in these regiments. Their behaviour upon the whole throughout the war, whether in quarters or in the field, had been admirable.

SIR GUY CARLETON

Early in the winter Carleton received permission to return home, so soon as Lieutenant-General Grey, appointed in his place, could relieve him. But peace now seemed so certain that Grey was withheld and Townshend wrote to Carleton, "Let me earnestly entreat you to remain at this important moment for the evacuation of New York and distribution of His Majesty's troops. So much less brilliant but none the less difficult and important; a great and complicated business, removal and distribution of troops, security and disposal of public property, liquidation and adjustment of accounts, the care, support and assistance of Loyalists, all claim your attention. The justice of your claims to return home are obvious. If His Majesty could find any man on either side of the Atlantic as much trusted he would not press this so urgently."

There is no space here for any catalogue of Carleton's manifold duties through this busy and anxious winter of 1782-3. Arrangements were being pushed forward in Nova Scotia, which then included New Brunswick, for the reception of Loyalist emigrants, and Carleton among other things protested with success against the saddling of uncleared forest lands with quit rents. At another time we find him restoring the bells of Charleston which some fervent refugees had included among their baggage, at another endeavouring to recover six thousand pounds worth of clothing which American underlings had appropriated on its way to the prisoners in Pennsylvania.

CESSATION OF HOSTILITIES

And amid these and innumerable other minor matters, outside the care of a large garrison, the bitter cry of refugee arrivals was always in his ears.

At the end of March, 1783, arrived the news that the preliminary articles of peace were signed. The opposing generals complimented one another, and Washington issued orders for an absolute cessation of any hostile acts. But the French government were ill pleased. The capture of American trade had been with them a leading object, and as one means towards it they hoped to secure terms so favourable for the Loyalists that they would remain in the country, assist in its progress, and look to the French as benefactors. Dr. Franklin and Oswald had upset all this and, what was more, the Loyalists now learned to their dismay that any hopes they still cherished of getting some reasonable guarantees in the treaty were dashed to the ground. Congress had no power, so it declared, to take any action in this matter. All it could do was to undertake that a recommendation should be made to the different states to show consideration for their late enemies. The British ministers, who, to do them justice, had struggled in vain for something better than this, hoped that even so much might have some mitigating effect. The wholesale confiscation of property at the close of a civil war fought out for a principle between neighbours of the same race, blood, and faith, was unknown among civilized people in modern times, certainly among Britons.

SIR GUY CARLETON

But the Loyalists knew the temper of their people better and prepared forthwith to depart. On April 17th five thousand five hundred and ninety-three refugees were embarked for Nova Scotia as a first instalment. "Many of these," writes Carleton to Governor Parr, "are of the first families and born to the fairest possessions, and I beg therefore that you will have them properly considered."

On May 6th Carleton met Washington and Clinton, the governor of New York, at Tappan and discussed the exchange and liberation of prisoners. Carleton's vessels were in such demand that it was necessary to march the prisoners overland to New York, and the management of this business was entrusted to Colonel Alured Clarke, whom we shall meet again later in Canada. About six thousand altogether had to be thus brought by road, some from as far south as Charlottesville in Virginia. Those who have read Captain Anbury's journals may well fancy that they shook the red dust of that now delectable and always most beautiful Virginia district off their ill-shod feet with heartfelt relief. A week later proclamations were sent out by both governments dissolving the officers' paroles. By the terms of the treaty the British were to evacuate New York, the only spot in the country except the far western posts that they now held, with as much despatch as possible. Nothing was actually said about the Loyalists going with them; but Carleton to his honour determined to interpret the clause this way,

TRANSPORT DIFFICULTIES

and, as time went on and the bitter feeling towards them more fully revealed itself, his resolution in regard to this became immovably fixed and proof against the constant complaints of congress at the delay. His transport facilities were quite unequal to the great demands made on them. From the time that peace was proclaimed fresh refugees, who had made brief experiments at home of what peace meant, came thronging in. As fast as any new supply of transports gave promise of meeting the demand these refugees increased and occasioned further delay. The whole proceeding took over six months, and from July onwards Carleton was constantly importuned by congress to fix some precise limit to his occupation. He replied shortly, but always courteously, that he was quite as anxious as they were to finish the business, that it was purely a matter of transport, that in the collection of this his utmost endeavours were engaged and that no man could do more. To their objections that the Loyalists were not included in the agreement Carleton replied that he held opposite views. In any case he regarded it as a point of honour that no troops should embark until the last Loyalist who claimed his protection should be safely on board a British ship. He requested congress to appoint agents that they might see for themselves how zealous he and his officials were in their endeavours. By September, when there were still numbers to be moved, Carleton got rather short in his replies to these importunities,

SIR GUY CARLETON

and at last on being requested to name an outside date he honestly declared that he could not even guess when the last ship would be loaded; but he was privately resolved to remain until it was. He informed them, moreover, that the more the uncontrolled violence of their citizens drove refugees to his protection, by so much the longer would his evacuation be delayed.

The American government were greatly concerned lest property belonging to their friends should be included in the Loyalists' baggage. By far the most difficult property to classify were the negroes, mostly refugees like the others. Who of these were bond and who were free, and if the former to whom did they belong and what course was the correct one to pursue, was a problem such as no fair-minded British commander, except Leslie at Charleston, has probably ever been confronted with. The Ethiopian's affidavit, then as now, was hardly reliable. For that matter few white men would be willing to swear away their liberty. Then again the question whether a negro escaping from a rebel master to a government at the time locally supreme and who had thus obtained his freedom should be returned as a chattel, which according to strict law and the treaty he should have been, was really a complicated question. It must be remembered that the British flag did not legally mean freedom in 1783 as Canada did half a century later. Carleton was utterly loath to send these people back

NEGROES

to masters who would not unnaturally receive them with more or less harshness of treatment. He requested, therefore, that commissioners should be appointed to take full particulars of every negro that was shipped, and wherever there was any case for compensation it should be registered for after consideration. This plan was adopted, and elaborate registers were made of all the identified negroes, describing their appearance, sex, age and owner. These may be read to-day among Carleton's papers, where they are described in hundreds as "likely fellows," "stout wenches," "likely lads," "incurably lazy," "stout fellows," and "wornouts." To any one familiar with southern life immediately after the late Civil War, as is the case with the present writer, these phrases have a curiously suggestive ring, though the Pompeys, Cæsars, Jupiters, Princes, and Dianas that figure in Carleton's lists had then almost wholly given way to less classical appellations.

Elaborate lists still remain to us of the officers of the Loyalist corps put upon half pay, and among the letters to Carleton from various provincial officers one is surprised to find that the custom of purchase apparently flourished even in these locally raised regiments, three hundred pounds being mentioned as having been paid for a company, and two hundred and forty pounds for the quartermaster's berth in a New Jersey volunteer corps. The most pathetic portion perhaps of Carleton's papers consists of letters from widows of Loyalists whose husbands had fallen,

SIR GUY CARLETON

explaining their wretched circumstances in detail, and petitioning for pensions which seem to have been always allotted to them. Six Loyalist corps numbering about one thousand five hundred men were disbanded and settled in Nova Scotia, and several Hessian officers with small fortunes applied to Carleton for similar privileges, which were, of course, granted on the same scale of acreage as that allotted to British officers. But I must not drift into the affairs of the Loyalist refugees so voluminously set forth in the Carleton correspondence, and of such abiding interest to most Canadians. It will be enough to say that the bulk of these shipments went to the Maritime Provinces, including Cape Breton and Prince Edward Island, whose proprietors had made considerable, though to them profitable enough, concessions. A few went to both Upper and Lower Canada to swell the numbers that then and afterwards resorted thither overland, and these last included many Americans other than Loyalists frightened out of the neighbouring states by the bogey of taxation which was now provoking disturbances all over the country. The number of Loyalists whom Carleton actually embarked it is difficult to estimate with any accuracy. The number expected was twenty-seven thousand, but this was probably in excess of that which actually sailed. It was the end of November before the last British drum beat its farewell on the battery, and the last British red-coat filed into the boats. On November

THE LAST DESPATCH

29th Carleton wrote his last despatch on board the *Ceres* anchored in the harbour. It supported a final petition of Loyalist widows for pensions, and included the fact that "His Majesty's troops and such remaining Loyalists as chose to emigrate were successfully withdrawn on the 25th inst., from the city of New York in good order, and embarked without the smallest circumstance of irregularity or misbehaviour of any kind." Thus dropped the curtain on Carleton's second period of laborious and distinguished service to his country, as it also dropped on one of the most fateful and pregnant struggles in the world's history.

CHAPTER XI

DORCHESTER'S RETURN

AFTER two years spent in England, which, so far as we know, were uneventful ones to Carleton save that he was created Baron Dorchester, he was offered and accepted the chief-governorship of Canada at the beginning of 1786. With the sudden influx of Loyalist refugees variously estimated at from thirty to fifty thousand, a third of whom perhaps would be in Canada proper, the equilibrium, social, political and religious of that country, bade fair to be considerably upset. New cleavages, new issues and new difficulties were imminent within the province. Without it France was in a highly electrical condition, while one of the two great parties into which the United States was now divided was actively hostile to Great Britain, and sore at the failure to include Canada in their new republic. Indeed the immediate future of Canada promised to tax the capacities of the ablest ruler, and the British government at this crisis seems to have turned naturally to Carleton. Domestic legislation of a thorny kind and danger from without was the almost certain lot of the next occupant of the Château St. Louis, and it would seem that some pressure was put on Carleton in the matter and that he went out rather from a sense of patriotism and duty than personal inclination.

SIR GUY CARLETON

However unemotional his temperament, the feelings of Dorchester, as we must now call him, may well have been stirred as he again beheld the spires and rooftrees and batteries of Quebec ascending from the water line to their high protecting fortress, and as he climbed once more the steep familiar streets, every turn of which he had such good cause to know. When eight years previously Haldimand had arrived to take his place, the two had met in brief interchange of courtesies. This time Dorchester had renewed Haldimand's acquaintance in London before sailing, and was received at Quebec by Hope, the lieutenant-governor, who had acquitted himself with sufficient credit in the interval. His government had been marked by comparative domestic peace, pending the advent of so renowned an arbiter of Canadian friction. "We must preserve Quebec even if we have to send Carleton himself," Shelburne had written with scant courtesy and, one might add, scant gratitude, to Haldimand, whose biographer in this series has freed the memory of that excellent official from a good deal of ill-judged and unmerited censure.

Events of incalculable significance to North America, and to the world for all time, had happened since Carleton left Quebec in 1778. A new nation had arisen to the southward and had thrown off inadvertently the germ of another. A new and invigorated Canada had been born, which through the crucial fever of racial discord was to emerge at last into a power of such proportions as few of its most

UNITED EMPIRE LOYALISTS

ardent friends had ever dreamed of; but Dorchester was among those few.

He had now to face the incipient difficulties of this upheaval as it affected Canada. The shaggy wilderness along the Upper St. Lawrence and the north shore of Lake Ontario, that had been in his former reign but a forbidding barrier cutting him off from the western posts, was now gradually opening to the light before the axes of the first United Empire Loyalists. Dorchester's trouble with the earlier handful of British Americans in their inequitable claims to a monopoly of power must have recurred to him as he looked over the correspondence relating to thousands of these men, whereas before there had been only hundreds. But the latter, by no stretch of imagination, could have been regarded as picked men. These others Dorchester, from his New York experience no doubt, knew well were persons for the most part of another calibre, and yet this very fact may have seemed to make the future problem of Canadian government the more difficult.

That Dorchester had to report his reception as a warm one goes without saying. His reputation had probably increased in his absence, not only by that automatic process by which time enhances the virtues of the virtuous and the vices of the vicious, but by comparison with other rulers who even if misjudged and underrated were at any rate not Carletons. He had, moreover, a host of old friends

SIR GUY CARLETON

in the country, or perhaps having regard to the popular governor's temperament, admiring acquaintances would be the better word. The "friends of congress," or those advocating the most exclusive Anglo-Protestant pretensions were doubtless not so enthusiastic in their greeting.

Dorchester had come out with wider powers than any previous governor. He was not only the ruler of Canada, but had chief authority, when called upon to exercise it, over Nova Scotia, New Brunswick, and Prince Edward Island. The latter, hitherto under an administrator directly responsible to the Crown, was now, though vastly increased in population through United Empire Loyalist immigrants, under a lieutenant-governor. New Brunswick, just created a province, was for the same cause similarly administered. The Loyalists in the district of Montreal and those already at Kingston on the shores of Lake Ontario numbered from five to ten thousand and were steadily increasing. There was not now to be another Livius, for this time Dorchester had brought out his own chief-justice, William Smith, son of a New York judge and himself once chief-justice of that important province. Taking the loyal side he had retired to England with Carleton who held him in high regard. Both of them had been much in conference while in London with Lord Sydney, now a secretary of state, as to the future conduct of Canada, and Dorchester's after correspondence with that nobleman bears small

LEGAL CHAOS

resemblance in tone to the perfunctory and peppery despatches between Germain and himself.

Dorchester was at once confronted with the old difficulty of the French and English laws in Canada, which the Quebec Act had theoretically settled by giving the criminal courts to the one and the civil courts to the other. Some, however, of the ordinances of the Quebec Act were not final, and had to be renewed every two years, which in such cases gave rise to much discussion. But though the English criminal law commended itself to all, English litigants in matters not affecting land constantly rejected the French code. This, being a mixture of the old French and Roman law, with much that custom alone had improvised and sanctioned, presented a Herculean labour for the English advocate to grapple with. French justices it was complained still followed French, and English justices English law, precisely as they chose, to the confusion of all litigation. Smith showed his predilection at once for a loose interpretation of the Quebec Act, and a leaning towards the royal proclamation of 1763, and gave official utterance to it in reversing a judgment of the Common Pleas that came to him early in his first term. Indeed the confusion had become so great that one of Dorchester's first acts on calling the legislative council together was to appoint a committee to inquire into the matter and report upon it.[1]

[1] See appendix U.

SIR GUY CARLETON

Committees were also nominated to report on the commerce, the police and the education of the province. Commerce was almost wholly represented by Montreal and Quebec, both now about the same size, and each containing about eight thousand souls. Their merchants, being mostly British, drew up a report on the confusion of the existing laws, which Dorchester's committee in turn strongly recommended to his "most serious consideration and reflection." Trial by jury in civil cases had, since Dorchester's former rule, been introduced with the limitation that it was optional with the litigants. Smith now brought a new bill into the council continuing the ordinance in all civil affairs, and establishing trial by jury between "merchant and merchant, and trader and trader," as well as in the matter of "personal wrongs" proper to be compensated in damages, "with certain other clauses intended to cure some of the disorders now prevalent in the courts." This, however, was rejected by the committee. The opposing party now brought in a fresh bill, but in the words of one of the others it merely retained the name of jury lest the advantages derived from that "glorious institution" should be wholly lost. The merchants prayed to be heard by council against the bill, and were so heard through the mouth of Attorney-General Monk for six hours. In his peroration Monk exposed such a confused state of justice that he "astonished the whole audience." These disclosures moved Dorchester to ap-

EDUCATIONAL CONTROVERSIES

point a committee under Chief-Justice Smith to investigate into the past administration of the laws as well as into the conduct of judges in the courts both of Appeal and of Common Pleas. Every leading person was examined, and such a state of confusion was shown to exist, says a legal chronicler as no other British province ever before laboured under, "English judges following English, French judges French law, and what was worse some followed no particular laws of any kind whatsoever."[1]

The committee called to take evidence on the schools and education of the province, and to form an opinion as to founding a university, produced no definite result, like the others, in view of the great general changes involved in the division of the country by the Canada Act of 1791. But it produced a pretty controversy between Hubert, the Bishop of Quebec, and his coadjutor Bailly, who was a highly polished cleric, a *persona grata* at the Château St. Louis, and had gone back to England in 1778 as tutor in Carleton's family. Their respective replies in answer to questions make instructive reading. It need only be noted here that the bishop was in favour of an improved education in theory only. He enumerated the various seminaries, such as that at Quebec for the higher education mainly of priests, and the other at Montreal which was merely a large free school—besides its college. The bishop proceeded then to mention the various convents,

[1] See appendix V.

SIR GUY CARLETON

such as the Ursulines, and the nuns of the General Hospital who gave education free or otherwise to girls. It seems clear from his manner of reply that virtue and respect for religion were the main things imparted to the young ladies at these teaching centres, which he considered more than adequate. He certainly gives the impression that he thought nothing else much mattered. But this was not what the committee were sitting for. Neither any lack of virtue or religion had caused concern to the governor and his council, but rather the want of educational opportunities for all classes. When the bishop was asked if it were true that only three or four persons in each parish could read and write, his Lordship repelled the insinuation as "a wicked calumny started by bad men" which had even reached his own sacred ears. Thirty, he declared, was more like the average number, but anticipating perhaps some measure of scepticism on the part of the committee, about half of whom were French, he qualified the estimate by admitting the larger portion of these select ones to be women. "The country curés," he protested, "do their utmost to spread education in their parishes." With regard to a university presided over by men of unbiased and unprejudiced views he opined that that sort of men had generally no views of any kind on sacred matters. As to the demand for a university, he thought that the farmers with so much land to clear would prefer, until that was accomplished, to keep their sons at home to help

EDUCATIONAL CONTROVERSIES

to clear it, rather than spend hard-earned money in sending them to gain education at Quebec.

M. Bailly, the coadjutor, who for various reasons was on the worst of terms with his ecclesiastical chief, but who was an abler and broader-minded person, then proceeded to demolish the bishop's statements in relentless fashion, under the specious pretext that some malevolent person had foisted the paper on the committee as the bishop's with design to injure him. He sarcastically depicted the bishop as arguing that till Canada was cleared up to the polar regions the education of its inhabitants must be left in abeyance. His further enthusiasm for non-sectarian education is eloquently expressed and covers several pages. It was pointed out by him and others that the new provinces of Nova Scotia and New Brunswick would contribute students to such a university increasingly as time went on.

The finding of the committee was under six heads, which in general terms may be described as in favour of free common schools in every parish and a secondary school, to use a modern phrase, in every town and district, and lastly of a non-sectarian college from which religion was to be rigorously excluded. As regards the last proposition, this committee of 1787, judged by the light of the intervening period, may be regarded as a singularly sanguine body.

As a Canadian historian has well said, these gen-

SIR GUY CARLETON

eral inquiries on commerce, law and education, if they served no other purposes, succeeded in illustrating in a high degree the passions and prejudices that distinguished the province at that day. The income of the Jesuit estates was regarded by most people as a natural source of revenue for any fresh educational enterprises. Four aged members of the fraternity alone survived, and at their death the property passed away from the order. The balance of the income, after their frugal wants had been supplied, had been hitherto devoted to the maintenance of the seminary. But another claimant had to be considered, for the estates had been either granted or promised to Amherst about the time of the conquest, and he now urged his rights. Perhaps these had not been formally established or defined; in any case the Canadians, as was natural, in view of the scarcity of money and lack of educational facilities strenuously objected and presented a petition to the Crown which Dorchester forwarded early in 1788. The weakness of Amherst's claim, if otherwise valid, lay in the fact that the Jesuits held the estates in the light rather of trustees than of owners, and that the property was originally given for the education of Indians and Canadians. The matter was not finally settled until 1888.

Other interests, however, were moving. In his first year Dorchester was approached by the Vermonters in the person of Silas Deane, who had been mooting the subject in London, in regard to an outlet for

THE INDIAN QUESTION

their trade by the St. Lawrence. Vermont, not admitted as a state till 1791, as readers of Haldimand's life will know, had been prompted by various reasons during the war to coquet with British rule through the medium of Quebec. Now, however, it was a commercial matter and all above board. Free trade with Canada had been suggested long before and the Green Mountain men were now anxious to combine with the British province in circumventing the rapids of the Richelieu between St. Johns and Chambly—for this was then their natural trade outlet—by a canal. Dorchester, who had already discussed the matter in London, was favourable to the scheme. It seemed feasible and would have promoted friendly relations, a motive always powerful with Dorchester. But this also fell through, and was not achieved for fifty years.

What gave the governor most concern, however, was the critical state of the Indian question in the far West. The moment he landed this was pressed upon him by letters from Sir John Johnson who was in charge of the western districts. These posts, stretching southwards from Detroit to the Ohio and northwards up the shores of Lake Huron to Michilimackinac, had been retained by Great Britain as security for certain concessions on the part of the United States to the Loyalists. The Indians had been ignored altogether in the treaty of peace through timidity, or oversight, or a feeling of helplessness, and those whose hitherto recognized territories were being invaded right and left by adventurers over whom an inevitably weak congress had no control, were loud in their protests. The forts were feebly garrisoned, the Indians were losing faith in British compacts and friendship, while something approaching war on a considerable scale and of a quite lawless kind was setting the West on fire. The Alleghany frontiersmen, who mainly composed the vanguard of these new Ohio settlers and would-be settlers, were a fine and virile race with a prevalent strain of Ulster or Scotch-Irish Presbyterian blood. The defenders of the Sault-au-Matelot at Quebec in 1775 had felt their courage, and the sentries on the walls had suffered much from their deadly aim. But they had their failings, chief among which perhaps was an impatience of outside control and a contempt for distant governments, natural enough to men who had not merely to carve out, but to fight for their own homes. Historians and contemporary despatch writers speak of them as Virginians and Pennsylvanians, but such a definition is purely technical and due to the fact that they lay at the back of and within the parrallels of these and other states. They bore indeed slight resemblance to the normal Virginian or Pennsylvanian, had little intercourse with them, and flouted both them and their governments whenever it suited. For the weak authority of the much harassed congress they had no regard whatever, unless it was backed by sufficient troops. Some acquaintance with

ALLEGHANY FRONTIERSMEN

their descendants still living rude lives in the wilder portions of their ancient haunts helps one to realize how hopeless it would have been, except by force, to impress upon such people the equity of distant treaty rights and above all the rights of Indians, whom they held as vermin, though they respected them as warriors. To hold back men of the type of Boone or Brady, of Clarke or Logan, of Shelby or Sevier, from the edge of a boundless wilderness by parchment documents, was a practical impossibility even if such treaty rights had been clearly defined. Behind these born frontiersmen followed clouds of only less hardy and reckless settlers from the eastern provinces, and soldiers lately disbanded from Washington's forces. The Indians' territory was invaded at all points on the upper Ohio and to the south of the lakes, and sanguinary skirmishes were of constant occurrence. St. Clair, who had commanded and evacuated Ticonderoga before Burgoyne's advance was sent as governor to the new territory, and did his best for peace, but the Indians told him that they could no more restrain their young men than the Americans could hold their own wilder spirits. The British agents in the meantime could give no assistance, while the small British garrisons on the edge of the struggle were weak to futility.

The Indians were clamouring to know whether the British posts were to be given up to "the Yankees,"[1] and threatened to visit Dorchester at Quebec,

[1] See appendix W.

SIR GUY CARLETON

and get to the root of the matter. Indeed these unfortunate people may well have fallen into a state of bewilderment as to who was now their "Father," a third claimant having appeared as candidate for this disinterested relationship. In the meantime they continued to interchange scalps with the western frontiersmen who burnt their villages and council halls, till the American regular troops were called into the field to the number of two thousand three hundred and received one severe defeat at the hands of as many Indians. But this was not till 1791.

It was no desire of wounding British susceptibilities or infringing British rights that prompted this forward movement on the American frontier so far as the government was concerned. On the contrary, there was a general appreciation of the advantages of English over-sea trade after its long cessation, and the trans-Alleghany people saw that their only outlet was by the Mississippi through Spanish territory. There was, therefore, a strong feeling that this magnificent waterway must be opened to them willingly or unwillingly. The backwoodsman's views on foreign politics were crude and are sometimes only less so now. The feelings of Spain would not have been much considered had the power been theirs, as the darker schemes of Aaron Burr and Wilkinson and their unfortunate dupe Blennerhasset a few years later give ample evidence.

It was natural for every reason that Dorchester should wish to visit his sub-governments of Nova

PATTERSON'S HOBBY

Scotia and New Brunswick as soon as possible, having in view the interesting situation and rapid development brought about by the Loyalist refugees. Almost immediately on landing he informed Parr, the lieutenant-governor of the former province, that he hoped shortly to be with him, and to include the islands of St. John and Cape Breton in his tour. The former, at that time scarcely giving promise of the importance it has since attained as Prince Edward Island, was under a lieutenant-governor named Patterson, who on being superseded by the home authorities in the autumn of Dorchester's arrival, refused to give up his post to his successor, Fanning, whom they had sent out. He writes his reasons to Dorchester, which were in effect that the island had been his hobby. He had given it its laws, its roads, its inhabitants, its separate legislature. He had made his home there and his interests were such that they could not be managed by another. He could not go to England to answer charges of which he knew nothing, as when he was in Europe he obviously could not collect evidence in the island. At present he was condemned unheard and for what he did not know, so he proposed to remain until further light was shed upon the matter. His people were apparently with him, so Mr. Fanning's immediate prospects of administering the fertile little island were poor, though that well known Carolina Loyalist and the majesty of the law prevailed in the end. This incident is a fair illustration of the enor-

SIR GUY CARLETON

mous difficulties which the size of the country presented to its administrators of that day.

Nova Scotia, before its division and the Loyalist influx, had contained about fifteen thousand inhabitants. In a couple of years over thirty thousand had been added to them. A monthly mail packet was established from Halifax to England, and Dorchester set to work to organize a land express from Quebec to the winter ports. It sounds strange now that the most effective method of transit was found to be on foot! Speaking generally there were two distinct waves of Loyalist immigration. The influx of 1783 has already been alluded to. It was the immediate result of the close of the war and included disbanded Loyalist regiments as well as people of all sorts and conditions for whom a residence in the new republic was either impossible, unsafe or unpalatable. Later arrivals consisted of those who might have gone in '83 but were deterred not merely by the reported rigours of the climate and infertility of the soil, which was a common impression to the south, but by their fears of the Quebec Act and of strange laws, and the absence of representative government. All the Loyalist and militia corps were of course in the first batch, over six hundred for instance having been settled by Butler and de Peyster at Niagara, and about five hundred on the Crown seigniories of Sorel, and others near Montreal, Chambly and St. Johns. Nearly four hundred, of whom a considerable part were Loyalist soldiers and Rangers, were provided for

LOYALIST SETTLEMENTS

in the district of which the modern Kingston is the centre. It was quite obvious that ex-American colonists would not be satisfied to hold land under seigniorial usage, and it was necessary to go outside the line of the seigniories. There was little difficulty in finding land in the Richelieu country and to the west of Montreal, and of course, none whatever in the virgin wilderness up the St. Lawrence towards Lake Ontario or on the Canadian shore at Niagara, nor for the few score families who settled as far down the St. Lawrence as Gaspé and the Bay of Chaleurs. That this large necleus of settlement soon manifested an impatience of those French laws which still perplexed was not unnatural. Settlers also kept dropping in from the States, where there was much friction and discontent, and swelled the cry for constitutional changes and above all for that elective assembly which they had been accustomed to regard as the one thing essential to the happiness of all freeborn men.[1]

Dorchester recognized all this to the full, and warned the home government that fresh concessions in this direction were inevitable. But he confessed himself at a loss for a plan, so complex had the matter now become. "In a country," he writes, "where nine-tenths of the people do not yet understand even the nature of an assembly, any such scheme should be fully explained to them and they should be given ample time to digest it."

[1] See appendix X.

SIR GUY CARLETON

The organizing activity of the Kingston Loyalists was early astir. For while they were still petitioning Dorchester for another supply of provisions pending the gathering of harvest, they prayed that the English and Scottish Churches might be established among them, and that they should be assisted to erect a schoolhouse in each neighbourhood. They also petitioned for a supply of clothes, and it must be remembered that scarcely any of these people, gentle or simple, were able to bring much more with them than they could carry upon their backs. The story of their fight with poverty and the primæval forests, with the plague of insects, which then made life almost intolerable during the summer months, with sickness beyond reach of doctors or drugs, is both a pathetic and a noble one, above all when one remembers the physical comforts and social distinction which had been the former lot of so many of them. But all this has been told elsewhere many times. Dorchester did what he could. He sent them food and clothes and such medical assistance as the province, itself poorly provided in that respect, could spare. He eventually went to see them himself, though his visit was delayed for a season by the arrival of Prince William Henry.

He found them, however, the following year, progressing favourably. Settlers were shortly expected on the American shore of the St. Lawrence and Lake Ontario, and the United Empire Loyalists were influenced by a not unworthy ambition to show them

THE LAND DIFFICULTY

that they were finding material as well as sentimental consolation beneath the British flag. The land tenures, however, were still giving much anxiety, for the owners of seigniories French and English, of which last there were now a few, objected to the government selling wild lands in free and common socage. It contrasted too favourably with the position of their own *censitaires* and would thereby tend to depreciate their own estates. But the division of the province was already in the air, and settlers from the south were flocking steadily into it, some attracted by the easy terms of land, and others the objects of ill usuage at home; for the soil of Upper Canada had proved fertile beyond expectation, and all could now see that the idea of a virtually homogeneous French Canada under British rule was shattered. The Quebec Act, which in any case was not regarded as final, would soon need amendment under the pressure of developments due to peculiar causes that no human eye could have foreseen at its enactment.

Still, even a division of the province would by no means dispose of the land difficulty. The British-American settlers on the Richelieu and Lake St. Francis already numbered some thousands and would absolutely reject the French method of tenure and inheritance, as they had already substituted the acre for the *arpent* and the square survey for the narrow strip wherever possible. The Eastern Townships of Quebec to-day still in part illustrate the

SIR GUY CARLETON

contrast between the two races in their ideas of survey and settlement. Nor again is it realized in Great Britain, and not fully perhaps even in Canada, what a large admixture of German blood went in with these United Empire Loyalists. One entire German Loyalist regiment settled in the Kingston district, and on the roster of another corps one finds a thick sprinkling both of Dutch and German patronymics.

As already mentioned, in the August of 1,787 Dorchester's intended visit to the Maritime Provinces was postponed by the arrival of Prince William Henry, the future King William IV. in command of H. M. S. *Pegasus*. With Judge Prowse's[1] entertaining account in mind of the cheerful and popular manners of the sailor prince during his long stay in Newfoundland, one can well believe that he repaid the enthusiasm with which the Canadians greeted him in hearty fashion. De Gaspé tells us what despair he caused Lady Dorchester at her balls by choosing his partners where he listed rather than where ceremony required. On his way up from Quebec to Montreal, whither the governor preceded him, he stopped at Sorel where government had encouraged the beginnings of a town and shipyards. The leading inhabitants were so delighted with the friendly young man that they violated their past and exchanged the old name of the place for that of William Henry. But

[1] Prowse's, *History of Newfoundland*.

FIRST BISHOP OF NOVA SCOTIA

time had its revenge. Sorel, if but a mushroom townlet then, had graven its name deep in the story of two wars and after a few years only officials in public documents remembered its second baptism, till even they wearied of the farce.

A French marquis on his travels was soon afterwards sent to Dorchester with introductions from leading Englishmen, but the governor privately begged that these visits of foreigners should not be encouraged, for the political state of the country made them embarrassing. But a more useful arrival now put in an appearance, namely, an Anglican bishop for British North America; the first of a long line of distinguished prelates that have served that Church on both sides of the border. This was Charles Inglis, who was to take his title from Nova Scotia and reside there, but to have jurisdiction over Anglican Quebec. He had distinguished himself in New York both as an earnest churchman and evangelist, while later as a zealous Loyalist and rector of Christ Church he had aroused the enmity of the patriot party by his inconvenient eloquence. He left New York with Carleton at the evacuation and proceeded to Halifax, where his abilities gave him the first claim to the new see. In 1789 the bishop visited Quebec and ascended the river to Montreal, warmly welcomed everywhere by officials and Anglicans. The latter at Montreal had hitherto been indebted to the courtesy of the Récollets for the use of their church. Dorchester now granted and had restored

SIR GUY CARLETON

for them the derelict church of the suppressed order of Jesuits. In this same August the first Episcopal conference of the Protestant Church and the first confirmation was held in the Récollets' church at Quebec.

It is curious in Sydney's official letters to Dorchester to read of a notion prevalent in England that America was going to apply for a monarch of the House of Hanover! The minister also deprecates any idea of contracting a commercial treaty with Vermont and represents the London merchants trading with Quebec as greatly annoyed at the want of gaols in Canada for the confinement of debtors. In short the Coutume de Paris seemed to the British merchant a monstrous anachronism. The British minister, however, writes that he does not see why the Canadians should not have their own laws if they chose.

Dorchester in this same year (1788) sent back the 29th, 31st and 34th Regiments and received instead the 5th, 26th and the first battalion of the 60th, so he had now, in view of possible complications with the United States, some two thousand troops spread over one thousand one hundred miles of frontier, and an extremely unreliable militia. The late success of the Americans had undermined British prestige in the eyes of the Canadian masses. The Canadian militia, now grown more than ever averse to thoughts of war, would feel that the regulars supporting them were not infallible and were at any

POSTAL ARRANGEMENTS

rate under a cloud. During 1788, however, Dorchester did his utmost to give efficiency to this service, and instructed the lieutenant-governors to have the forces of their several provinces set in order, for even if peace were maintained with their neighbours, war with France might break out at any moment. He sent to England for thirty thousand stand-of-arms and other war material, which Sydney promised him by the following spring. The postal arrangements too were completed at the same time, and it is curious to find, even in these early days, Halifax and St. John worrying Dorchester with their rival claims as open ports for a quick passage. This was to be made twelve times a year by a sailing packet and the Quebec letters were to be delivered by a walking postman till roads could be cut! The dispute was settled by dividing these substantial favours alternately between the rivals, and Finlay of Quebec as postmaster-general had to see them carried out.

The expense of forwarding heavy packages may be gathered from the post-office charges of £28 16s. on the transport of a petition in a box from Montreal to Quebec addressed to Dorchester, which the latter refused to accept on the reasonable pretext that a continuance of so expensive a correspondence would be an intolerable burden on all concerned.

Adam Lymburner, a Quebec merchant, and described by Dorchester as "a quiet, decent man not unfriendly to the administration" had been already sent to England with a petition from the Quebec

SIR GUY CARLETON

merchants for a change in the constitution. But the Loyalist influx had introduced silent arguments for this departure far more potent than the somewhat poor ones hitherto advanced by the old British faction in Quebec.

In the summer of 1788 the notorious and energetic Ethan Allen, whose ardour had been in no wise cooled by his long confinement in a mediæval British fortress, again approached in diplomatic form the personage who had captured him and had been the means of his unwilling visit to Europe. His brother had been Dorchester's correspondent in the previous year and his letters had merely related to the free shipment of goods from Vermont to the St. Lawrence, and those commercial affairs which Silas Deane, it will be remembered, had in hand. Ethan Allen certainly bore no malice, for this curious document is little short of a proposal to return to the British fold. His hatred of the new federal government, together with the commercial advantages of the British alternative, was no doubt the inspiring motive of Allen and the party he represented. Vermont had not yet become a state and owing to many causes a considerable party within her borders had no longer any wish that she ever should. Her proximity to Canada, wrote Allen, made her an object of suspicion and jealousy to the new government, but if the latter tried to force itself upon them there were fifteen thousand able-bodied Vermonters more than equal to a similar number of

VERMONT'S PROPOSALS

United States troops. Their objection to joining the new confederacy was that it would expose them to the displeasure of Great Britain, ruin their commerce and involve them in debt, if not insolvency. The differences of the confederacy owing to diversity of climate and their licentious notions of liberty imbibed in the course of the revolution operated against successful combination in government. Allen urges Dorchester not to undervalue Vermont on account of her geographical limitations. Immigration adds to her strength, as the people continually coming in want "property not liberty."

During the last three years of the war Allen pointed out that there had been practically an alliance of neutrality between Vermont and the British. "If the latter," he declared, "could have afforded them protection at that time, the Vermonters would readily have yielded up their independence and have become a province of Great Britain. Should the United States now attempt to coerce them they would doubtless do the same if British policy harmonized with the idea. The leading men of Vermont are not so sentimentally attached to a republican form of government, yet from political principles are determined to maintain their present mode of it till they can have a better, or until they can on principles of mutual interest and advantage return to the British government without war or annoyance from the United States." Allen was an able, if somewhat unscrupulous, man. Schooled by a gene-

SIR GUY CARLETON

ration or two of partisan warfare against the French-Canadians the Vermonters were the best irregular soldiers in the United States, with the exception perhaps of the Alleghany mountaineers.

While Lymburner was on his way to appeal to the British government and the House of Commons on the question of obtaining an elective assembly and diminishing the scope of French laws, a petition concluding with sixteen pages of French-Canadian signatures was presented to Dorchester protesting against the aforesaid appellant as professing to represent the new Canadian subjects as well as the old. The former, they declared, greatly demurred to any further change in their ancient laws, while as for a House of Assembly they rather objected to one than otherwise.

Dorchester's plan for overcoming the inefficient state into which the militia had subsided was to call out three battalions for two years service, replacing them at the end of the term by others, but retaining the officers in permanent commission to take over each fresh corps as it came up. Le Comte Dupré was at this time colonel of all the militia of the town and district of Quebec and we find him corresponding direct with Sydney, describing his efforts to put his men on a good footing and asking for flags, uniforms, etc., and also a salary for himself as an encouragement to other Canadian officers.

Through the whole of 1788 and 1789 Dorchester shows his keen interest in the curious drift of Am-

AMERICAN POLITICS

erican politics beyond the Alleghanies, in Kentucky, and towards the Mississippi. The links of the confederacy were just now dangerously loose, as the Vermont incident alone would illustrate, but greater issues seemed at stake in the south-west. The latest plan reported to Dorchester was for Kentucky to secede and join Spain, though it was suspected that her true intention was to declare independence of the union, seize New Orleans and then look to Great Britain for assistance. Letters from Kentuckians to Dorchester are extant speaking even then of the inevitable separation of the west from the east, the need of the former for foreign protection with the right of navigating the Mississippi and the alternative of an appeal to Spain or Britain. The latter country was advised to form connections with western men of influence and capacity. A few weeks later particulars are forwarded to Dorchester from Kentucky of a scheme to induce France to seize New Orleans with offers to put Great Britain in her place, to make Dorchester an active agent in the matter supplying in his turn arms and ammunition. Any objection on account of the present peaceful relations with Spain it was urged might fairly be waived, as that power had supplied money and material to the rebellious colonists of Britain. These matters interested Dorchester and he sent most of the documents to Sydney, stating, however, that he had declined to assist or even to give his opinion on the merits of the scheme. The French minister to the United States,

SIR GUY CARLETON

Count Moustier, at this moment asked leave to cross the border at Niagara and make the round tour by Montreal and down Lake Champlain, but Dorchester with all politeness possible felt himself obliged to decline the honour for reasons politic.

At Christmas, 1789, Dorchester received from Grenville, who had taken Sydney's place at the colonial office, the first draft of a new bill for the better government of Quebec, the object of which was to assimilate the constitution to that of Great Britain so far as circumstances would allow. Consideration for the French, said Grenville, had received great weight in the adoption of the new plan for dividing the province. Dorchester himself thought that the few thousand Loyalists at present settled to the west of Montreal hardly justified immediate division. He seems to have underrated, which with his level head and wide experience is singular, the great influx there would be from the States so soon as the fear of French laws and customs was removed. Respecting the boundaries of the two provinces, they were to be left blank in the draft of the Act. Members of the legislative council were to be honoured with baronetcies, and perhaps higher distinctions, if sufficient wealth flowed in to sustain them. The view of the Quebec British is expressed in a letter from Finlay, the deputy postmaster-general, to the home government. He professes not to know Dorchester's private opinion. Indeed the latter's reserve was notable till he came to act; but the writer gives a

THE WESTERN POSTS

receipt for converting the Canadians into Englishmen—a very old one it is true, and its possible efficacy at the time is still a matter of speculation, if a futile one, with some modern writers. The seigniors would certainly oppose any proposal to change the old system, and cherished, according to Finlay, mistaken ideas of their own importance.

Hope, the lieutenant-governor, was now dead, and Dorchester urged the need of a good sensible man of some rank to take his place. In answer to this Grenville offered the succession to Dorchester's brother, now lieutenant-governor of New Brunswick, but if he preferred remaining there, which for somewhat obvious reasons he very sensibly did, Colonel Alured Clarke who had done well in Jamaica should be sent, as he ultimately was. Grenville approved of Dorchester's interest in the Kentucky movements. He commended his caution but suggested certain advantages that might arise from the threatened split in the confederacy. But the governor's interest in western matters was by no means an academic one, for the responsibility of the western posts, still held as a point of honour by Great Britain, to the resentment of the republic, lay heavily upon him. At any moment the American troops, traders and settlers, might become involved in a great Indian war. In such case the weakness of the posts would invite seizure by American forces heated with battle and exasperated with losses, and the seizure of the posts would inevitably lead to the very conflict from which Dorchester by all reasonable means was anxious to save the British government. Danger came too, in 1790, from another quarter, in the shape of what is known in the troubled history of Pacific coast treaties as the "Nootka incident." The enormous distance which at that period separated Quebec from Vancouver Island may well seem to have removed this affair completely from Dorchester's sphere of anxieties. But it had its bearing on the western posts from the fact that it nearly provoked war with Spain, and Spain, as we have seen, was somewhat closely involved with that westward movement of the Americans which President Roosevelt in his notable volumes on the subject has aptly and euphoniously termed, *The Winning of the West*. But Spain, who had seized British vessels trading from a British post on Vancouver Island and by refusing all demands for satisfaction had brought the two countries to the brink of war, yielded at the last moment when France, being in no mood or condition for a great war about nothing, refused her support.

CHAPTER XII

THE CANADA ACT

LYMBURNER in the meantime had arrived in England, during the summer of 1789, to represent the views of the British-Canadians and of a fraction of the French who were against partition and in favour of an elective assembly. He somewhat ignored the paucity of his French supporters in urging the wishes of his fellow-colonists on the British government, but otherwise was a sensible and clear-headed man. Reforms of some kind were impending and inevitable, and it was only right that his party should be heard, particularly as many of their claims had become reasonable through altered circumstances and unforeseen developments. How plainly one seems to see this old faction-riven Quebec in the voluminous correspondence of the time—sometimes preserved in the original handwriting, French or English, crabbed or ornate, scholarly or illiterate, of the men who so unconsciously tell us its story, interleaved here and there with criticisms on the enclosures or characteristic disquisitions by governors and lieutenant-governors on the state of the country.

As one follows the arguments of these various advocates and puts oneself for the moment in their respective situations, it is sometimes difficult to

SIR GUY CARLETON

preserve a judicial twentieth century attitude and stamp them as the mere outbursts of prejudice or faction. Even those seemingly arrogant all-British fanatics that Dorchester so snubbed, and the congress sympathizers whom in duty bound he treated still more severely, had some justification. They were for the most part Americans, to use a convenient and significant designation. They were accustomed to democratic usages, such as had spelled prosperity for the communities that had produced them. Few of them had basked in the sunshine of those little vice-regal circles which had tempered the republicanism of a favoured group in each colony. They had been invited, under definite promises as they supposed, to Canada, a province that they had directly or indirectly helped to conquer with a great expenditure of blood and treasure. Eighteenth century conquerors had not attained to altruistic ethics, and they well knew that if the kings of France or their proconsuls had been in a similar position might would assuredly have spelled right. We may recall Frontenac's merciless intentions towards New England and New York, if support of such an unanswerable argument were needed.

Their case would appear less offensive to us moderns if they had simply demanded that the colony should be administered by the governor and council in the interest of British settlers, till these last assumed proportions that should make popular government restricted to themselves seem reasonable

AN OPEN QUESTION

to current opinion. But it was the cant cry of popular government, where current figures made mockery of the term and only spelled the tyranny of an ill-instructed few in naked characters, that has put the would-be-legislators of 1763 and 1787 so hopelessly out of court with most historians even of their own race. The downright policy of forcibly anglicizing the colony would have been at least honest and logical and not out of harmony with those times, if distasteful to ours; but not surely under such a caricature of popular freedom as their scheme involved.

It is still sometimes argued, and indeed quite open to argument, that sixty thousand scattered peasants might have been turned into freeholders, to their immediate relief; that some thirty or forty seigniorial families (there were twenty-seven officially returned in 1787) of small rent rolls might have been made permanently happy or at least comfortable, whether as exiles or otherwise, for a trifling sum in commutation. Religion might have been left severely alone, with stringent precautions against external intrigue through its means—easy enough to effect in an isolated country with an unhampered government. British settlers, it is argued, would have poured in freely. In a few decades a Protestant parliament would have been at least as representative of the country as that Protestant assembly dissolved in 1800 was representative of Ireland, and for having deprived them of which Irish Catholics abuse England in such unmeasured terms. The effect of such a policy towards the Canadian peasantry firmly and benignantly administered by men like Carleton, or approximating to his likeness, might or might not have saved Canada from the racial friction that distracted and weakened her for so long, though at the expense of the French spirit and nationality which is nowadays such a factor in a peaceful land. It is quite easy to argue either its success or failure in convincing fashion. Putting political morality as we now hold it and race sentiment out of the question, it is an interesting if futile subject for reflection. Great Britain, to her credit, proved superior to the ethics of her day and in advance of the times—in advance indeed of her own offspring who held themselves to be the vanguard of political liberty. Happily the retort, possible at almost any other moment, that Britain in this generous action was influenced by fear of France is impossible, for in 1763 France was crushed, humiliated, and bankrupt, and her rival at the very zenith of her power. Nor does the more enlightened French view that Great Britain only did her duty, though in most creditable fashion, seem quite adequately to express the measure of her merit. Nor again should it be forgotten that her first viceroys, in the teeth of unceasing opposition, acted not only in the letter but in the spirit of their generous instructions.

But there were cleavages other than racial in this

CAUSES OF DISCONTENT

little dominion of Dorchester's, if not such violent ones. Conflicting views and interests stand out plainly in the current literature and correspondence of the time, and contribute to its history. Scarcely any one, it must be remembered, was rich; nearly all were poor. A still infant trade was harassed by wars and rumours of wars. The incomes of *rentiers*, professional men and office-holders were small, and the struggle for place and position proportionately keen. Numbers of deserving people had lost much or all of their property in the invasion of 1775-6. The seigniors, as we have seen, had lost, as a class, their hold on the peasantry. A few of them, both before and after the conquest, had been extortionate in the matter of rents, to which there was no legal limit, and their *censitaires* proportionately irritated. Lanaudière, Dorchester's aide-de-camp, had offered his seigniory of thirty square leagues to the government for settlement with freeholders, but the rest opposed all change in land tenure for reasons already stated. To the British such obstacles to the free purchase and exchange of land proved an irritation and inconvenience, but still more they militated against the development of the country. The seigniories had been devised to keep a docile peasantry on the land, to prevent restlessness, and to preserve discipline; and the seigniors themselves had been instituted as trustees for the common weal rather than as ordinary landowners.

A seigniory could be sold only in bulk, but a fifth

SIR GUY CARLETON

of the purchase money went to the Crown. A tenant again or *censitaire* could sell his holding, but was liable always to the annual rent of a few *sous* an *arpent*, the seigniorial mill rights and, what was more serious still as an obstruction to ready transfer, liable also to the *lods et ventes*—by which a twelfth of the purchase money went to the seignior, including of course a twelfth of the improvements. In the neighbourhood of towns these restrictions with many minor ones almost strangled the sale of land. A prosperous trader in Quebec, to give an example, could not buy a country place a mile or two out of town untrammelled by these curiously belated and un-American burdens. The inrush of Loyalist settlers could be accommodated only outside the seigniories, which not merely pressed them back with their improvements into less accessible regions but left a vast amount of available wilderness almost indefinitely wild. As free and common socage was the only tenure acceptable to these American or British newcomers, another set of land laws was required within the province. The complications were even greater than a modern reader might suppose, and there is neither space nor need to elaborate here the many minor details that now confronted the administration. When a thousand or two townsmen represented and seemed likely for some time to represent the British element, there would have been small wisdom in rooting up the Canadian land system, seeing that toleration of it had been formally accepted. But now fresh developments

IMPORTATION OF PRIESTS

compelled some modification of this archaic survival and created a situation which may well seem extraordinary in a vast and almost virgin country, carrying, even in 1791, but some one hundred and thirty thousand souls. The notaries, it might be added, by education and identity of interest and a natural preference for their own laws, were mostly with the seigniors in their attachment to the system.

The clergy appear to have outlived such little unpleasantness as the American sympathizers had stirred up between them and their flocks anent the legalizing of the dime. There had been some difficulty too about a supply of priests since the connection with France had been severed, the local supply qualified for the more important offices proving short. Importations from old France had been interdicted for obvious and sufficient reasons, while permission to introduce priests from the Catholic provinces of central Europe seems to have been little if at all utilized. Bishop Hubert indeed intimated to Dorchester that the plan was not agreeable, though he had recognized as reasonable the veto against the introduction of ecclesiastics from the dominions of the House of Bourbon. Those who most objected to the proposed partition of the province were naturally the British residents within what would be the limits of the old one, and who saw the recent and unexpected addition to their ranks, with the hopes thus raised, in prospect of being in great part wrenched away. Lymburner, as we have

SIR GUY CARLETON

seen, was their eloquent advocate and pleaded their cause for many hours before a committee of the House of Commons. Dorchester's objections, already quoted, to the partition were less fervent and due to another cause, namely a distrust of the ripeness of so small a community for self-government. Perhaps his experiences of the British politicians of Quebec and Montreal had influenced his judgment.

In March, 1790, however, he sent home a list of suitable persons for seats in the legislative and executive councils of the two proposed provinces of Upper and Lower Canada. For the former he mainly relies on the judgment of Sir John Johnson, whose services entitled him to be its first governor. But before his letters were received in England Simcoe had been already appointed. It seems that the home government considered Johnson's private interests in western Canada as too considerable for the detachment of mind necessary to their representative in the new province. These details were arranged in the spring of this year, as it had been intended to pass the bill through during the session. Dorchester was anxious to go to London himself, both on private accounts and for the better conduct of a measure fraught with so much importance to Canada. But now as ever, placing his country's interests before his personal inclinations and convenience, he accepted at once a hint of Grenville's that it would be acceptable to the king if he would remain at his post while the state of the West continued so critical. It is true that

SIMCOE'S APPOINTMENT

his agents in the United States, who always kept him well informed, reported that no attack would be made on the British posts that year, but then the Spanish trouble over the Nootka Sound was brewing, and Dorchester foresaw complications on the western frontier should war break out with that power.

Dorchester did not receive the news of Simcoe's appointment with complacency. The bill had been postponed in the session of 1790, and he wrote again to Grenville in September urging the claims of Sir John Johnson, his distinguished services, and the discontent which their non-recognition would arouse among the Loyalists of his country. He again urged that Johnson should be appointed governor of the new province and colonel of the militia, while Simcoe could with advantage take charge of the Indian department. The non-acceptance of Dorchester's views on this point was the key no doubt to the uneasy terms upon which he stood towards Simcoe when the latter eventually took office. The former's views, as communicated at length to the government, did not approve, as we have seen, of an immediate concession of popular government. He proposed that the four western districts should be placed under a lieutenant-governor, and that a firm and benevolent government should be established. He had always rejected the idea of high-sounding hereditary rank among the colonists. He had strong leanings, however, towards some sort of aristocracy for the new settlements, and made the proposal so often alluded

SIR GUY CARLETON

to in modern times that the Loyalist immigrants should have the right and their children after them to affix the letters U.E. to their names. But he objected to all proposals for making the office of legislative councillor hereditary—knowing better than the home government the fluctuations of fortune in colonial life. This plan was adopted, however, and embodied in the Act, though common sense and experience endorsed Dorchester's views and kept it a dead letter. His notions of an aristocracy were of a wider and less conspicuous kind. He could not guess how completely Upper Canada, without the aid of any outward marks of distinction, would develop his theory, though not altogether perhaps upon the lines he would have appoved of or with as much success as he anticipated.

The western boundary of the proposed new province also perplexed him not a little. To include the western forts, such as Oswego, Niagara, Detroit, and Michilimackinac, would be to encroach on territory ceded to the United States by treaty and provoke their hostility at once, while to leave them out of British jurisdiction involved complications. The result was that no definitions of the western and southern limits of the province were included in the Act at all. In general terms Dorchester held to the principle that had marked both periods of his administration. "A considerable degree of attention," he wrote, "is due to the prejudice and habits of the French inhabitants who compose so large a propor-

VIEWS OF THE CHIEF-JUSTICE

tion of the community, and every degree of caution should be used to continue to them the enjoyment of those civil and religious rights which were secured to them by the capitulation of the province, or have since been granted by the liberal and enlightened spirit of the British government." Every active mind had some suggestions to make at this important moment, and Dorchester's chief-justice, Smith, not always in agreement with his friend and superior, put his contribution to the literature of the movement in the governor's hands for transmission to England.

Smith heartily concurs in the partition of the province but would fain do more than this. As an old and leading member of the former colony of New York he dreads the weakness inherent in a group of democratic assemblies all pulling different ways in time of danger—for he knew well that nothing but the fortunate combination of a Washington, the French alliance and the Germain-Howe insanities, could have saved the revolting colonies from disaster. He had seen them recently, at the close of a successful war, doing their utmost to stultify its results by fatuous quarrelling, bickerings and jealousy of each other and of all authority. Smith, in short, was nearly a century before his time and advocated nothing less than a combination of all the British North American provinces, Newfoundland included, under a central administration and a federal assembly. " I am old enough," he writes, " to remember what we in the Maritime Provinces dreaded from this French

SIR GUY CARLETON

colony and what it cost to take away that dread which confined our population to the edge of the Atlantic." He adds to a long and interesting letter, ten clauses embodying his scheme as additions to the new Canada Act. Upon the whole we may credit Chief-Justice Smith with the gift of foresight in no ordinary degree.

The introduction of the Canada Act had been deferred on account of the threatened war with Spain, whose territorial interests were so interwoven with American western progress. Throughout the first half of 1791, while the Act was passing through the British parliament, Dorchester remained in Canada, though he had been invited[1] by the ministry to come over in March and assist in the completion of the bill. Faction and agitation were lulled by the impending change in the constitution, but it was a busy enough season for the governor, as his official correspondence plainly shows. Every matter of the smallest moment from Detroit to Gaspé seems to have come under his notice, and many matters also which were by no means small. The constant friction upon the western frontier, the appeals of traders and Indians, the reports of agents and officers—full of rumours, false and true, of warlike encounters between Indians and Americans—were always with him, while the various surveys, charters, grants, and the infinite minutiæ inevitable to the settlement of thousands of people at widely

[1] See appendix Y.

THE CANADA ACT

scattered points added to the complexity of his responsibilities. Clerical matters, too, had to come under his surveillance, both Catholic and Protestant, for the newly organized Church of England was now concerned with the building of churches and rectories and the acquisition of lands, while the chronic question of the Jesuits' estates was always in the front.

But we must leave Dorchester to these multifarious duties of no special moment to our story, and follow as briefly as may be the fortunes of the Canada Act in its by no means tranquil passage through the British parliament to the royal desk.

On March 4th, 1791, the bill was introduced in the House of Commons by Mr. Pitt, and on the twenty-third Mr. Lymburner made the long address to the members already alluded to. He opposed the bill in its present form. As representative of the British Quebec interest he pleaded for a total repeal of the Quebec Act and against the partition of the province. He told the story of inefficient judges and miscarried justice and the general confusion in all legal matters which Dorchester's commission, it will be remembered, exposed in somewhat dramatic fashion. He alluded to the proposed partition as a "violent measure," and thought that if the parts were separated any future attempts to combine them would be hopeless. He was also of opinion that the country beyond Niagara, which

SIR GUY CARLETON

in no long time became the garden of Canada, could never be of much importance on account of the barrier to transport offered by the Falls. He was emphatic, where Dorchester was only doubtful, as to the difficulty of finding sufficient capable men who would leave the clearing of their farms for legislative duties. Lymburner being a Scot, not an American, failed to realize what experience and talent existed among the United Empire Loyalists. Having delivered these and many other destructive arguments, he then proceeded to the constructive theories of his party, modified in some particulars by concessions to the inevitable.

A House of Assembly was naturally in the forefront, though the admission of Catholics was at last recognized as unavoidable. Its sessions should be triennial. There should be a legislative council of life members. Hereditary seats in it, however, like every sensible man in Canada, he would have none of. He advocated the criminal law of England, together with the same code of commercial law and the *habeas corpus*, while in the matter of land, marriage settlements, dower and inheritance, the law of Canada might be retained so far as Quebec, Three Rivers, and Montreal were concerned. In the rest of the provinces the common law of England should prevail, and he argued that there should be power when petitioned for to accept the surrender of the feudal grants of a seigniory and to re-apportion the land in free and common socage.

BURKE'S SPEECH

Soon afterwards the merchants trading with Canada presented a petition against the Act, on the ground that the measure would be damaging to the commerce of the colony. Fox spoke against the bill, urging that it was not sufficiently liberal. Towards the end of April it was in committee. The attendance, as usual in colonial matters of a peaceful nature, was scanty, and an adjournment was asked for and refused by Pitt. Burke took part in the debate to declare against the division of the province, and also to air his strenuous views on the French Revolution, and to provoke the famous quarrel and final breach between Fox and himself which here took place. Canada and her affairs were nearly lost sight of through the irrelevancy of Burke's peroration, which was made the object of outcries from the floor, and sharp reminders from the chair. Indeed, the colony seems to have been chiefly serviceable to the great orator in this debate as an excuse for indulging in sonorous adjectives that invited alliteration, though "bleak and barren" were not felicitous ones for a country of universal forest and considerable fertility. That, however, did not much matter in the House of Commons, nor perhaps would it now. The opinions of the numerous private members of parliament who expressed themselves with much complacency upon a question which was still a source of some doubt and perplexity even to Dorchester are of no consequence. Their votes were, however, of consequence, and the

SIR GUY CARLETON

Act was carried through both Houses, and became law on May 14th, 1791.

The intention of the Act was to assimilate the new constitution of the two Canadian provinces as nearly as possible to that of Great Britain. The legislative council of Quebec, or Lower Canada, was to consist of not less than fifteen members, its elective assembly of not less than thirty, half of whom were to form a quorum. The minimum strength of the council and assembly of Upper Canada was fixed at seven and sixteen respectively. The preponderating wealth and intelligence of the British merchants was partly recognized by the allotment to the towns of Quebec, Montreal, Three Rivers, and Sorel of two members apiece. The provinces were to be divided into electoral districts based so far as possible on population, and not on geographical area. The qualification for both voters and candidates was liberal, providing they were of age, and either born or naturalized subjects. A forty shilling freehold, or its equivalent, was the qualification in the country, and in the town the ownership of a house worth five pounds a year or the occupancy of one producing twice that amount. The Crown withdrew all right to taxation except as regards such duties as it might be expedient to impose for the regulation of commerce, the net produce of the same to be applied in every case to the use of the province they were collected in.

There was provision, too, for the exchange of the

CLERGY RESERVES

seigniorial tenure into freehold on petition. It was by this Act, too, that one-seventh of the Crown lands was set apart for the "support of a Protestant clergy." This apparently comprehensive term was defined in another clause more precisely. This last empowered the erection of parsonages when required in each township of the English district "according to the establishment of the Church of England," and endowed them with the reserved lands of that particular township. In the long disputes which this measure gave rise to in after years, the first part of the ordinance was loudly quoted by the non-Anglicans without its supplement, which leaves no doubt of the intention of the Act, whatever its wisdom. The boundary between the two provinces was virtually the same as to-day.[1] The western bounds of Upper Canada, however, were left undefined for good reasons, as we have seen; those between Quebec and New Brunswick were deferred for local settlement. The Crown reserved to itself the fullest powers of veto and appointment. The governors of Lower Canada, however, still retained as before the suzerainty, to use a convenient term, over all the other provinces and their lieutenant-governors, Upper Canada of course included.

[1] This Act did not divide the country into Upper and Lower Canada. This was done by order-in-council, August 24th, 1791, after the Act was passed.

CHAPTER XIII

A NEW SITUATION

DORCHESTER sailed for England on August 18th, 1791, leaving Sir Alured Clarke, the new lieutenant-governor, in charge. Clarke had gained some reputation in the West Indies, and sustained it by his conduct in Canada. It was his privilege to inaugurate the first step in constitutional government, though perhaps of a more apparent than actual kind, the Act passing into effect with much ceremony and festivity on December 26th. The council remained much as before:—Chief-Justice Smith (Speaker), St. Ours, Finlay, Baby, Dunn, DeLongueuil, Panet, Mabane, DeLevy, Harrison, Collins, Lanaudière, Pownall, de Boucherville, John Fraser and Sir John Johnson, the first eight composing the executive. The House of Assembly did not meet till the following December, 1792, when fifty members took their seats, two from each district, or county. The names which Clarke applied to these newly created countries are not felicitous. Buckinghamshire, Hampshire, Bedford and Surrey had not been wholly inappropriate to the broad fields of the once Church and king-loving Anglo-Virginian squires, and, indeed, in due course acquired something of the very atmosphere suggested by

SIR GUY CARLETON

these time-honoured names. But their sudden application to this northern land of French Catholic peasants is something of a shock even to the reader a century afterwards, though curiously characteristic of that inartistic side of the British character which covered the backwoods and prairies of the United States with embryonic classic cities. How these amazing designations fared at the hands of the *habitants* we may not know—still worse even than William Henry (*vice* Sorel) no doubt.

As Dorchester was absent and my space is dwindling, I must not linger over Clarke's two years of office; nor dwell further upon the still seething dangers of the West, with open war raging between the Americans and Indians, and disasters to the former, which increased his correspondence and kept him anxious and busy. Nor is it possible to draw any picture of this first mixed assembly of thirty-four French and sixteen British representatives of the people, with the lingual and other little difficulties, the one to be perennial, the others merely those of inexperience. It should be noted as a social incident that Prince Edward, our late Queen's father, arrived with his regiment, the 7th Fusileers, at Quebec just before Dorchester left, and as a political one that Simcoe, the first lieutenant-governor of Upper Canada, landed in November, 1791, on his way to his official duties. His first despatches, a business at which he was notoriously prolific, do not suggest much political acumen, for

DORCHESTER'S RETURN

he had formed the opinion that Hamilton was anxious for war with England, and he did not himself think much of Washington's character. But Simcoe was both an admirable man and a good administrator, as readers of these volumes know.

War had been declared by France against Great Britain and Holland some six months prior to Dorchester's return to Canada. When he landed at Quebec, after just two years of absence, on September 23rd, 1793, it was not before his presence was required. A new situation had to be faced, for no one could guess what the attitude of the French-Canadians would be when Great Britain and their own mother country were engaged in deadly strife. That the quarrel was with the government of the Revolution and not with that of the old régime might or might not mitigate the situation. Racial sentiment would be equally powerful in both cases, but the Church and upper classes would have been more dangerous in the former, the peasantry in the latter, as was soon apparent.

Quebec greeted its old and much loved governor with a general illumination. Bishop Jacob Mountain, too, arrived soon after Dorchester to be the first prelate of the Canadas, for hitherto they had been in ecclesiastical dependence on the but little older see of Nova Scotia. Dr. Mountain had been a fellow of Caius College, Cambridge, tutor and private secretary to Pitt, rector of a Norwich parish, and was now to imprint his name worthily and indelibly on Canadian records. There were now about a dozen Anglican clergymen altogether in the two Canadas, but in Quebec neither church nor rectory, service being still held in the chapel of the Récollets.

The crisis of the Revolution and the fall of the French monarchy had occurred during Dorchester's absence. The American republic was quivering with excitement, further stimulated by French agents, and the ripples of the tumult were being felt in the heart of the French-Canadian parishes. The old adage that imitation is the sincerest form of flattery accounted, no doubt, for part of this exuberance. The wave of Gallican sentiment that swept over the Southern and Middle States is perhaps the most extraordinary and, in some ways, unaccountable movement in the history of the country. Carolina, Virginia and Maryland planters whose only acquaintance with privilege and tyranny was such as they had themselves exercised over their own negroes—who were not, by the way, included in this saturnalia of freedom and license—danced wildly about crowned with caps of liberty like emancipated slaves, and exchanged the modest courtesies of American democratic life for the fantastic crudities of French *sans-culottes*.

The notorious and impossible Genet had landed at Charleston, a few weeks before Dorchester left England, as minister of the French republic, and executed a triumphant overland progress to Philadelphia. The exuberant and exotic mummery which

GENET IN AMERICA

lined the country roads and dragged the chariot of this ridiculous Jack-in-office through the towns, brings a blush to the cheek of the modern American as he reads of it. Never, probably, did a sane and sensible people give way to such an exhibition of far-fetched and misplaced banality. Jefferson pulled the strings of his puppet till the latter's caperings broke them and left that vain and crafty demagogue cursing his own lack of discrimination. The leaders of the Federalists and all sensible men looked on aghast. Washington and Hamilton did more than look on, for Genet fitted out privateers in American ports and seized British shipping actually in American estuaries. Every one knows how the story ended, and how after insulting everybody all round, Washington and even Jefferson included, this unique specimen of a diplomat was sent about his business. Fearing to go home he became naturalized as an American, and died in the country forty years later.

With all his feckless effrontery, Genet had been dangerously active, during the few months he was at large, in his endeavours to drag America into a war with England. His agents were in every direction and were busy intriguing among the Canadians. The French Revolution was even a better card for such men to play than the two clauses of the Quebec Act utilized for the same purpose in 1775. Moreover, on this occasion it was Frenchmen appealing to Frenchmen, for many of these emissaries were Canadians who had deemed it prudent to leave the country after

SIR GUY CARLETON

the 1775-6 troubles, and had gathered much worldly wisdom in the wider atmosphere of the American republic. A French Utopia, where everything was to be had for the asking and vexatious laws and burdens swept away, presented, moreover, at the hands of a French fleet or army, was a much more alluring programme than the more doubtful promises of the Bastonnais in 1775. France no longer represented the very mixed blessings that its re-adoption implied in the days of the monarchy. Seigniors, tithes, taxes, *corvées* and soldiering had no place in the new order, so they were told with more grain of truth than the Bastonnais Utopia had contained. One need not say what the priests thought of all this, nor yet the seigniors for whom a red republican army, even a French one, had small attraction. Some of the notary and doctor class, themselves derived from the peasantry and from whom alone in French Canada political adventurers could spring, seem, however, to have regarded the new gospel with less repugnance. Besides all this, one of the two great parties in America, that of Jefferson and Madison, crafty and ill-balanced leaders who had never themselves smelt powder, and the former of whom was sometimes even credited with a lack of normal physical courage, was breathing fire and slaughter against England and all belonging to her in senseless and suicidal fashion. The South, as the more ignorant section, formed the main strength of their party, while the provinces bordering on Canada supported

THE DUKE OF KENT

Washington, Hamilton and Jay in their efforts to maintain neutrality and their predilections for Anglo-Saxon ideals with a qualified friendliness for Great Britain.

Such was the highly charged atmosphere in which Dorchester once again found himself, and now, as ever, with but a handful of troops and an unreliable militia. One knows nothing definite of how he had passed his time in England, nor does it signify. He kept in touch with his deputy at Quebec and the British government, but otherwise, no doubt, was taking that well-earned rest which his advancing years and his labours past and to come made requisite; for he was now nearly seventy, and had lived a strenuous life. He had by this time, too, a large family, and so far as we know was a domestic man with no taste for staking his patrimony at Brookes's, nor for the deep potations of Fox and Pitt. Nor, again, had his health in Canada been always of the best.

Prince Edward, afterwards Duke of Kent, was still at Quebec, and remained there in command of the 7th Regiment until the January following Dorchester's arrival. He had made himself extremely popular with all classes, and only left for active service in the West Indies. Kent House, above the Montmorency Falls, still serves to remind us of a prince who is chiefly interesting, perhaps, as Queen Victoria's father, though he has some special claim to notice from the fact that he held commands in

SIR GUY CARLETON

British North America for seven years, the last four of them being spent at Halifax. Dorchester had on this occasion to reply to the many addresses of regret at the prince's departure which reached Quebec. The latter had left in a hurry to reach the scene of action, and while travelling on the ice over Lake Champlain the sleighs containing all his personal effects disappeared down an air-hole and were seen no more. At Boston we are told he had to ship in a small vessel of six guns, which ran the gauntlet of the French cruisers and only escaped by its fast sailing powers, though it received their fire.

The first news Dorchester had to send home was the failure of the peace conference between the American commissioners and the Indians, including both those of the West and the Six Nations, who demanded that their territory as far as the Ohio should remain inviolate. On November 11th, he opened the second parliament of Lower Canada, with Panet as speaker of the assembly. He urged the necessity of passing laws for the administration of justice, and he laid stress on the inadequate means of defence against foreign enemies. The finances too came up, and may serve to show the extraordinary disproportion between revenue and expenditure, so great, indeed, as to throw four-fifths of the cost of government (which was about twenty-five thoussand pounds a year, while the revenue was only five thousand pounds) on the Crown. This condition of things contributed to stultify the power

THE MILITARY PROBLEM

of the popular assembly.[1] The veto of the upper chamber and the Crown could be exercised without any fear whatever of consequences. The one effective weapon of a parliament, namely, the withholding of supplies, was unavailable when the supplies were mainly furnished by the British government, while in regard to the legislative council, though its members held their seats for life, that very fact inclined them against popular departures and to sympathy with the governor. French influence, though not yet aggressively developed, was naturally in the ascendant from its great numerical preponderance. Both languages were used in debate, and the services of an interpreter were regularly employed. In this first session of Dorchester's, Panet was made judge and de Lotbinière was chosen speaker. In November Dorchester issued a proclamation in English and French requiring magistrates, captains of militia, and all good subjects to seek and secure persons holding seditious discourses, spreading false news, or publishing libellous papers. He turned his attention also towards improving the defences of Quebec, and passing a militia bill.

Indeed, the military problem was upon him again in all its seeming hopelessness, and the dangers from within and without as imminent as ever. He issued orders for the embodiment of two thousand militia; but though the British, who were now more numer-

[1] See appendix Z.

SIR GUY CARLETON

ous than formerly, came forward "with alacrity," the *habitants* objected strongly to the service. French and American intriguers had played upon this string among others, and had succeeded in convincing the peasantry that to be balloted as a militiaman implied military service for life. "Nothing," writes Carleton, "is too absurd for them to believe." The first day they were called out to furnish their proportion of the two thousand to be enrolled for service they broke into a mob, and refused to be balloted for. Two were sent to prison for riot and the country parishes threatened to rescue them. The British proportion of militia was only seventy out of two thousand, and this, said Carleton, did not escape their observation.

Monk, whose voluminous correspondence with Nepean has been preserved, speaks of the alarm created among the merchants by Dorchester's speech in March. He, too, tells of the general spread of French principles, and speaks of the whole country as so infested with them that it was found on calling out the militia that there was scarcely a hope of assistance from the new subjects. Threats, he writes, were used by the disaffected against the few who were found loyal. "It is astonishing to find the same savagery exhibited here as in France in so short a period for corruption. Blood alliances do not check the menaces upon the non-complying peasants. These include the burning of houses, death, embowelling, decapitation and carrying heads

INTRIGUE

on poles, as the depositions show, besides throwing off all regard for religion." The intrigues were traced to Genet and the now numerous French consuls. Correspondence had been carried on between Canadians in the United States and the disaffected in Canada, and French emissaries had been sent in to prepare the people to follow the example of France. Monk thought that nothing less than five thousand troops in Canada till the war was ended would secure the country. An address entitled, *Les Français libres à leurs frères les Canadiens*, was read at a church door, and circulated as a pamphlet. In this the people were urged to "follow the example of France and the United States, and to upset a throne so long the seat of hypocrisy and imposture, despotism, greed, and cruelty. Their assembly is a mockery, and secret machinations are employed everywhere to upset its efforts at better laws. Canadians, arm yourselves, call your friends, the Indians, to your assistance, count on the sympathy of your neighbours and of the French." Everything in short was to be abolished, and the *habitants* would find themselves in the delightful position of an independent nation in league with France and the United States, and would immediately rise to the blessings of that liberal education and establish those institutions for science and the higher arts for which they had been pining, and the free prosecution of that ocean commerce to which their genius and inclinations were so inclined. Even the *habitant*, accustomed as he must now have been to broadsides of unintelligible bombast, must have rubbed his eyes at the burning ambitions with which he was here credited. The prospect, however, of getting everything for nothing was plain enough amid the cloud of verbiage, and to an illiterate peasantry this fact has seldom failed to appeal.

CHAPTER XIV

CLOSING YEARS

IN this war with the French republic the situation was in some respects more serious for British interests in Canada than it had been when the former country was actually allied with the Americans in the revolutionary struggle; for France was at that time still a monarchy, and her emissaries, even with the utmost exercise of casuistry, could hardly make much of the retrospective blessings of the ancient régime as a stimulant to Canadian discontent, while the seigniors and the Church, who might have been susceptible, had been attached to the British connection by practical, and to them beneficent, measures. Washington, too, in those days, as may be remembered, had been entirely opposed to a resurrection of French power in Canada. Now, however, France was a republic, and though war against Great Britain was never declared by the States it was regarded in 1793-4 as imminent, and it would have been promoted by a party that had an almost fanatical affection for its sister republic, short-lived though this affection proved.

Jefferson, Madison and Randolph were possessed of an insensate hatred of Great Britain and were followed in this by their fellow Southerners, the least instructed and most excitable portion of the republic in foreign affairs. Moreover, the indebtedness to Great Britain throughout this section was much greater than in any other, and the temptation to wriggle out of these debts by a war which would be much more keenly felt in the North was great to a population whose notions of financial morality make the speeches in the Virginia assembly of that day instructive reading. No people more profoundly ignorant of France and Frenchmen could have been found in the world than the noisy factions who were then clamouring for a warlike alliance with her against Great Britain. Dorchester thought war was certain, and at this moment he had occasion to harangue the Miami Indians in a speech which created considerable excitement in the United States. He remembered very well, he told them, the line they had pointed out three years ago, just before his last departure for England, as the boundary they desired between themselves and the States, and how he had promised to represent their situation and wishes to the king, and expressed his hope that all the grievances they complained of on the part of the United States would soon be done away with by a just and lasting peace. Dorchester went on to say that he had waited long but had not yet received one word of satisfaction from Americans, and from what he could learn of their conduct

SPEECH TO THE INDIANS

towards the Indians, he would not be surprised if the English were at war with them during the present year, and then a line must be drawn by the warriors. "What further can I say to you? You are a witness that on our part we have acted in the most peaceable manner and borne the language and conduct of the people of the United States with patience, but I believe our patience is almost exhausted."

The report of this address having been obtained by American sympathizers in Montreal, was forwarded to congress and published in the American papers. Jefferson's party made the most of it, and appealed to Hammond, the English minister, denouncing Dorchester's speech as "hostility itself." Hammond reported the matter to Dundas, the secretary, and Dundas wrote to Dorchester in a tone bordering on reproof, for the treaty which the Federal party were labouring to make with Great Britain was now in progress and Jay had made a favourable impression in London. Nothing was known, however, of these improved prospects on the western frontier in the summer of 1794. Reports had just come in that Wayne's army to the south of Lake Erie was two thousand strong, besides five hundred more in garrison. Forty dollars was being paid for scalps, and one thousand dollars was offered for Simon Girty's, a famous British scout who had cut some figure in the old French wars. War with Great Britain was regarded as in-

SIR GUY CARLETON

evitable, and Wayne was only waiting to advance against the Indians till their corn was ripe. Dorchester replied to Dundas's letter expressing a wish to resign. In another letter, assuming some freedom of speech as the *doyen* of colonial governors, he replied that no secretary was long enough in office to acquire sufficient knowledge of a colony. He might well have said more, and to the effect that no minister in London was qualified to direct every movement and interfere in every detail in a distant country whose political, physical and social atmosphere was so hopelessly outside his vision. Such, however, was the deplorable custom of that time. But the Duke of Portland, taking alarm at the prospect of losing a man who for the apparently impending crisis was their only hope, wrote denying that any reproof was implied. On the contrary, he thought Dorchester had been quite right in the Miami matter.

This affair was by no means confined to Dorchester's oration, but included the rebuilding of a fort by Simcoe, with his approval, in the Indian territory some fifteen miles south of Lake Erie, on the Maumee. This had been done in the preceding spring. Indeed the station had been fortified and occupied by British detachments ever since the close of the war, but a year or two previously, trade having left it, it had been abandoned. But now with a fresh war impending, it was rebuilt as a defence to Detroit, and, under legal guise, as being in Indian territory

TROUBLE WITH VERMONT

not yet, at least, surrendered by treaty to the States. The action, however, made some little stir in the latter country as an invasion of territory. Dorchester had much trouble, too, with the posts on Lake Champlain, occupied just now by small detachments. The Vermonters, who at one time had professed such partiality for British rule, had changed their minds completely, and had given both Alured Clarke and Dorchester the utmost annoyance by petty insults and outrages on their small outposts. They had even made an offer to congress to conquer Canada unaided. It may be remembered that heady Vermonter, Ethan Allen, had undertaken to do the same with Montreal, and had found his way instead to a prison in Cornwall. American historians for the most part insist that the commander of the western British posts encouraged the Indians in their resistance to the United States! Well knowing that this meant a general war and almost certain destruction of these weak isolated forts as well as the probable conquest of Canada, we are asked to suppose that Sir John Johnson, Butler, Hamilton, McKee, Campbell, and above all the less prominent officers in lonely and remote commands, were nothing less than madmen. Dorchester's dread of war is conspicuous in all his western instructions.

The voluminous correspondence of his officers is eloquent of their precarious position should war break out. To allege that St. Clair's defeat had not given them satisfaction would be to write them down as less than human, but to picture them as stirring up a bloody war with France and the United States combined, is to suppose them men wearied of life, of liberty, of employment, even of patriotism. One can only suppose that American writers, who follow one another in such statements, have not read the redundant correspondence that for many years passed between the western posts and Quebec, and in these, at least, there was sufficient plain speaking. Young subalterns and captains may—nay, we know from these letters they did—reply to the bombastic defiance of irresponsible Kentucky riflemen under the walls of their own forts with spirit, but no responsible officer did, or could do, otherwise than dread a war which would almost certainly have landed them as prisoners in the United States. To do them justice, most of their contemporaries in rank on the American side kept well within the letter of their instructions, which was to refrain from all offence. But Wayne summoned Fort Miami to surrender as being a re-constructed post outside what he considered to be Canadian territory. Major Campbell, however, refused, and there was some acute correspondence between them. The former had just shattered the Indian resistance at Fort Recovery, though at a loss to himself of two hundred and fifty men.

Jay's Treaty was negotiated in the year 1794, though only ratified in the next, amid the uproar of the Jeffersonians, then known as the Republican party. Washington and Hamilton, his good political

AMERICA AND FRANCE

genius, if we may say so, were determined to keep on terms with England and avoid entanglement with France, whose wrath knew no bounds on publication of the treaty. That England was prepared to meet them at least half-way, the private correspondence of British ministers and their American and colonial representatives is better evidence than the noisy turbulence of provincial demagogues, politicians, and land-grabbers. Under the circumstances, France may be pardoned her ebullition of feeling, which sent the American envoys within her gates to the right about, and treated Americans and American ships with a harshness that would have provoked actual war if retaliation had been decent or prudent. But the Federal party, all the more that their gratitude to the France of 1778 was still strong within them, saw more clearly the drift of republican France, and amid the passions of virtual civil war could not forget that Americans were by race, blood and language, and every instinct that guided their political and domestic life, Englishmen and not Frenchmen. A sanguinary and domestic struggle could not change their flesh and blood, their traditions of centuries, nor ally them in anything but the mere link of friendly treaties to a nation stranger to them even than to the English of old England. Hamilton said Talleyrand was "the first American to divine Europe," and upon the rhodomontade of hot-blooded but intensely provincial Anglo-American farmers and planters, Hamilton looked with the disapproval and contempt of a cool-headed and far-sighted man.

In May, 1794, Dorchester succeeded without difficulty in getting an Alien Act passed by the assembly, for all sorts of people were coming and going in Canada. In spite of the threatened war, emigrants, from the States chiefly, were pouring in steadily, attracted by easy terms of land and favourable reports of its fertility. Many of these no doubt looked ahead and calculated that Canada in a short time and without much disturbance would be included in the republic. There was beyond doubt, too, an element, particularly in the Eastern Townships of Quebec, whose motives and sentiments, without being, perhaps, clearly defined, were widely different from those of the Loyalists. To this day the old British population of the Townships, in part at least, suggests that ancient affinity with the frontiers of Vermont from whose overflow it drew so many of its earlier settlers; men not at that time greatly concerned with flags, politics and boundaries, but with a keen eye for a stretch of alluvial river bottom and a slope of hardwood timber facing the sun.

The Alien Act was lengthy and elaborate. It will be enough to say here that it was enacted against the danger arising at this inflammable time from the settlement of persons not British subjects. Each captain had to give a list of foreigners on board his ship, while the passengers in their turn

PRECAUTIONS

had to prove their identity. In cases of treason or suspicion the Habeas Corpus Act could be suspended, and "assemblages of people, seditious discourses, false news" were to be carefully watched, and if needed the Act was to be suppressed. It was to be enforced for a year. The time was one of imminent peril, and no well-intentioned subject, French or English, was going to split hairs over such reasonable methods of precaution. They were not directed at such domestic matters as were then at issue, for these at the moment were not very acute and in any case had become of minor consequence. Indeed, the attitude of a large part of the peasantry had become so serious, not merely about Montreal, which was always the storm centre, but even in parishes adjoining Quebec, such as Charlesbourg and Beauport, that prominent men of both nationalities formed societies for the public safety and sank their civic differences. Monk, who was very useful in organizing them, writes to Dundas that by the suggestions of Dumontier a number of officials and friends of government had been marked for assassination in case of a successful invasion.

Arrangements, too, had been permitted for settling refugees from France, and Dorchester found this used as a vehicle for introducing Frenchmen of another kind and with other objects. The distinction was not easy to draw. The Duc de La Rochefoucauld-Liancourt visited the colony in the summer of 1795 and remained for some time as

SIR GUY CARLETON

Simcoe's guest in Upper Canada. But Dorchester felt it prudent to forbid him access to the Lower Province lest his presence should be taken for an expression of active sympathy on the part of France for the malcontents.

Dorchester kept in close touch all this time with the Maritime Provinces, and there was a good deal of correspondence going backwards and forwards between himself and his brother in charge of New Brunswick, and with Wentworth, lieutenant-governor of Nova Scotia. In the former province a regiment of six hundred men was raised. In 1795 the cost of government for the year was, in round numbers, twenty-five thousand pounds, while the net revenue had risen to ten thousand pounds. The customs for both provinces were levied in Quebec, and the estimated proportion, one-eighth, due to the Upper Province was paid over to it. The crops for the above year, too, were very short, and it was necessary to call on England for grain, a proceeding quite unusual since the old French days when the necessity was almost perennial. By this year, however, things began to quiet down. A draft of Jay's Treaty had been forwarded to Canada and copies were circulated not only in the east but in the west. It had yet to be ratified, but still the mere fact of its being drafted had a good effect. The militia, however, were called out as a test and their reluctance to serve well justified the dread of war. It was not only the intrigues of outsiders that had

FEES AND PERQUISITES

brought about this insubordination. What Dorchester had written ten years before during the American invasion might have been repeated now with even greater force: "A people so disused to military service for twenty-seven years do not willingly take up the firelock and march to the frontier when their passions are not strongly agitated." The constitutional associations of the upper classes, however, had done much good, and Dorchester was able to report an improved condition of affairs. Moreover, in the course of 1795, Jay's Treaty was ratified, and it was definitely agreed that the western posts were to be given up in the following year, peace being made in the meantime between the Indians and the United States.

Dorchester had waged continual war against those fees and perquisites which he considered brought the officials of the province into disrepute, lowered the dignity of government, and created justifiable discontent. Osgoode, who had been made chief-justice of Quebec in 1794, received the appointment on the understanding that it no longer carried any of these emoluments. There was a great deal of official work going on, too, in connection with the allotment of lands to the new settlers, and the same opportunities occurred to unscrupulous officials in Canada as in a more wholesale and shameless way were being embraced on the other side of the boundary. These lapses, however, became more flagrant, and expanded into more open scandals,

SIR GUY CARLETON

with their inevitable exposures, in the days of Dorchester's successor. Fees to the governor would seem to have been, formerly, quite usual in connection with land grants, but Dorchester voluntarily surrendered his, and was cordially thanked by Portland for so doing. He felt strongly, too, the iniquity of men in England being planted on a colony which they never saw, and having their duties performed by deputies. It was these absentees who were often the worst offenders, for they took no interest whatever in the work done by their deputies, but only an abiding one in the fees accruing therefrom. In a letter to Portland, Dorchester regrets that gentlemen in England should look to America for compensation for their petty political services. It had produced a sufficiently evil effect in the revolted colonies, and would have the same in those that were still left to the Crown. These persons, he ventured to suggest, should receive such remuneration in their offices as to place them above pecuniary speculation in the colonies, and Dorchester had earned the right, if any one had, to speak plainly on the subject. For though by no means a rich man, and with a large family, his long rule in Canada had been distinguished not merely by scrupulous honesty, but by a self-abnegation in money matters rare enough in those days.

The treaty with America brought on the question of settling large numbers of the Indians on British territory. The details of this distribution, however,

FRICTION WITH SIMCOE

fell to Simcoe and his officers, though Dorchester was insistent for information concerning them, and did not allow Simcoe to forget that his immediate chief was at Quebec and not in the British colonial office. This brings us to the misunderstanding between these two admirable and faithful servants of the Crown. It belongs, however, to Simcoe's story rather than to that of Dorchester, and has been treated at length by his biographer. A brief summary of the dispute, and the occasions that lead to it, is perhaps necessary, since it was partly owing to this unpleasantness that both of the parties to it resigned their posts, and left Canada almost at the same time. Neither conceived himself properly treated by the home government, but Dorchester's attitude was indifferent, and his views slightly contemptuous. Whether right or wrong they were based on the long experience of an elderly and well-tried public servant, who had no fear for his reputation, and was in any case weary of office and anxious for home and rest. Simcoe's feelings, on the other hand, were tinged with the disappointment and soreness of a man still full of work and in mid career. Dorchester had always been an advocate for a clearly defined amount of central authority. He considered that the American colonies had grown into the condition that encouraged rebellion by the careless manner in which they had been allowed to drift. The fact that when rebellion came this very aloofness proved their chief stumbling-block was not to the point.

SIR GUY CARLETON

Dorchester's mind travelled back rather to the origin of things, and in the matter of defence against foreign aggression his experience in the Seven Years' War was wholly in favour of his argument.

Simcoe found himself in a remote wilderness of a most promising nature. He was not hampered by the race question. His people were energetic and mostly loyal Britons. He himself was of a practical turn of mind, and took an immense and praiseworthy interest in the material beginnings of what was obviously destined to be a great province. He was a voluminous despatch writer, and inclined to forget in certain matters that Dorchester was his chief. Two or three Indian appointments were made, not merely without consulting the latter but with some attempt to sustain them in the face of his objections, and Dorchester was an extremely punctilious person, exacting in the support of his theories of a limited but firm centralization. He had never fallen out with lieutenant-governors in New Brunswick or Nova Scotia, but there was marked friction in Simcoe's case, though it was purely personal between the two men; nor were the causes of disagreement of a nature, as it so happened, to create material mischief. Simcoe thought a military post was the best nucleus for an industrial centre. Dorchester thought otherwise; nor could any one nowadays with the light of a continent's development to guide him hesitate as to which was right. Simcoe wanted

CAUSES OF FRICTION

to create a capital and centre for the western district of modern Ontario on the spot where London now stands. Dorchester favoured York (now Toronto), and insisted upon it. Simcoe thought the latter should be made the naval base of Lake Ontario; Dorchester considered Kingston as at that time the best point. It would be purposeless here to argue in favour of the foresight of one or the other. It is difficult for us nowadays to appreciate the arguments that would have operated in 1794 and 1795 with either of them. But a more immediate cause for friction lay in the question as to whether the larger force of troops was required in Upper or Lower Canada. Simcoe, in short, asked for more men and Dorchester would not spare them. They were a pitiful handful in all, some two thousand three hundred, to wrangle about. At one time Upper Canada was the most threatened point, but then at a desperate moment, like the one in question, Quebec was the key of Canada. So long as she remained unconquered the colony was not lost. This was a recognized axiom in North America and no one had better cause to know it and hold it than Dorchester. Simcoe though he had done gallant service in the Revolutionary War as colonel of the New York Loyalist regiment, the Queen's Rangers, had not been at quite such close quarters with the Quebec theory. But apart from these general arguments, at the moment when Simcoe was most sore about the refusal of men from Dorchester's slender stock, the danger from the Americans, which had seemed to lie on the lakes, was being greatly lessened by the attitude of Jay in London, unknown to Simcoe, while the danger from France was somewhat growing on account of the schemes she was concocting with that volatile factor, the state of Vermont, of which a few words later.

When the treaty with America was ratified, Dorchester's intention, as he wrote to Simcoe, was to bring down most of the troops to Lower Canada, the danger in the west being at an end, while the French danger in the east was growing, for reasons already given. But Simcoe with his pet theories of developing material prosperity by military posts, seems to have lost sight of the danger of foreign invasion in the more exposed parts of the colony. He had corresponded directly and voluminously with Dundas and somewhat overlooked Dorchester, to whose conspicuous personality, years, and long service in North America, was due perhaps something more than perfunctory official recognition. In November, 1795, Dorchester wrote to Portland that the enclosures turned on the question whether he was to receive orders from Simcoe or Simcoe from him, and that the latter must have had expectations of an independent command in the upper country and even beyond. The situation of Nova Scotia and its dependencies did not permit Lieutenant-Governor Wentworth to extend his control to Quebec, and according to Dundas's letter regarding Simcoe this

A LONG SERVICE

independence of his command was established. "All command, civil and military, being thus disorganized and without remedy, your Grace will, I hope, excuse an anxiety for the arrival of my successor, who may have authority sufficient to restore order, lest these insubordinations should extend to mutiny among the troops and sedition among the people." This is plain speaking enough. Dorchester, who had already taken umbrage at the reproof in the matter of the Miamis, felt that this tendency to ignore the central authority made it impossible for him any longer to retain office as governor and commander-in-chief in North America. It will be remembered, too, that he had been against the division of the provinces, which were to be re-united in 1841, only to be separated again when the federal authority had been established over the whole of British North America.

But the misunderstandings that led to Dorchester's retirement are of slight consequence. It was thirty years since he had first entered upon his task. He was weary and he was getting old, and had vastly exceeded in length of service any other Canadian governor before his day or after it. He felt, no doubt, that he was getting out of date, or rather out of tune, with certain phases of administration, and wholly disapproved of them. But his work was done, and there was no special reason for extending still further an already quite exceptional length of responsible public service. The crisis with

SIR GUY CARLETON

America and the long strain, which his presence alone of living Englishmen had tempered on both sides of the Atlantic with some measure of relief, were over for the present. What might have followed had Jefferson been elected in 1797 one cannot guess, but his defeat by a solid vote of the Northern States showed unmistakably the sentiments of Canada's more immediate neighbours, sentiments which they never wholly abandoned, since the War of 1812 was resented by most of them, and was mainly the work of Jefferson's party and the South. There now remained only France to settle with, for Spain had proved innocuous as a source of strife between Great Britain and the States, the motives being conflicting, and the factor of sentiment as in the case of France being entirely absent; indeed, there seemed a fine quarrel brewing between France and the United States, as represented by the Federal party. The latter, soon to be committed to another period of power, had already begun to discover that thirteen states and an ungovernable West were a sufficiently restive team to handle, and had abandoned not merely the intention but even the desire to attach another partly hostile and generally uncongenial province by force of arms. They had come to the conclusion that Great Britain on the St. Lawrence was infinitely preferable to France, whose not unnatural schemes in that direction were looked upon with disapproval.

Vermont, however, had been always troublesome

VERMONT AGAIN

and restless. The water route from Lake Champlain to the St. Lawrence, her natural outlet as she regarded it, and soon to be improved by the canal that Vermonters had so much at heart, was a source of dispute which twisted her political sympathies this way and that, made her factious in her domestic, and unstable in her outside, relations. She was now a state. Her ostensible leaders, who had formerly been quite ready to play the part of Arnold towards the republic, were now the principal channels of French intrigue, and could they have done so would have dragged the neighbouring colonies into war with Britain, not, however, from political passion or from broad general principles such as are permissible to nations, however mistaken, but for mere purposes of local trade. The Southerners, who sported liberty caps and sang the "Marseillaise," to the edification of their own slaves, men who, to quote the words of an unknown historian, "could not have pronounced two French words correctly to save themselves from hanging," were inspired by ignorance and hatred of the mother country and a further hope of shuffling out of their debts to her people. The Vermonters, with Ira Allen at their head, were cool calculators. As the scheme of gaining their trade route by remaining British had failed, the alternative was to make Canada either French or American, and achieve their object in that way.

Adet, the French minister from the revolutionary government, was recalled soon after Dorchester had left Quebec. His methods and his manners had not helped the cause of France with the American government. But what is more to the point, he had set his heart on regaining Canada for France. He had engaged the whole new consular service of his country in this task, and we have seen the trouble his emissaries had caused Dorchester during these last years of his government. Though the latter sailed in July, 1796, he retained his office till the following April, when Prescott, his successor, was appointed, and it was during this winter of his administration that Ira Allen sailed from Ostend in the *Olive Branch* with twenty thousand stand-of-arms, besides artillery and ammunition. The ship was captured and brought into Portsmouth. Allen professed that this prodigal supply of arms was for the militia of Vermont, which it would have provided four times over; but certain people who were behind the scenes assured the Duke of Portland that they were designed for the invasion of Canada. Vermont at that time had certainly no other use for such a prodigious armament.

It is perhaps needless to state that the Federal government had neither cognizance of, nor sympathy with, such adventures. Adet, it appears, had himself written some of the proclamations with which Canada was deluged during Dorchester's last two years of office. These were supported by canards regarding French victories on sea and land and the immediate approach of French fleets. At

FRENCH INTERFERENCE

one time, the precise date at which the French troops would enter Canada had been injudiciously fixed. Though the ratification of Jay's Treaty removed these enterprises from the domain of such probability as they ever possessed, they produced a little crop of arrests in Prescott's first year and the dramatic hanging and quartering of a certain weak-minded McLane in the presence of the civil and military population of Quebec. A month after the expiration of Dorchester's government about forty French-Canadians were arrested, most of whom were convicted on light sentences. There were also attempts by French emissaries to stir up the Indians to an attack on Western Canada. A French agent, Jules de Fer, employed by Liston, the British minister at Philadelphia, a year later to sound the feelings of the French-Canadians, reported that there was a considerable sentiment in favour of being re-annexed to France, but that few would move unless success was quite assured by the landing of a large force. The emissaries of the directorate, whose ability for intrigue seems always to have far exceeded their judgment, reported to their government with characteristic exaggeration that the French-Canadians were burning to risk life and fortune in the cause. There is no evidence that any French-Canadians of education or influence felt anything but repugnance to a renewed connection with their mother country, as now remodelled.

SIR GUY CARLETON

It is melancholy that two such faithful, and in their different ways capable, administrators as Dorchester and Simcoe should have embittered each other's closing years of office. Most of their correspondence is very acrid. Simcoe thought the Indian department should be in his immediate hands and not in those of a superintendent. The absence of the latter, Sir John Johnson, in England, no doubt aggravated certain abuses, usually financial ones, that created constant scandals in a service which afforded enormous temptations to dishonesty. The conflicting views of the two men as to the founding of provincial capitals and harbours and the methods of settling a new country have been alluded to. Simcoe writes: "Stations for the king's troops judiciously selected is, in my opinion, the only basis on which towns will arise to the great benefit of the service." Dorchester replies: "The impolicy of placing so many troops out of the way, and the enormous abuses in the public expenditure for twenty years are not the only objections to this method of encouraging settlements. The principle itself is erroneous, as evinced by the improvements in provinces where no extraordinary expenses were incurred nor troops were employed for civil purposes." Simcoe poured out his grievances to Dundas and Portland, while Dorchester curtly intimated more than once, as we know, that if a divided authority was to be the method of government in British North America it was time he took himself off.

SAILS FOR ENGLAND

Dorchester had met his last parliament on November 20th, 1795, and it had continued sitting till May 7th. Among its duties was the alleviation of distress, owing to a bad harvest, and the governor laid an embargo on the exportation of wheat. The last occurrence during his long term of residence was the withdrawal of the British troops in June from the western forts, which were to be formally occupied by the Americans in August. Dorchester sailed for England on July 9th, the lieutenant-governor, Prescott, also in command of the military forces, remaining his representative till the spring of the following year, when he formally took his place as governor-in-chief. Addresses of affection, respect and regret were presented to the departing governor by the people both of Quebec and Montreal, coupled with expressions of devotion to the Crown and "the happy government under which it is our glory to live." The high example set by the private lives of himself and his family were gracefully alluded to. Dorchester knew now that he was leaving never to return, and his feelings of regret mingled with the yearning for peace and rest inevitable to his now abundant years and the strenuous fashion in which most of them had been spent.

Guy Carleton must be judged mainly by his works. He has left no private correspondence to help us, for his wife destroyed it all after his death, nor has the contemporary gossip of Quebec sent down to us any very lucid pictures of the man in his hours of ease among friends or family. Happily his official correspondence, spread over sixteen busy years, reveals much of that side of his character which is most vital to the appreciation of a great proconsul. His jealousy for the honour of the British Crown and impatience of everything mean, dishonest or unjust that would cast a slur on it, was a leading note in his career. His kindness of heart was a byword, while his fair and liberal treatment of the king's new subjects, in accordance, as he thought, both with policy and justice, never wavered, though it often brought him temporary unpopularity with one side or the other. For this, however, or its opposite, Dorchester cared very little. Of strong personality and extreme independence of character, he was never swayed for a moment by what men might say or think of him; but his instincts were true and his heart was sound. Even those who suffered, as a rule justly, from the first never denied the second. Though distinctly a *grand seigneur* and with a reserved manner, his qualities of head and heart must have been all the greater to procure for him the large measure of affection and esteem with which he was generally regarded. And this reputation, it should be remembered, was steadily maintained through two long terms of eight years apiece, so widely sundered that they almost represented two different generations of Canadians. No cases of undeserved hardship or neglected merit seem to have been too insignificant

HIS CHARACTER

for Dorchester's attention, and when rebuke was required he cared little for the rank of the transgressor, as might be inferred from the candour of his communications even to secretaries of state.

Against jobbery, whether in the grasping of fees, or in that odious, and then too common, custom of foisting incompetent deputies on the colony while politicians at home shared the plunder, he waged incessant war. We have plenty of evidence that the Château St. Louis was, during Dorchester's tenancy, the centre of a graceful and dignified hospitality. He desired to be fair to the French-Canadians and thus frequently laid himself open to the accusation of a bias in favour of that nationality. But if he ever exceeded equity and prudence in this particular he was heavily punished by the ready surrender of the Canadian peasantry to the wiles of outside intrigue; for there is no doubt he felt it bitterly. He unquestionably modified his earlier views of the British trading community, probably from the fact that as time went on they justified his better opinion. They, no doubt, themselves acquired greater discretion and gradually absorbed from outside a better and wiser element. Above all, the trials of 1775-6 divided the sheep from the goats, and inclined a better feeling between the educated English and French who shared a common peril and fought side by side against a common enemy. It had been Dorchester's lot to govern Canada through periods of

SIR GUY CARLETON

great political stress and in some moments of extraordinary peril. That he saved her to Great Britain in those years would alone entitle him to the perpetual gratitude of Canada and of the empire. But this achievement, conspicuous though it was, is very far from comprising the whole debt under which he has laid posterity. It was but a crowning incident in many years' record of less showy but valuable service. Mistakes he doubtless made, though it is not easy to put one's finger on them, amid the personal feelings and faction which distinguish that little nucleus of a coming nation over which he ruled and which fifty years later Lord Durham still called, "Two nations warring within a single state." Dorchester, however, had to face the further disadvantage that these domestic distractions were carried on under the very guns, either active or threatening, of two powerful enemies.

The frigate *Active*, which carried Dorchester and his family from Quebec, was wrecked on the Island of Anticosti, near the mouth of the St. Lawrence. Happily no lives were lost, and the party were conveyed by coasting vessels to Percé on the Gaspé shore. A ship was sent for them from Halifax, and they sailed direct for England, arriving at the end of September. Dorchester retained his governorship for six months longer, when Prescott succeeded him in the titular honours of office as he had already done in its actual duties. Dorchester was now seventy-two, and spent the remaining twelve years

HIS DEATH

of life left to him in rural retirement, first at Kempshot, near Basingstoke, and later at Stubbings, near Maidenhead, where he died suddenly on November 10th, 1808. These years, as may be imagined, were quite uneventful ones. Dorchester left a numerous family, and his title descended in the male line till 1897, when it became extinct. It was revived, however, in the person of the present Baroness Dorchester, a cousin of the last lord and descendant of the governor, and passes to her son, Dudley Massey Carleton. There are a great number of living descendants of the famous governor, and among these, it may be interesting to note, are several groups of a family directly descended from him, and well known to the writer, long settled in Virginia.

Stubbings, where Dorchester died, had been his first purchase. He bought Greywell Hill, near Winchfield, in Hampshire, which is now the chief home of the family, from the trustees of Lord Northington. Lastly, he bought Kempshot, near Basingstoke, where he himself chiefly lived, as has been stated, an uneventful life, interesting himself much in the breeding of horses, of which he had always been fond. Among other distinguished guests who occasionally visited him in his country home was the Prince Regent.

Six of Dorchester's sons died from wounds or disease on active service. The death of the eldest in 1786 was both singular and sad. Dorchester was actually on the sea, bound for his second term of

SIR GUY CARLETON

office in Canada, when the youth landed at Plymouth on sick leave from the continent. Those were queer times, and though heir to a barony as he was, this young British officer seems to have been so friendless and hard put to it for clothes that he was nearly hanged as a French spy. However, he contrived to reach London, and being at once taken ill again with camp fever seems to have been quite stranded in the great city. The only person whose name he could think of was Mr. Pitt, and he applied to that minister, who secured him quarters in Westminster, where he died.

A picture of the siege of Bergen op Zoom, where Carleton, it will be remembered, was wounded, hangs in the dining-room at Greywell Hill. By a remarkable coincidence another son of Carleton's met his death there carrying the same sword with which his father had so distinguished himself on the former occasion. Among the other treasures here is the wooden bedstead with curtains which the general used in Canada and on all his campaigns, and on which he died. As it is scarcely more than five feet long, and was curtained all around, it is assumed that the owner, a tall man, must have habitually rested in a doubled-up position. There is also preserved a handsome carved horn, presented by the Western Indians to the governor while in Canada.

Lady Dorchester lived to a great age, and plenty of people not long dead remembered her perfectly. Though a small woman she was awe-inspiring to a

LADY DORCHESTER

degree in the extraordinary ceremony she observed and exacted, and the hauteur of her bearing, her own family being included in this attitude. When visiting her son-in-law, Lord Bolton, of Hackwood, so an eye-witness used to relate to present members of the family, her entry to the dining-room at meal hours was a prodigiously solemn affair and never occurred till all the family and guests were assembled. Her hair at this time, 1830, was lifted high up with lace and scarlet ribbons, her dress costly and elaborate. She wore scarlet shoes with very high heels and gold buttons, and carried in her hand an ebony cane. On entering she would bow graciously to the assembled company, and no one thought of sitting down till she herself was seated. Such was the lady who some fifty-five years before had come almost as a bride to preside at the Château St. Louis, Quebec.

APPENDICES

APPENDICES

A

The English-speaking traders were invited to Canada by the army leaders. Though they came from the American colonies, only a very small number of them were born there. This mercantile minority received less than justice then, and has received little more since. Murray and Carleton were strongly prejudiced against them, and their opinion has been uncritically accepted by later writers. Many of them were excellent citizens. Only some were truculent. This was due not solely to native perversity but also to the treatment which they received at the hands of the authorities in the colony.

B

All the seigniors were not members of the *noblesse*, and social distinctions in Canada never approximated conditions in old France. See W. B. Munro, "the Seigniorial System in Canada," Longmans, 1907.

C

Amherst's reply to the demand for a continuance of French law was that the Canadians became subjects of the king. This was not a denial, but only a shelving of the question.

D

William Gregory was the chief justice. After his dismissal he practised at the Canadian bar. The attorney-general was George Suckling, who came from Nova Scotia where he had been a member of the Assembly. He knew a lot of law, but little of human nature. For an illustration of his pedantry, see "Canadian Historical Review," vol., 3 p. 253.

E

The one French Canadian in Murray's council was François Mounier, a Protestant who had come from France just before the fall of Canada. A Roman Catholic could not take the oaths required of a councillor until the Quebec Act was passed.

F

Murray's ordinance of September 17th, 1764, establishing civil courts, waived the religious disqualifications of English law on only two points. Canadian lawyers were admitted to plead in the court of common pleas, and juries were thrown open.

G

Murray was recalled to answer a swarm of complaints from Canada, many of which were backed up by London merchants. His explanatory letters were always slower in reaching the board of trade than were the accusations of his enemies, and he was suspected as a creature of the Earl of Bute. He was finally cleared of all charges by an order-in-council of April 13th, 1767.

H

This version of the remonstrance incident is based solely on Carleton's statement, which was very wide from the truth. Carleton called together a truncated council and with it reversed the decision of a previous full council. The aggrieved councillors drew up such a mild remonstrance that Carleton was able to misrepresent it to the home government. Carleton tried vainly to squirm out of the

APPENDICES

awkward position in which he found himself as a result of his illegal action. Having turned the majority of his council against himself, Carleton dared not meet it until he found an opportunity for cutting off the heads of the opposition by dismissing Irving and Mabane, thereby reducing the rest to submission. Throughout the whole incident, he consistently deceived the home government. "Canadian Historical Review," vol. 4, p. 321, A. L. Burt, Sir Guy Carleton and his First Council."

I

Carleton did not object to this action of Irving and Mabane at the time. His objection arose some days later when he discovered in the incident a plausible excuse for dismissing them from the council. See article quoted in note "H" *supra*.

J

These changes in the judicial system were effected by two ordinances published before Carleton's arrival and with which he had nothing to do. That of July 1st, 1766, which had been prepared by the home government, re-enacted the admission of Canadians to all juries, to remove a prevailing doubt, and enacted that suits between Canadians should be tried by Canadian juries, suits between British-born by British-born juries, and suits between Canadians and British-born by mixed juries. A third term was added by the ordinance of July 26th, 1766.

K

Murray issued no proclamation in 1762, but if he had it would not have applied to Three Rivers or Montreal, for at that time he was only military governor of the Quebec district.

The whole legal system of Canada rested on insecure

SIR GUY CARLETON

foundations for the following reasons. (1) The royal proclamation of October 7th, 1763, was so vaguely worded that it produced grave differences of opinion over its interpretation. Did it sweep away all French law or only part of it, and if the latter what part? (2) This proclamation promised an assembly and Murray's commission, of subsequent date, empowered him to legislate with the assistance of a council and assembly. But all legislation in Canada down to the Quebec Act was by governor and council without an assembly. The only authority for this was in Murray's instructions. Hence arose two serious doubts, whether the king alone could delegate legislative authority to the governor after he had promised an assembly, and even if he could do this whether the instructions conferred any power not expressly granted by the commission which preceded it. Thus the English-speaking merchants in Canada could say that "the ordinances are not worth a farthing," which of course included the ordinance establishing the courts of justice and all their judgments.

L

Cramahé's lieutenant-governorship of Three Rivers was only nominal. On the establishment of civil government, August 10th, 1764, the military governors, Burton and Haldimand, were offered appointments as lieutenant-governors of Montreal and Three Rivers respectively. They refused and Murray nominated Irving and Cramahé in their stead. But these offices amounted to nothing and almost immediately disappeared.

M

The alternative of leaving the West "under temporary administration" had already been tried and found wanting, 1763-1774. There were several good reasons for extending the colony to include the country north of the Ohio, which

APPENDICES

was the meaning of the boundaries set forth in the Quebec Act. That country, set aside as an Indian reserve in 1763, was to have received a special government. As the plans for this never matured, the problem of preserving law and order in this territory remained unsolved. Indeed it was more acute in 1774 than it had been in 1763 because of the increasing activity of the fur traders. The simplest way to give this territory a government was to annex it to a territory that already had a government. Canada was the natural choice. The few settlers in this territory were French from Canada. The fur trade, its only economic interest, was focused at Montreal, and for this reason both the English and the French in Canada desired its annexation. Geography also suggested this solution, for in those days when waterways were the chief means of communication this territory was much more accessible from Canada than from any other colony. Moreover the native problem could be more effectively handled through the Canadian governor than through any other, who would be hampered by an assembly. Finally, had none of these causes existed, the mother country could hardly have been expected to give the keeping of this great land to any of the colonies on the brink of revolution.

N

Carleton violently warped the Quebec Act, giving it a meaning very different from that intended by the home government. The latter desired to give every just satisfaction to the English minority as well as to the French majority. Broadly speaking, trade was in the hands of the English, while real property was in the hands of the French. Though establishing French civil law for the sake of the French land-owners, the act was not designed to rob the English of the advantages of English civil law for their commerce. Indeed, trial by jury for civil matters was

SIR GUY CARLETON

agreed to as part of the act by Lord Chancellor Apsley, until he recalled an incident in the autumn of 1766 when a Quebec jury returned a verdict that undermined the revenue. Articles 12 and 13 of Carleton's instructions clearly reveal the purpose of the home government to satisfy the English mercantile minority by granting the right of habeas corpus, trial by jury for civil cases and English commercial law. The governor and council were to pass ordinances to this effect. Carleton, however, defeated this purpose by secreting these instructions and by concealing his disobedience from the home government. This wrought a grave injustice to the English minority without conferring any benefit upon the French majority. The law of Canada before the conquest was the custom of Paris and this contained no commercial law. There was little need for the latter until the conquest established commercial freedom. The consequent commercial development was the work of the English-speaking merchants who enjoyed English commercial law until the passing of the act. Thus Carleton robbed them of the body of the law which had regulated their business and imposed in its stead a body of law which they neither wanted nor understood, which had been little if ever used in the French period, and in which the French now were little interested because they did not possess ten per cent of the business of the colony. Carleton seems to have been actuated by blind prejudice. "Canadian Historical Review," vol. 1, p. 166, William Smith, "The Struggle over the Laws of Canada, 1763-1783."

O

By robbing the English minority of their commercial laws (see note "N" *supra*), Carleton left them with the impression that the British government had deserted them. Had it not been for this, there would have been less sedition amongst the English minority, and the door to American

APPENDICES

agitators would have been less widely opened. Thus Carleton was responsible for augmenting the danger in the impending crisis.

P

On September 21st, 1776, Carleton ordered Cramahé to quarter "all the recruits and drafts for the British regiments in the mutinous parishes on the north side of the river and let the officers remain with them to take care of them." (B. 39, p.177).

Q

On closer examination, this incident "of a staff appointment" reveals Carleton in a less favourable light. The "new arrival" was not Germain's appointee, but Carleton's. He was the latter's own brother, Major Thomas Carleton, who came to the country for the purpose of accepting the appointment. Germain's "protégé' was an "old timer" and had the further advantage of superior rank, Lieutenant-Colonel Gabriel Christie. The office in dispute was that of quartermaster-general. Carleton filled it under the authority of a letter from the under secretary, Sept. 8th, 1775, before Germain was appointed secretary of state. Germain seems to have been innocent of this arrangement. He cancelled the appointemnt of Christie as soon as he received Carleton's remonstrance. (Q.11, p. 217; Q.12, pp. 62, 90, 105ff.)

R

Howe was informed of Burgoyne's plan of campaign but was left to form his own plans. (See Egerton, "The American Revolution," pp. 120, 121.) On June 10th, 1777, Carleton forwarded to Burgoyne a letter from Howe, New York, April 5th, in which the latter not only stated that he expected to be in Pennsylvania but also offered general advice upon the course Burgoyne should follow. (Q. 13,

SIR GUY CARLETON

pp. 237, 240). Too much reliance was placed upon expected aid from loyalists along Burgoyne's line of march and upon Burgoyne's capacity in an emergency.

S

The quotation about Germain's nominees, Livius and Owen, turning out two judges at Montreal is mistaken. Carleton could never accuse Germain of this for Livius and Owen were Dartmouth's nominees. The next quotation does not allude to Livius but to Southouse. (Q. 14, p. 267. In the "Canadian Historical Review," vol. 5, p. 198, n. 4, it is erroneously stated that the reference was to Owen). Livius did not supplant Grant. The latter was never on the bench in Canada. He was acting attorney-general for a short while until James Monk was appointed to the office. The displaced Montreal judge to whom Carleton referred was John Fraser, and Carleton himself was partly responsible for Fraser's predicament. The picture of Livius in the quotation is quite unreliable. It was drawn by Carleton after Livius had caught him in wrongdoing, after he had dismissed Livius in a high-handed manner and was trying to justify himself against his accuser and victim. See *infra* note "T" and footnote, p. 188.

T

An examination of Carleton's correspondence with Germain over civil appointments does not reflect discredit upon Germain. In his first letter to Germain on civil matters, August 10th, 1776, (Q. 12, p. 119) Carleton criticised a number of appointments made by Germain's predecessor, Lord Dartmouth. Owen had arrived in the fall of 1775 with a commission as judge of Detroit, but Carleton, attracted by his quality, had appointed him to the bench at Montreal in the place of John Fraser then a prisoner in the revolted colonies. A certain Mr. Gordon had arrived

APPENDICES

at the same time, bringing a mandamus to be clerk of the crown and pleas, which Carleton now pointed out included five distinct offices some of which were incompatible and were moreover already filled satisfactorily. Livius had also arrived in the previous autumn with a commission of vice-admiralty and a mandamus to be judge of the common pleas at Montreal. Carleton now complained that his own nominee as surrogate of the vice-admiralty court was thus displaced and that Livius turned out one of the Montreal judges. As a matter of fact, Livius replaced Marteilhe on the Montreal bench, and Marteilhe was already permanently incapacitated by illness. (Q. 14, p. 265) Carleton also denounced fees.

Germain replied, March 26th, 1777, (Q. 13, p. 90) to only two points in this letter. Having learned indirectly that Carleton had objected to Gordon's warrant as incomplete, he had compared the establishment agreed to while Carleton was in England and found that Gordon's office corresponded with it, had consulted Dartmouth out of courtesy, and finally had sent out a new corrected warrant. He continued that he would never have agreed to the appointment had he been aware that this one office had branched out into so many. Though he did not say it, Germain implied that all would have been well if Carleton had reported directly upon his refusal to admit Gordon and his reasons for so doing. The second point was fees. Germain denied that there had been an agreement at the time of the Quebec Act to exclude fees from the courts, for that would have slowed up the course of justice.

The only appointments made by Germain were notified to Carleton in a letter of August 22nd, 1776. (Q. 12, p. 92) Chief Justice Hey, refusing to return, was succeeded by Livius. Southouse, who had just been appointed attorney-general upon the death of Kneller, was promoted to take the place Livius was vacating, and James Monk, solicitor-

SIR GUY CARLETON

general for Nova Scotia, succeeded to Southouse. In the same letter, Carleton was informed that Owen's appointment to Detroit had been a mistake for Montreal and was now corrected.

In acknowledging this letter, May 23rd, 1777, (Q. 13, p. 160) Carleton said:—"I have only to observe thereon that Your Lordship has turned out of their employment two men of abilities and good character. Mr. Grant has acted as Attorney-General ever since Mr. Kneller left the Province; and Mr. Fraser, as Judge of the Common Pleas at Montreal, ever since the first establishment of the Civil Courts of Justice in 1764. These gentlemen have both exposed their lives more than once to oppose rebellion; Mr. Fraser, for the same cause, has suffered in his property, been personally insulted, and is still detained a prisoner by the rebels. The power I have not; I am at a loss to know, after the fate of these gentlemen, how I can even talk of rewarding those who have preserved their loyalty, without an appearance of mockery. Of this you may be assured, that such things will occasion no small exultation among the King's enemies."

This reply was certainly querulous. There was nothing to criticise in Livius' promotion. It and more had been promised by Germain's predecessor, and Livius was undoubtedly the best lawyer in the colony. Nor could Carleton object to Owen's nomination to the Montreal court,—he had already done it himself. There remained only the appointments of Southouse and Monk. It will be observed that they were made to fill vacancies created by action in London.

Germain replied, July 25th, 1777;—(Ibid., p. 182) "In all this no increase was made in the number of appointments from hence, and how it should happen, as you say it did, that I turned out of their employments two men of abilities and good characters, I am unable to comprehend. It

APPENDICES

however gives me concern to find that two gentlemen, who have both exposed their lives and suffered in their fortunes, by opposing the rebellion, are disappointed in their expectations of reward from the crown: but as things are circumstanced I can only say that as you have now for the first time made me acquainted with their names and merits, I will not fail to take the first fit occasion of recommending them to His Majesty, for some mark of His royal favor."

Germain was right, and the only points which Carleton could make in his rambling reply of October 15th, 1777, (Q. 14, pp. 264) were that he had ordered Cramahé to recommend Grant as a successor to Kneller, and that Southouse did not know the French language or law. He even stated that Southouse turned out Fraser, apparently forgetting that he himself, more than a year previously, had put Owen in Fraser's place. He should have limited himself to denouncing Southouse's incompetence, for Southouse was a complete failure on the bench.

U

The appointment of the committee referred to was made not in the legislative council but in the council upon state business, the "privy council" which was no longer "privy," on November 6th, 1786. Four committees were then appointed to report on: (1) the courts of justice, (2) the militia, the highroads and communications; (3) population and agriculture; and (4) external and internal commerce and the regulation of the police. These committees were all appointed to collect the information necessary to guide the home government in resettling the constitution of the country.

V

The "fresh bill" was introduced by St. Ours before Smith's bill was lost. Some days later it ousted Smith's bill and

SIR GUY CARLETON

seemed about to carry. This threw the merchants into a panic, for the bill if it became law would have robbed them of two precious rights secured in 1785, English rules of evidence for the trial of commercial cases and optional juries for the trial of commercial cases and torts. The appearance of Monk, the attorney-general, on behalf of the merchants was quite regular. According to the custom of that time, he could practice privately when (a) the government was not interested and (b) he secured permission from the governor or lieutenant-governor. Both these officials had given their consent. Monk's speech on April 14th, 1787 was followed by a week of angry debates in the council, some demanding an investigation into the conduct of the judges, the others demanding that the investigation be into the behaviour of Monk. Dorchester did not "appoint a committee under Chief Justice Smith," because the members of the council were themselves implicated as members of the court of appeals. He commissioned the chief justice to conduct the investigation. This investigation by the chief justice should not be confused with the work of the committee on the courts of justice referred to above. That committee was composed of the chief justice and five other members of the council. It reported three months before Monk made the charges that gave rise to the chief justice's investigation. Monk was dismissed for his attack on the judges, but he was soon afterward reinstated.

W

Dorchester did not know whether the British government intended to keep these western posts or to abandon them. If they were to be retained, he urged that they be strengthened. If they were to be given up, he advised that they be destroyed rather than be handed over as they were. (Q. 27-1. p. 34, Dorchester to Sydney, Jan. 16th, 1787). If the Americans were to seize the posts, Dorchester was instructed

APPENDICES

to recapture them if he could. Sydney regarded the Indians' friendship as most important for holding the posts, for protecting the fur trade, and for defending the colony. Therefore he increased the quantity of presents for the Indians and instructed Dorchester to supply them with such "ammunition as might enable them to defend themselves" against the Americans. (Ibid. p. 47; Q. 28, p. 30).

X

There were political reasons for settling the loyalists beyond the old seigniories. (See McIlwraith, "Haldimand," appendix "S") The loyalists in Canada did not receive their lands in freehold tenure. This was one of the reasons for the Constitutional Act.

The loyalists took little part in the agitation for an assembly, the centre of which was the mercantile interest of Montreal. The merchants of Quebec, though joining, were not so aggressive as those of Montreal.

Y

Dorchester was not invited home. On Feb. 8th, 1790, he requested leave to return for a few months on private affairs. On May 6th and again on June 5th, Grenville discouraged Dorchester's desire on the ground that he was needed in Canada. On August 4th, Grenville wrote permitting his return when the new lieutenant-governor, Clarke, had arrived,—but only on condition that circumstances would permit. This reached Dorchester in the middle of October. As it was too late to return that season, Dorchester said that he would come in the spring.

Z

The territorial revenues and the duties collected under the Quebec Revenue Act were not at the disposal of the

SIR GUY CARLETON

assembly. It could claim control only over the revenue raised by the authority of the local legislature. The first revenue act which it passed was in 1793 and produced only £905 during the ensuing year. Upon securing the approval of the home government, Dorchester inaugurated the practice of submitting for the information of the assembly a complete statement of revenue and expenditure. The assembly made no effort to secure control of public finance for more than ten years after Dorchester departed. "Canada and its Provinces," vol. 4, pp. 491-518, Duncan McArthur, "History of Public Finance, 1763-1840."

INDEX

INDEX

A

ALLEGHANY frontiersmen, their characteristics, 232
Allen, Ethan, captures Ticonderoga and Crown Point, 83; deserts Fort St. Johns on the approach of the British, 84; his foolhardy attempt to capture Montreal, 98, 99; taken prisoner and sent to England, 99; his correspondence in the Vermont negotiations, 244, 245
Allen, Ira, captured with arms for the supposed invasion of Canada, 300
Allsopp, member of the first legislative council, 91
Americans, besiege Quebec, 114-26; the killed and wounded, 131; evacuate Canada, 146, 147; battle for the naval supremacy of Lake Champlain, 154-7
Amherst, General, Canada surrendered to, by Lévis, 2; conditions of the surrender, 10
Anderson, Captain, British officer, killed at Quebec, 130
Arnold, Benedict, his parentage, 104; marriage, 104; business, 104; character, 104; captain of the "Governor's Guards," 105; receives the commission of colonel from the Massachusetts committee, 105; joins Allen as a volunteer in the attack on Ticonderoga, 105; captures an armed sloop at St. Johns, 105; resigns the service of the Massachusetts committee in a huff and enlists with Washington, 105; appointed commander of the expedition against Quebec, 105, 106; his force, 106; sails from Newburyport for the mouth of the Kennebec, 106; his historic march to Quebec, 107-9; arrives at Point Lévis, 109; holds a council of war and decides to advance on Quebec, 109, 110; congratulates Montgomery on the capture of St. Johns and outlines his prospects of capturing Quebec, 110; lands at Wolfe's Cove, 110; sends a summons to surrender to Cramahé which he refuses to receive, 111; moves his troops to Pointe-aux-Trembles, 111; joined by Montgomery, 116; driven from his headquarters in St. Roch, 121; on the march to Sault-au-Matelot, 127, 128; wounded, 128; transferred to Montreal, 132, 135; repulses Forster at Lachine but is forced to retire from Vaudreuil, 142, 143; leaves Canada, 147; sells for his own benefit military supplies obtained in Canada, 147; defeated by Carle-

329

ton on Lake Champlain, 155-7; his losses, 155; burns the buildings in Crown Point and proceeds to Ticonderoga, 156

Asgill, Lieutenant, a victim of retaliation, 198-200

Assembly, House of, the agitation for, 55, 56, 60, 61; withheld for the present, 64; the demand for, 237, 264; its first meeting, 269

B

Bailly, M., bishop coadjutor, 227; opposes the bishop's views on better education, 229

Ball, Miss, wife of Christopher Carleton, and mother of Lord Dorchester, 29; afterwards marries the Rev. Thomas Skelton, 29

Barnsfare, Captain, in charge of the battery at Près de Ville, 127

Barré, Colonel, 67, 69

Belette, Captain, engages the enemy at Sorel while Carleton proceeds to Quebec, 113

Boston, evacuated by Howe, 134, 159

Bouchette, skipper, pilots Carleton from Sorel to Three Rivers, 113

Bouquet, Henry, Colonel of the 60th, his victories in "Pontiac's War," 6; made a brigadier, 6; his death in Florida, 7; bequeaths his papers to Haldimand, 7

Bourinot, Sir John G., quoted, 63

Briand, Monseigneur, appointed bishop and sent to Canada, 23; his simple life, 58; his efforts to rouse the patriotism of the *habitants*, 87

British colonists, their ideas on the subject of land tenure, 12, 13; monopolize trade and stir up strife with the French-Canadians, 16, 17; forward a petition for Murray's recall, 17; their discontent with Murray, 23; censured by Murray, 24; present petitions for a House of Assembly, 60, 61; express their satisfaction with the Quebec Act, 78, 79

Burgoyne, Sir John, arrives in Quebec with troops, 144; sent to recover Chambly and St. Johns, 146; finds them deserted, 146; agrees with Carleton in postponing the siege of Ticonderoga, 158; returns to England, 163; back in Canada, 171; to make a junction with Howe's army at the south and fight his way to Albany, 171, 172; his birth and early military life, 175; marriage, 175; in the House of Commons, 175; a dramatist and versifier, 175; as a soldier, 175, 176; his personality, 176; his army, 176, 177; defeated and forced to retreat, 180; his mistakes, 181, 182; defends himself, 182

Burke, Edmund, takes part in the debate on the Canada Act, 265; his quarrel with Fox, 265

Burr, Aaron, Montgomery's aide, 106, 122, 234

Burton, Sir Francis, lieutenant-governor at Montreal, 21

INDEX

Butterfield, Major, surrenders with congress forces at the Cedars, 142

C

CALDWELL, COLONEL, 111; commands the British militia, 115; his house burnt by Arnold, 121; leads a company to defend the second barrier, 129; with Carleton in his attack on the rebels, 138; sent to England, 138

Campbell, Captain of the 27th, arrested for participation in the Walker outrage, 36-8

Campbell, General, commissioner in the matter of cartels, 207, 208

Campbell, Major, refuses to surrender Fort Miami, 286

Canada Act of 1791, 227; the bill introduced in the House of Commons by Pitt, 263; the debate upon, 263-5; becomes law, (May 14th, 1791), 266; its provisions, 266, 267; comes into effect, (December 26th, 1791), 269

Carden, Major, sent to Long Point to dislodge Ethan Allen, 98; killed, 99

Carleton, Christopher, father of Lord Dorchester, 29; death of, 29

Carleton, Sir Guy, afterwards Lord Dorchester, his birth and parentage, 29; early military life, 30; military preceptor to the Duke of Richmond, 30; is refused permission to accompany Wolfe on the Louisbourg expedition, 31; after three appeals accompanies him to Quebec as quartermaster-general, 31; wounded at the battle of the Plains of Abraham, 32; returns to Europe and sees active service, 32; appointed to succeed Murray at Quebec, 32; his arrival and welcome, 32, 33; an incident of his independence, 34; relinquishes all fees and perquisites attached to his office, 35, 36; the object of his first mission, (1766-78), 39; of his second, (1786-96), 39, 40; writes to Shelburne explaining his adherence to the French civil code, and gives a sketch of the province, 43-8; allays the anxiety of the home government as to French plans of revolt, 48, 49; foresees the revolt of the American colonies, 50, 51; has a new ordinance passed for the administration of justice, 54, 55; returns to England in 1770 and remains four years, 59; his report on manufactures, 59, 60; deeply involved in the drafting of the Quebec Act, 63, 68; the story of his marriage, 75, 76; returns to Canada (1774), 75; receives addresses expressing satisfaction with the Quebec Act, 78; instructions from Dartmouth, 81; reports the loss of Ticonderoga and Crown Point to Dartmouth, 85, 86; calls out the militia, 86; when returning to Quebec is entertained at Three Rivers by Tonnancour, 89; opens the first legislative council, 90; hurries

331

SIR GUY CARLETON

back to Montreal on hearing that the rebels are again on the Richelieu, 91; his army of defence, 93; orders Walker's arrest, 100; makes every effort to raise the siege of St. Johns, 102, 103; writes Dartmouth the reasons of his failure, 103; attempts the convoy of his force from Montreal to Quebec, 104, 112, 113; prepares to face the siege, 114; receives a letter from Montgomery, 118, 119; learns that the first barricade has been fired, 129; attends Montgomery's funeral, 132; receives reinforcements from England, 137; attacks and puts to rout the rebels, 137, 138; his humanity towards the fugitives, 138, 139; meets Burgoyne at Quebec, 144; improves the defences of the country, 150, 151; re-establishes courts of Quebec, 151; defeats the congress fleet on Lake Champlain, 154-7; reviews the situation and decides not to attack Ticonderoga in the face of the coming winter, 157-9; returns to his civic duties in Quebec, 159; his opinion of the Canadians, 161; gives a dinner and ball on New Year's Eve, 162; sends his plans for the coming campaign to Germain with Burgoyne, 163; superseded in command by Burgoyne, 163, 164; writes Germain, 165-9; sends in his resignation, 169; remains in office another year, 171; his plan of campaign, 171; compelled to sanction a *corvée*, 178; receives discouraging messages from Ticonderoga, 179; Powell applies to, for instructions, his reply, 180; his appointments in the courts, 183; disapproves of Livius as chief-justice, 184; disapproves of Germain's colonial appointments, 185, 186; calls out the militia, 187; his kindness to American prisoners, 188; last letter to Germain, 188, 189; returns to England, 189; appointed peace commissioner, "general and commander-in-chief, etc.," 193, 194; sails for New York, (1782), 193; receives addresses of welcome, 195; confronted with the Philip White incident, 198-200; instructed to propose negotiations of peace with the Americans, 200; asks to be recalled on hearing that complete independence is to be ceded to the Americans, 203; corresponds with Washington about the Loyalists, 206; appoints a commission to meet Washington's representatives, 207, 208; discusses the matter of cartels with Washington and Clinton, 214; superintends the transportation of the Loyalists and evacuates New York, 214-19; after two years spent in England returns to Canada as governor-general (1786), 221; created Baron Dorchester, 221; his warm reception, 223, 224; his powers as governor, 224; appoints committees to report upon the legal

INDEX

code, commerce and education of the province, 225, 226 ; finds the Indian question in a critical state, 231 ; establishes a postal service, 243 ; receives a petition from the French-Canadians protesting against Lymburner's mission, 246; his efforts to maintain the efficiency of the Canadian militia, 246 ; receives the first draft of a new bill for the better government of Quebec, 248 ; his objections to the division of the province, 248 ; favours Sir John Johnson's appointment as lieutenant-governor of Upper Canada, 258, 259 ; his multifarious duties, 262, 263; sails for England, 269 ; returns to Canada, 271 ; reports the failure of the peace negotiations between the American commissioners and the Indians, 276 ; opens the second parliament of Lower Canada, 276 ; faces the militia problem again, 277, 278 ; harangues the Miamis, 282, 283 ; correspondence arising from the event, 283, 284 ; wages war against fees and perquisites, 291, 292 ; his misunderstanding with Simcoe, 293-8, 302 ; wishes to resign, 297; sails for home, 300, 303, 306 ; a summing up of his character and work, 303-6 ; his remaining years and death, 307 ; the death of his sons, 307, 308

Carrol, Charles, appointed congress commissioner to Canada, 135

Carroll, Father, afterwards archbishop, accompanies congress commission to Canada, 135

Caughnawagas, serve with the Canadians against the rebels, 88 ; desert Preston at Fort St. Johns, 100

Chambly, defended by Major Stopford, 93 ; the fall of, 99, 101

Château St. Louis, 144, 162, 221, 305, 309

Chaudière, River, 106, 107, 108

Clarke, Colonel Alured, 214 ; appointed lieutenant - governor of Quebec, 249 ; left in charge during Dorchester's absence, 269

Clinton, Governor of New York, meets Carleton to discuss the matter of cartels, 214

Clinton, Sir Henry, returns from his command at New York, 192

Committee on education, appointed by Dorchester, 226 ; the finding of, 229

Congress, its attitude towards the Quebec Act, 70-3 ; matters precipitated by the seizure of Ticonderoga and Crown Point, 95; undertakes the invasion of Canada, 96 ; appoints a commission to investigate the military situation of Canada, 135 ; reports it as hopeless, 136, 137 ; violates a compact for the exchange of prisoners, 143 ; controls the entire open country, 196 ; called upon to settle the Philip White incident, 198-200 ; receives the proposed terms of peace with bad grace, 207

333

Conolly, William, "patron" of Guy Carleton and his brother, 30

Contrecœur, M. de, member of the first legislative council, 91

Cornwallis, Lord, his surrender at Yorktown, 191

Cramahé, Hector Theophilus, member of the executive council, sent on a mission to the British government by Murray, 16, 59; appointed deputy governor in Carleton's place, 59; attends the first meeting of the legislative council, 90; in command at Quebec, 109; hears of the approach of the Americans under Arnold, 109; refuses to receive Arnold's summons to surrender, 111; improves the defences of Quebec, 117

Crown Point, seized by the rebels, 82; Arnold burns all the buildings in, 156; British advance to, 157; left unprotected, 159

D

Dambourges, Lieutenant, serves in defence of Quebec, 129

Dartmouth, Lord, succeeds Lord Hillsborough as colonial secretary, 77; sends instructions to Carleton, 81; receives Carleton's report of the loss of Ticonderoga and Crown Point, 85, 86; receives from Carleton an account of the reasons of his failure to raise the siege of St. Johns, 103

Digby, Hon. Robert, Carleton's naval coadjutor, 194

Disney, Captain, of the 44th, arrested for participation in the Walker outrage, 36-8; "most honourably acquitted," 38

Dorchester, Baroness, maintains the title, 307

Dorchester, Lady, *see* Howard, Lady Maria

Dorchester, Lord, *see* Carleton, Sir Guy

Drummond, Colin, member of the first legislative council, 91

Duggan, Jeremiah, a partisan of Montgomery's, 120

Dunning, Mr., as a witness for the Quebec Act, 65

E

Easton, Colonel, disputes Carleton's passage at Sorel, 112, 113

Effingham, Earl of, father-in-law of Lord Dorchester, 75

Elliott, Mr., commissioner in the matter of cartels, 207, 208

Enos, Colonel, refuses to proceed with Arnold on his march to Quebec, 108; afterwards court-martialed and honourably acquitted, 108

F

Fanning, Mr., appointed lieutenant-governor of Prince Edward Island in Patterson's place, 235

Finlay, Hugh, member of the first legislative council, 91

Forster, Captain, stationed at Oswegatchie, 142; successfully attacks Major Butterfield at the Cedars, 142; marches on to Montreal but

INDEX

has to retire to Vaudreuil, 142; repulses Arnold and makes a compact for the exchange of prisoners which is broken by congress, 143; retires to Oswegatchie, 143

Fox, Charles James, Right Honourable, his objections to the Quebec Act, 66; secretary of state under Rockingham, 192; opposes the Canada Act, 265; his quarrel with Burke, 265

Franklin, Benjamin, sent as congress commissioner to investigate Canada's military situation, 135; his opinion of the Walkers, 136; interviewed by Oswald in Paris, 192, 213

Fraser, Captain, involved in the Walker affair, 19; threatens to resign, 19; arrested and tried for participation in the Walker outrage, 36-8

Fraser, Captain Malcolm, of the Royal Emigrants, 112, 124, 130; in command at Three Rivers, 144; repulses Thompson, 145, 146

Fraser, John, member of the first legislative council, 91

French-Canadians, the, a superior class, 10; opposed to English laws, 14; forward a counter petition protesting against Murray's recall, 18; the question of their religion, 21, 22; Murray's flattering description of, 24, 25; rumoured plans of revolt, 48; forward a petition to the Crown referring to matters legal and lingual, 61; pleased with the Quebec Act, 77, 78; enroll as volunteers, 84; eight are elected to the legislative council under the new Act, 90

G

GAGE, GENERAL, requests Carleton to send him reinforcements at Boston, 78; sails for England, 92

Ganesvort, U.S. officer in possession of Fort Stanwix, 173

Gates, General, occupies Ticonderoga, 157

Genet, Edmond Charles, French minister at Philadelphia, his career in America, 272, 273

George III., his proclamation regarding his new subjects, 7-9; refuses to allow Carleton to accompany the Louisbourg expedition, 31; after three appeals appoints him quartermaster-general with Wolfe against Quebec, 31

Germain, Lord George, his career as Lord George Sackville, 148; character, 149; the cause of his malevolence towards Carleton, 163; appoints Burgoyne to supersede Carleton, 163, 164; Carleton's reply to, 165-9; receives Carleton's resignation, 169; a contemporary statesman's opinion of, 170; his prejudice against Carleton, 170; his plan of campaign. 171, 172

Gladwin, Major, his defence of Detroit, 5

Glapion, M. de, superior at Quebec,

petitions the king for the re-instatement of the Jesuits, 35

Gordon, brigadier, shot by Lieutenant Whitcomb, 152

Graves, Admiral, in command of the fleet, 92; refuses to send transports to Quebec, 92

Greene, General, 197, 204

Grey, de, solicitor-general, report of, 62

H

HALDIMAND, GENERAL SIR FREDERICK, bequeathed Colonel Bouquet's papers, 7; governor at Three Rivers, 21; appointed Carleton's successor, 183; arrives in Quebec, 189, 222; exchanges prisoners with Vermont, 207

Hamilton, Alexander, 106

Hamilton, Captain, of the *Lizard*, 130

Havana, Cuba, the siege of, 32

Hazen, Moses, 84

Heath, General, Washington's commissioner in the matter of cartels, 208

Henderson, Captain, assists in the defence of Quebec, 112

Hey, chief-justice, tries prisoners accused in the Walker affair, 37-9; renders assistance in drafting the Quebec Act, 63, 68; comes to Canada as chief-justice, 81, 91; shames the British into serving as volunteers, 88

Hillsborough, Lord, secretary of state, correspondence with Carleton, 50, 51

Howard, Joseph, arrested for participation in the Walker outrage, 36-8

Howard, Lady Anne, refuses Sir Guy Carleton and marries his nephew, 75, 76

Howard, Lady Maria, wife of Lord Dorchester, 75; personal appearance, 77; returns to Canada with her children, 162; characteristics, 308, 309

Howe, General Lord, evacuates Boston, 134, 159; occupies New York, 160; his futile and ineffective pursuit of Washington, 160; his social festivities in New York, 160; ordered by Germain to send a force up the Hudson to meet Burgoyne but never receives his instructions, 172

Howe, Sir William, appointed to command in America, 92

Hubert, Roman Catholic bishop of Quebec, approves of better education in theory only, 227, 228

Huddy, Joshua, hanged in retaliation for the death of Philip White, 198

Hunter, war-sloop, fires on Arnold, 110, 114

I

ILE-AUX-NOIX, 98, 152

Indians (see also under names of tribes and nations), chiefly valuable as scouts, 88; ordered to watch the Americans at Ticonderoga, 88; forty of them join Arnold, 110; with Forster at the Cedars, 142; at the battle of Oriskany, 174; desert from Bur

INDEX

goyne's army, 178; ignored in the treaty of peace, 231; their territory invaded by the Alleghany frontiersmen, 233, 234; wage war upon the Americans, 270; failure of their peace conference with the American commissioners, 276

Inglis, Charles, first bishop of Nova Scotia, 241; has jurisdiction over Quebec, 241

Iroquois, the, swear allegiance to Carleton, 151

Irving, Colonel, appointed deputy-governor in Murray's place, 23, 24, 33, 34; dismissed from the council, 39

J

JAY's Treaty, 286, 290, 291, 292, 301

Jesuits, the, petition the king for their re-instatement, 35, 58; the claims upon their estates, 230

Johnson, Guy, nephew of Sir William, leads the Six Nations, 88

Johnson, Sir John, raises a battalion known as the King's Royal Regiment of New York, 151; at the battle of Oriskany, 173; informs Dorchester of the critical state of the Indian question in the West, 231; his disappointment at not being appointed lieutenant-governor of Upper Canada, 258, 259

Johnson, Sir William, quiets the discontent of the Six Nations, 5, 6

K

KENNEBEC River, 106, 107, 108
Knox, General, Washington's commissioner in the matter of cartels, 208

L

LA CORNE, SAINT LUC DE, arrested for participation in the Walker outrage, 36-8; a member of the first legislative council, 91

Lake Champlain, 82, 146; its fleet, 149; a description of, 153; battle for the naval supremacy of, 153-7

Lake George, 153, 157

Law, English civil, 10, 11; futile attempts to enforce it in matters connected with property, 13, 40

Law courts, established in 1764, 13; the king's bench, 13, 14; common pleas, 14; trial by jury, 14; justices of the peace appointed, 14; the first presentment of the grand jury, 14-16; French dissatisfaction at the delays and costs of, 41; Masères' four suggestions for the improvement of the legal code, 41, 42; a new ordinance passed for the administration of justice, 54, 55; Dorchester appoints a committee to report upon the legal code, 225

Laws, Captain, despatched to attack Arnold in the rear, 129; puts Arnold's men to rout, 130, 131

Legal difficulties in Canada, Morgan commissioned to investigate, 43, 51; abuses in the administration of justice, 51-4; a new ordinance passed, 54, 55; Dorchester appoints a committee to report upon, 225

Legislative council, the first under

the new Act, 90, 91; members of, 269

Leslie, General, at Charleston, 197, 204

Lévis, Chevalier de, surrenders to Amherst, 2

Life of Shelburne, quoted, 170

Lippincott, Captain, executes Joshua Huddy in retaliation for the death of Philip White, Loyalist, and the consequences of his act, 198–200

Livingstone, Robert, Montgomery writes to, 115, 116

Livius, Mr., appointed chief-justice at Montreal, 184; airs his importance, 187; not included in Carleton's council, 187; appeals to the privy council and is deprived of his office, 188

Lizard, frigate, defends Quebec against Arnold, 110, 114, 130

Lotbinière, M. de, renders assistance in drafting the Quebec Act, 63, 68

Loyalists, the, recommended to Carleton's "tenderest and most honourable care," 194; refugees keep pouring into the British lines, 202; regiments of, under Carleton, 202, 203; petition Carleton for protection, 206; arrangements for their reception in Nova Scotia, 212, 214; their transportation to the Maritime Provinces, 214-19; the immigrations of 1783 and later, 236, 237; Simcoe proposes that they be allowed to affix the letters U. E. to their names, 260

Lymburner, Adam, Quebec merchant, sent to England with a petition for a change in the constitution, 243, 244, 251, 257, 258; pleads for the repeal of the Quebec Act and against the partition of the province, 263, 264

M

MABANE, ADAM, dismissed from the council, 39; member of the first legislative council, 91

M'Govoch, of the 28th Regiment, a witness in the Walker outrage, 36; presented for perjury, 38

McLean, Allen, commands the Royal Emigrants, 93; at Quebec, 112; on the number of killed and wounded, 131; with Carleton in his attack on the rebels, 138; receives reinforcements at Quebec, 144

Marriott, Dr., advocate-general, as a witness for the Quebec Act, 62, 69

Martial law, proclaimed, 86

Masères, attorney-general, prosecutes for the Crown in the Walker outrage, 37, 38; his four suggestions for the improvement of the legal code, 41, 42; investigates the legal difficulties with Morgan, 51; sails for England with reports on the state of the province, 56; his objections to the Quebec Act, 62, 63, 68

Megantic, Lake, 107, 109

Miami, Fort, rebuilt by Simcoe, 284; its surrender demanded, 286; refused, 286

Miamis (Indians), addressed by Dorchester, 282, 283

Minorca, surrender of, 28, 191

INDEX

Monk, solicitor-general in Nova Scotia, 186; represents petitioners against jury ordinance, 226; his report on the state of feeling of the French-Canadians, 278, 279

Montgomery, General Richard, his parentage, 96; education, 97; gazetted to the 17th Foot, 97; takes part in the conquest of Canada under Amherst, 97; sells his commission and goes to New York, 97; marries a daughter of Judge Livingstone, 97; personal appearance, 97; succeeds Schuyler in command on Lake Champlain, 97; despatches Ethan Allen to cement the friendliness of the *habitants*, 98; upbraids Carleton for putting Allen in irons, 100; besieges Fort St. Johns, 100-2; leads the main attack on Canada, 106; receives communication from Arnold, 110; sums up his chances of success, 115, 116; his familiar boast that he will eat his Christmas dinner in Quebec or hell, 116; joins Arnold at Pointe-aux-Trembles, 116; takes up his quarters at Holland House, 118; his letters to Carleton and the inhabitants, 118-20; his plan of attack, 122; spends Christmas Day in Holland House, 123; the plan of attack altered, 125; on the march from Wolfe's Cove, 125; the attack, 126; his death, 126, 132; buried in a hollow under the St. Louis bastion, 132

Montreal, its surrender in 1760; 2, population of, 9; meetings at, for the redress of grievances, 79; riots in, on the inauguration of the Quebec Act, 82; Ethan Allen's attempt to capture it, 98, 99; gaiety in, 162

Morgan, Captain, assumes command in attack on Quebec when Arnold is wounded, 128; his gallantry, 130

Morgan, Maurice, commissioned to investigate the legal situation in Canada, 43, 51; sails for England with reports on the state of the province, 56; his contributions to the archives as Carleton's secretary, 203

Morris, Colonel, head of the department of claims and succour, 202; his marriage, 202

Mountain, Jacob, first Anglican bishop of Canada, 271; early career, 271

Murray, General, as governor of Canada, 2, 4, 9; quells a mutiny among the troops, 4; his trouble with the English settlers, 9; establishes friendly relations with the French-Canadians, 10; discourages the attempt to enforce English civil law, 13; empowered to nominate a council authorized to make laws, 13; sends Cramahé to explain to the British government the state of affairs in Canada, 16; his recall asked for by the British settlers, 17, 18; goes to Montreal to quell the riots between the troops and magistrates, 21; summoned to London, 23; publishes a report of the colony,

24-8; his heroic but fatal defence of Minorca, 28; his proclamation of 1762, 42

N

NAIRNE, CAPTAIN, serves on defence of Quebec, 129

Napier, Captain, of the *Fell*, 113

New York, evacuated by Washington and occupied by Howe, 160; evacuated by the British, 214

"Nootka Incident," the, 250, 259

North, Lord, on committee of the Quebec Act, 63, 66, 68; defeat of his government, 191

O

ORISKANY, battle of, 173, 174

Oswald, Richard, sent to Paris to interview Franklin with a view to terms, 192, 213

Oswegatchie (Ogdensburg), 142, 143

P

PALACE Gate, Quebec, 122, 125, 128, 129

Parr, Governor, of Nova Scotia, 206; receives the Loyalists, 214, 235

Patterson, lieutenant-governor of Prince Edward Island, refuses to resign, 235

Payne, Captain, committed to jail by Walker, 19

Phillips, General, joins Burgoyne at St. Johns, 147; disapproves of leaving Crown Point unprotected, 152

Pitt, William, introduces the Canada Act in the House of Commons, 263

Point au Fer, 153

Point Lévis, 134, 138

Pointe-aux-Trembles, 32; Arnold's troops at, 111, 116

"Pontiac's War," 4; its cause and duration, 5, 6

Portland, Duke of, approves of Dorchester's action in the Miami affair, 284; hears Simcoe's grievances, 302

Powell, Brigadier-general, in command at Ticonderoga, 179; writes to Carleton for instructions, 180; abandons Ticonderoga and reaches St. Johns in safety, 180

Pownall, George, member of the first legislative council, 91

Prescott, Colonel, in command at Montreal, 89, 112; leaves with Carleton, 112; captured by the provincials, 113

Prescott, Robert, appointed governor-general in Dorchester's place, 300, 303, 306

Près de Ville, 118; the battery at, 127, 132

Preston, Major, despatched to St. Johns, but finds it deserted, 84; in command at St. Johns, 93; defends the fort against Montgomery, 100, 101; forced to surrender from shortness of food and ammunition, 102, 146

Price, a disaffected Montrealer, 122, 123

Prince Edward, Queen Victoria's father, visits Canada, 270, 275, 276

Prince William Henry (King William IV) visits Canada, 238, 240

Provincials, the, occupy Crown Point, 83; swarming in the coun-

INDEX

try, 103; clad in British uniforms, 120, 130; their hardships during the siege of Quebec, 123; put to flight, 138

Q

QUEBEC, population of, 9; its fourth and last siege, 114-26; last days of the siege, 127-39; the killed and wounded, 131; regiments at, 144; gaiety in, 162

Quebec Act, the, introduced in the House of Lords, 63; its delimitation of Canada faulty, 63, 64; sanctions existing usages rather than new ones, 64; the debate and passage of, 65; opinions for and against, 65-71; French and British settlers express their satisfaction with, 78, 79; two clauses of, misrepresented by the malcontents, 79, 80; comes into force on May 1st, 1775, 81; riots on the day of its inauguration, 82; the clause annulling all appointments held prior to it causes friction between Carleton and Germain, 183, 184

R

REGIMENTS, 10th and 52nd sent to Gage at Boston, 78; 7th and 26th at St. Johns, 93; 26th with Major Carden at Long Point, 98; 7th at Quebec, 112; 8th with Forster at the Cedars, 142; 29th and 47th with Carleton, 144; those sent back to England, 242; others brought out, 242

Riedesel, Baron, arrives in Canada in command of the Brunswick troops, 145; despatched to Three Rivers, 145; joins Burgoyne at St. Johns, 147

Rodney, Admiral, his victory in the West Indies, 195, 200

Royal Emigrants, afterwards the 84th Regiment, 93; at Quebec, 112

S

ST. JOHNS, Fort, 83, 84; deserted by Allen, 84; reinforced, 85; under Preston, 93; its position, 100; the siege of, 100, 101; forced to surrender, 102; its garrison marches out with the honours of war and is imprisoned in New Jersey, 102

St. John's Gate, Quebec, 120

St. Leger, Colonel, his unsuccessful siege of Fort Stanwix, 173, 174; retreats to Montreal, 174; despatched to the assistance of Ticonderoga, 179

St. Louis Gate, Quebec, 124

St. Maurice, the forges at, 60, 141

St. Roch, suburb of Quebec, 117, 120, 125, 127; its rebel battery captured, 130

Sault-au-Matelot, attacked by Arnold, 117, 125, 127; severe fighting at, 129, 130, 132

Savannah, evacuated, 204

Schuyler, General, takes command of the forces on Lake Champlain, 96; through illness is forced to resign, 96; during his command demonstrates against Fort St. Johns, has a skirmish with Carleton's Indians, and stations a

force at Ile-aux-Noix, 97, 98;
with Montgomery leads the main
attack on Canada, 106

Seigniorial tenure, 11, 255, 256

Senneville, M. de, joins Forster in
his attack on the Cedars, 142

Seven Years' War, closed by the
Treaty of Paris, 1

Shelburne, Lord, (Marquis of Lansdowne), Murray's report addressed
to, 24-8; sends Morgan to Canada to study the legal situation,
43; receives a sketch of the province from Carleton, 43-8; sends
Oswald to interview Franklin in
Paris, 192

Simcoe, John Graves, appointed
first governor of Upper Canada,
259; arrives in Canada, 270; his
misunderstanding with Dorchester, 293-8, 302

Six Nations (Indians), their grievances and discontent, 5; led by
Guy Johnson, 88

Skelton, Rev. Thomas, stepfather
of Lord Dorchester, 29

Smith, William, chief-justice of
Quebec, 224, 225; introduces a
new bill in relation to the legal
code, 226; appointed to investigate the legal administration of
the province, 227; his views on
the division of the province, etc.,
261, 262

Sorel, 112, 141, 145, 146; changes
its name to William Henry, 240;
its second baptism soon forgotten,
241

Stamp Act, the, 33, 57

Stanwix, Fort, its position, 173; St.
Leger's unsuccessful siege of, 173,
174

Stopford, Major, at Chambly 93;
his surrender after a thirty-six
hour siege, 101, 102, 146

Sydney, Lord, secretary of state,
224; his letters to Dorchester,
242

T

TEMPLER, COLONEL, in command at
Montreal, 84; despatches Major
Preston to St. Johns, 84; calls
for volunteers, 84

Thomas, General, takes command
in Wooster's place, 136; routed
by Carleton's army, 138; makes
a stand against Carleton at Sorel,
141

Thompson, General, U. S. officer,
attacks Fraser at Three Rivers,
145, **146**

Thompson, James, engineer, 117

Three Rivers, Carleton arrives at,
113; a dépôt of supplies, 141;
rendezvous of the troops, 144

Thurlow, Lord, attorney-general,
renders assistance in drafting the
Quebec Act, 62, 66

Ticonderoga, seized by the rebels,
82, 83; occupied by Gates, 157;
in command of Powell, 179; attacked by Seth Warner, 179;
abandoned, 180

Tonnancour, Colonel, entertains
Carleton, 89

Townshend, Charles, his comments
on the Quebec Act, 66, 67, 68;
his confidence in Carleton, 205;
requests Carleton to remain until
peace is declared, 212

INDEX

Treaty of Paris, closes the Seven Years' War, 7

V

VERGENNES, French minister, 192, 199

Vermont, approaches Dorchester in regard to an outlet for its trade by the St. Lawrence, 230, 231, 299; admitted into the Union as a state, 299; threatens to invade Canada, 300

Voyer, Colonel, commands the French militia, 115; at the defence of Quebec, 129

W

WALKER, a leading trader and magistrate in Montreal, 18; the billeting episode, 19-21; brought up for trial again, 36-9; refuses to join Ethan Allen in an attempt on Montreal, 98; arrested by Carleton's order, 100; entertains the congress commission, 136

Warner, Seth, heads a band of sharpshooters, 103; attacks Ticonderoga, 179

Washington, General, anxious to occupy Canada, 95; appoints Arnold to command the expedition against Quebec, 105, 106; evacuates New York, 160; retreats to Philadelphia, 160; recaptures most of Howe's posts, 160; corresponds with Carleton about the Loyalists, 206; appoints a commission for the exchange of prisoners, 207, 208; issues orders for a cessation of all hostile acts, 213; meets Carleton to discuss the matter of cartels, 214

Wayne, Anthony, congress general, summons Fort Miami to surrender, 286

Wedderburne, solicitor-general, renders assistance in drafting the Quebec Act, 62, 66

Wentworth, lieutenant-governor of Nova Scotia, 290, 296

Western Indians, wage war under Pontiac, 4, 5

West Indies, British losses in, 191

Whitcomb, Lieutenant, U.S. officer, shoots Brigadier Gordon, 152

White, Philip, Loyalist, his violent death and its consequences, 198-200

Wilkinson, Arnold's aide-de-camp, 147, 234

Wolf, manservant of Colonel Caldwell, escapes from prison and brings word of Montgomery's proposed night attack, 121

Wolfe's Cove, Arnold lands at, 110

Wolfe, General, his friendship with Carleton, 30; the king refuses his request to take Carleton with him on the Louisbourg expedition, 31; after three appeals has him appointed quartermaster-general on the Quebec expedition, 31

Wooster, General, U.S. forces, in command at Montreal, 116; replaces Montgomery, 132; recalled, 136, 138

Y

YORKE, attorney-general, report of 62

CANADIAN UNIVERSITY PAPERBOOKS

Other titles in the series

5. *Our Living Tradition* edited by C. T. Bissell.
13. *Champlain* by N. E. Dionne.
14. *The Life and Times of Confederation* by P. B. Waite.
16. *The Great Migration* by Edwin C. Guillet.
17. *A Prophet in Politics* by Kenneth McNaught.
20. *Testament of My Childhood* by Robert de Roquebrune.
21. *Count Frontenac* by William D. LeSueur.
27. *Wolfe and Montcalm* by Abbé H. R. Casgrain.
40. *Toronto During the French Régime* by Percy J. Robinson.
44. *Procedure in the Canadian House of Commons* by W. F. Dawson.

www.ingramcontent.com/pod-product-compliance
Lightning Source LLC
Chambersburg PA
CBHW030302080526
44584CB00012B/406